What is thoroughly enjoyable about this book is that although the premise is a review of Jamaican entrepreneurship, suggesting a stringent academic text, Dr. Laman's writing style is at once solidly analytical and entertaining. His entrepreneurs introduce us to the diverse and essential social, cultural and political elements that underpin the Jamaican experience.

These entrepreneurs, by their very character, defy the reality that surrounds them and single mindedly pursue their aspirations undaunted by obstacles, sabotage and failure but always supported by a nucleus of family and friends to cheer them on. They are like entrepreneurs anywhere, impacting our world but in a uniquely Jamaican way. This is an inspiring book that you will want to refer to again and again.

—Gloria Hobbins, Founder and President
Global Village Travels, Somerset, NJ

The success profiles were real page turners. Inspiring and motivating, they provide proof that you can rise above your circumstances and achieve success by determination, vision and hard work. *Jamaican Entrepreneurship* should be required reading for every student.

—Carole Brown, Retired educator, Montego Bay, Jamaica

Jamaican Entrepreneurship is a guaranteed addition to my library, and a must read for all worldwide!

—Gordon G. Harry, Chaplain, Atlanta, GA

Dr. Laman's very in-depth study of Jamaica's entrepreneurial achievements internationally, and at home, implies that Jamaica requires a new long-term economic strategy, one which is based on nurturing and fostering "opportunity" entrepreneurism throughout the island.

—George Meikle, Author, *In Praise of Jamaica*

I believe that my being asked to read *Jamaican Entrepreneurship* must have been part of a greater design. As part owner of a family-run business, the lessons I learned from the book kept me going when faith was beginning to waiver and my courage waning. It underscored the fact that entrepreneurship is not for the fainthearted and major success requires calculated risk, belief in self, great partnerships and hard work.

—**Maxine McDonnough, Manager**
Jamaican Epicurean Escape

This is a book with compelling stories of many Jamaican entrepreneurs who have started from humble beginnings, but with hard work dedication and a sense of hope and pride turned their passion and dreams into reality. It is a powerful case for micro, small and medium enterprises, with a bonus: It makes an interesting and motivating read. It is certainly a good guide for those people who want to make a difference in their lives by being independent and resilient and wanting to become an entrepreneur or a business owner.

I find this book to be a valuable and readable contribution to the growing and hot area of entrepreneurship and small business development. It clearly demonstrates some of the major characteristics and traits that it takes to be successful in business.

As a business and entrepreneurship educator, I am convinced that this book will assist in promoting entrepreneurism in students in any field of study regardless of their career aspirations. Hence I recommend this book as a useful and relevant supplement to the Entrepreneurship for the Caribbean Textbook that is being written for the Caribbean Advance Proficiency Examination course in Entrepreneurship.

This book will forever change your attitude about how to never give up and that one can be and do just about anything, if you put your mind to it. Enjoy and be inspired!

—**Mauvalyn M. Bowen, PhD**

Assistant Professor, Forbes School of Business
Ashford University, San Diego, CA

Former Head, Joan Duncan School of Entrepreneurship,
Ethics and Leadership, UTech, Jamaica.

Jamaican Entrepreneurship

A review of the characteristics, traits and ideas underlying the success of some of the island's most accomplished entrepreneurs.

Dr. Glen Laman

NATIONAL LIBRARY OF JAMAICA CATALOGUING-IN-PUBLICATION DATA
Laman, Glen
    Jamaican entrepreneurship: a review of the characteristics, traits and
ideas underlying the success of some of the island's most accomplished
entrepreneurs / Dr. Glen Laman
    p. ; cm.
Bibliography: p. - Includes index
ISBN 978-976-95693-1-7 (pbk)
1.   Entrepreneurship – Jamaica   2. Businesspeople – Jamaica
3.   Success in business – Jamaica
I.   Title
338.04   dc 23

Executive Editor: Lena J. Rose

Copy Editor: Maxine McDonnough

Book layout and cover design: Mark Weinberger

Published in Kingston, Jamaica by

minna
PRESS
www.minnapress.com

Printed in United States of America

Ordering Information
Quantity (Bulk) Sales. Special discounts are available on quantity (bulk)
purchases by corporations, associations, and others.
For details, contact the publisher: sales@minnapress.com

Dedication

To these wonderful women:

Adella, Maud, Hazel, Toni, Wendy, Brooklynn and Peyten.

They are my great-grandmother, my grandmother, my mother,

my wife, my daughter and my two granddaughters.

Acknowledgements

The foundation of this book is a set of profiles of successful Jamaican entrepreneurs. I am most grateful to those entrepreneurs who consented to be interviewed, making time in their busy schedules. Three profiles were compiled from published material and other sources—one is deceased while two were unavailable. I was inspired by their remarkable stories and it is my wish that others will be as touched by them as I was.

Hazel Robinson was especially helpful in introducing me to several entrepreneurs in Jamaica and even drove me to some interviews. I am grateful for her generosity. Pauline Laman helped me in contacting George Yap and Tesula Stewart-Miller put me in contact with Norman Wright.

I appreciate the help and support of my family: My wife Toni who read the material several times throughout the process also my children, Wendy and Brian who provided valuable input and support.

I am also grateful to the faculty and staff at the University of Management and Technology, especially for the help and encouragement of Dr. Yanping Chen, Dr. J. Davidson Frame, Dr. Robert Voetsch and Kevin Hagarty. Much of the research for this book was completed as part of my doctoral program at the university.

Finally, I am eternally grateful to the land of my birth, Jamaica: "All my days I will sing in praise of your forest waters and shining sand."

Contents

PART III—REVIEW AND ANALYSIS

RESOURCES

LIST OF TABLES

LIST OF FIGURES

Foreword

The Austrian economist, Joseph Schumpeter, is acknowledged to be the foremost prophet of entrepreneurship. While classical economists looked at economic activity as rooted in self-regulating markets, Marxists saw it as built on class struggle and neo-classical economists approached it as a science that should be modeled after physics.

Schumpeter recognized that the economic activity that transforms society is driven by a small cadre of non-conformist shock troops who possess a relentless drive to change the world: these are the entrepreneurs. His focus was on the *people* who make a difference, not on economic systems that work through the power of the marketplace to bring order out of chaos.

While traditional economics sought to understand equilibrium points in economic systems, Schumpeter addresses the *disequilibrium* entrepreneurs create through their innovations. He pointed out that economic progress rests largely on the *creative destruction* that is a product of entrepreneurial activity. He maintains that if we are to experience economic growth, the comfortable status quo must be regularly toppled by the destabilizing forces of entrepreneurial activity.

Schumpeter's startling insights are widely supported today—but chiefly in words, not action. You would be hard-pressed to find a CEO or government leader who disdains the contributions of entrepreneurship and innovation. Everyone sings praise to the entrepreneur. However, in practice, few business or political leaders truly support them, because *they are dangerous*. By upsetting the apple cart, they create problems that business and political leaders are not equipped to handle. They lead to uncertainty. Sure, they create great opportunities, but the handmaiden of opportunity is risk, and who wants to advocate more risk in life? Certainly, not most business and political leaders.

In *Jamaican Entrepreneurship*, Dr. Glen Laman examines the role of entrepreneurship in the Small Island Developing State (SIDS) of Jamaica. Looking at the impressive contributions of Jamaican expatriates throughout the world, he argues convincingly that there is something about Jamaican culture that supports an entrepreneurial outlook. He maintains that if Jamaican entrepreneurs could direct their energies and efforts internally—efforts employed so effectively abroad—Jamaica would experience a big economic boost.

In looking at entrepreneurship in Jamaica, Laman directs our attention to understanding three things: (1) the basic nature of entrepreneurial activity, which requires iconoclastic thinking and a willingness to march to the beat of a different drummer; (2) the social and business context of Jamaica, a tiny island nation that sadly has not been blessed by enlightened public policies since its liberation from British colonialism in 1962; and (3) the real world experiences of actual Jamaican entrepreneurs, all of whom overcame adversity to establish and run successful businesses.

While *Jamaican Entrepreneurship* is intended to be a practical, readable work designed to stimulate a sound entrepreneurial outlook among Jamaican citizens, business men and women, and policy makers, it is in fact the product of a doctoral research project carried out by Laman. The good news is that it is readable while, at the same time, carefully researched.

At the heart of the book is Laman's examination of 15 successful entrepreneurs. Through structured interviews and old-fashioned library research, he got their stories on what it took to be successful. In line with the findings of other studies of entrepreneurship, he learned that most of his subjects came from families where the parents functioned independently—they weren't the children of business or government bureaucrats. Like many of the world's most noteworthy entrepreneurs—Bill Gates, Steve Jobs, Larry Ellison, and Richard Branson—a notable portion of them stopped their formal education early. And, of course, success did not come easily—each entrepreneur had his or her daunting challenges to overcome.

I find the contributions of this book to be especially interesting because they shed light on a subject that receives scant attention: entrepreneurship in a small, less developed, island economy. For more than a century, the entrepreneurial contributions of people like Edison, Carnegie, Bolton, Watts, and Siemens have been recognized and praised. Contemporary entrepreneurs such as Mark Zuckerberg, Elon Musk, and the Google founders (Larry Page and Serge Brin) are folk heroes. Emerging countries like China, India, and Brazil are creating their own crop of widely-admired entrepreneurs.

While these people have personalities that are akin to what we find in the Jamaican entrepreneurs covered in this study, there is at least one big advantage they have had that the Jamaicans lack: they functioned in highly effective social, political, and economic environments, where governments promoted sound policies, investment capital was abundant, and the promise of success was great. Entrepreneurs in poor countries lack each of these advantages. Jamaica is particularly challenged because it is a tiny island with miniscule markets, an absence of raw materials, and heavy dependence on imported goods. Yet as Laman points out, it still has its success stories, and he offers insights into 15 of them.

This book is an optimistic one. Laman has carried out his examination of Jamaican entrepreneurship because he believes that if Jamaicans adopt an entrepreneurial spirit, they can thrive as a society despite the challenges they face being a Small Island Developing State. In writing this book, he gives cause for optimism: the subjects of his study offer palpable proof that with good business sense, a cheerful embrace of the unconventional, and unbounded energy, it is possible for a society to achieve great things.

J. Davidson Frame, PhD, PMP, PMI Fellow
Academic Dean
University of Management and Technology

Introduction

It has been said that entrepreneurs see opportunities where others see only problems. There are many problems facing the Jamaican economy. It therefore needs people—entrepreneurs—who can see opportunities among the problems and serve as sparks that ignite the economic engine and stimulate economic growth.

Entrepreneurship can play an important role in the market economy (Casson 2003). It can increase and spread wealth (Khalil, 2006; Nickels, McHugh, & McHugh, 2005). And yet, according to small business blogger and speaker Jay Goltz, writing in the *New York Times*:

> ...choosing entrepreneurship might be one of the most simple and pure adventures you can take. No permission needed, no essays to write, no tests to take, no interviews to get through, no one to tell you what to do or what not to do—and of course no one else to take the credit or blame (Goltz, 2012).

Entrepreneurship has been described as the most powerful economic force known to humankind (Kuratko, 2009). Much of the economic success of nations worldwide is the result of:

> ...encouraging and rewarding the entrepreneurial instinct...a society is prosperous only to the degree to which it rewards and encourages entrepreneurial activity because it is the entrepreneurs and their activities that are the critical determinant of the level of success, prosperity, growth and opportunity in any economy (Tracy, 2005).

High-intensity entrepreneurs can drive new growth. "For governments and foundations, this new breed of innovators provides the path to progress and prosperity." Countries that want to play in the global economy need companies like these, which are building and redefining industries that satisfy domestic demand and generate export income—not to mention create employment for the rapidly growing younger population" (Habiby and Coyle, 2010).

A distinction is made between entrepreneurs and small business owners and a discussion of the difference is provided later on. Entrepreneurs are of two types: "necessity" or "opportunity" entrepreneurs. The necessity entrepreneurs are the typical small business owners who start a business in order to provide income, not to pursue an opportunity or build an enterprise. The opportunity entrepreneurs are the main focus of this book. They are the ones who innovate to create jobs and help drive economic growth.

BACKGROUND

Fifteen Jamaican entrepreneurs from various industries were studied. The group is comprised mostly of leaders who have achieved success and have made significant contributions to the island's economy. Others provide valuable insights into Jamaican entrepreneurship. One small business owner or "necessity" entrepreneur is also profiled as her story is instructive in the differences between necessity and opportunity entrepreneurs. This study enhances our understanding of how these entrepreneurs were able to achieve success despite the many obstacles they had to overcome. At the same time, it provides a valuable documentation of the experiences of Jamaican entrepreneurs which currently does not exist in this format.

AN OVERVIEW OF JAMAICA

Jamaica is an island known for its warm, sunny climate and beautiful, white sand beaches. Despite its small size, the island has been making a disproportionate impact on the world stage in several areas and Jamaican culture is often regarded as the "coolest."

At the 2012 Summer Olympic Games in London, Jamaican athletes dominated the track and field sprint events for the second, consecutive Olympic Games. Jamaica could again boast of having the fastest man and woman in the world as Usian Bolt and Shelly Ann Fraser-Pryce both successfully defended their 100 meter Olympic crowns.

Jamaica made history when they qualified for the 1998 World Cup Soccer finals in France. The "Reggae Boyz," as the team is fondly known to the world, was the first English-speaking Caribbean team to qualify for the World Cup soccer finals. They gained numerous fans and were considered one of the most colorful and popularly supported football teams of the tournament.

Jamaica captured the world's imagination when it entered a bobsleigh team in the 1988 winter Olympics in Calgary, Alberta, Canada. Unlikely competitors though they were, the team quickly became the crowd favorite. In 2000, the Jamaican bobsleigh team won the gold medal at the World Push Championships in Monaco. The story of the Jamaican bobsled team was immortalized in a movie, *Cool Runnings,* loosely based on the actual story.

It wasn't much of a surprise then when in 2009, a Jamaican "dog sled" team, led by musher Newton Marshall, was the first team outside the temperate zone to compete in the Yukon Quest International Sled Dog Race, a 1000-mile race known for its grueling conditions.

Jamaica's reggae music is popular the world over thanks to the exploits of its most gifted and revered performer, the legend, Bob Marley. In 1999, *Time* magazine chose Bob Marley & The Wailers' *Exodus* as the greatest album of the 20th century.

And when it comes to beautiful women, Jamaica ranks with the best and currently ties with the US, Sweden and Iceland for third place in the number of times it has claimed the coveted Miss World crown in the international beauty pageant.

According to Jeremy Santos in an article for *Yahoo Voices*:
> ...part of the reason reggae shot to world popularity is its social themes...Reggae did more for the world by inspiring it to combat its own injustice. Bob Marley was honoured in Zimbabwe's 1980 independence celebration because his music has given inspiration to freedom fighters in the bush. Chinese students used the Wailers' "Get up, Stand Up" as their marching song in the 1989 Tiananmen Square demonstrations. In the Nicaraguan civil war, Marley's music was popular with both the contras and Sandinistas who were fighting oppression. And finally, another example of how reggae music has stretched out across the world and affected so many people is when the Berlin Wall fell; people stood up at the fallen rubble and sang "Three Little Birds" for hours. Reggae's contribution to the world is both musical and social and illustrates the power of people through music. Jamaica may be small but it's arguably the loudest island in the world (Santos, 2008).

Jamaica's cuisine has been described as a fusion of European, African, Spanish, Indian and Chinese flavors. Jerk, the most famous component of that cuisine, is now found the world over. It is a style of cooking in which meat is marinated with a very hot mixture of Jamaican jerk seasoning. Jerk seasoning has been traditionally applied to pork and chicken but has found application in other meats and seafood. Jerk seasoning features allspice and Scotch Bonnet peppers and includes other ingredients such as cinnamon, cloves, garlic, nutmeg, scallions, salt and thyme.

Jamaica Blue Mountain Coffee, Jamaican rum, and Red Stripe beer are also ambassadors of sorts for the island's vibrant culture and people. Many famous personalities can claim Jamaican ancestry or birth. See Table 1.

Jamaica is the largest English-speaking island in the Caribbean and it is the third largest English-speaking country in the Americas, behind the United States of America and Canada. It has a population of approximately 2.7 million people with a labor force estimated at 1.3 million in 2011. Jamaica, however, is struggling with chronic unemployment, poverty, high levels of debt, crime and other maladies. It seeks to develop its economy in order to combat these pressing problems.

According to Dennis Chung, CEO of the Private Sector Organization of Jamaica, when Jamaica gained independence from the British in 1962, it experienced a few years of high economic growth. During the 1970s, it saw significant declines in GDP following the initial growth period and only averaged two percent per annum for the period 1972 to 2007 (Chung, 2009).

AN OVERVIEW OF THE JAMAICAN ECONOMY

Jamaica is deep in debt. In 2011, its government debt was 138.8 percent of GDP (Collister 2012). According to a report by the Center for Economic and Policy Research:

> Jamaica remains one of the most highly indebted countries in the world. Interest payments as a percent of GDP were higher than anywhere else in the world in 2011, including crisis-ravaged Europe. This exceedingly large debt burden has effectively displaced most other public expenditure; debt servicing has taken up nearly 50 percent of total budgeted expenditures over the last four fiscal years while health and education combined have only been around 20 percent. This situation is very problematic for a country of Jamaica's income level, which should be able to invest in infrastructure and human capital, as well as have the financial flexibility to respond to frequent natural disasters and other external shocks (Johnston & Montecino, 2012).

Jamaica is considered one of the small island developing states (SIDS) by the United Nations. Along with these states, it faces various challenges in

TABLE 1	SOME FAMOUS PEOPLE OF JAMAICAN ANCESTRY	
NAME	**CLAIM TO FAME**	**JAMAICAN CONNECTION**
Diane Abbot	First black woman elected to British House of Commons.	Jamaican parents
Harry Belafonte	Singer, songwriter and social activist	Jamaican mother
Usain Bolt	World's fastest man	Born in Jamaica
Carla Campbell	Fashion model	Born in Jamaica
Naomi Campbell	Supermodel, actress and designer	Jamaican mother
Professor Anthony Chen	Winner of a Nobel Peace Prize in 2007, as part of a worldwide group, the Intergovernmental Panel of Climate Change	Born in Jamaica
Tessanne Chin	*The Voice* winner in 2013, an American television singing competition	Born in Jamaica
Jimmy Cliff	Musician, singer and actor	Born in Jamaica
Debra Ehrhardt	Actress, playwright and screenwriter	Born in Jamaica
Patrick Ewing	NBA Hall of fame basketball player	Born in Jamaica
Shelly Ann Fraser-Pryce	World's fastest woman	Born in Jamaica
Marcus Garvey	Pioneering civil rights activist and orator	Born in Jamaica
Malcolm Gladwell	Journalist, bestselling author and speaker	Jamaican mother
Kamala Harris	First female and minority attorney general of California	Jamaican father
Peter Blair Henry	Economist and dean of NYU's Stern School of Business	Born n in Jamaica
Michael Holding	Former West Indian cricketer and record holder	Born in Jamaica
Lester Holt	News journalist and NBC Today show anchor	Jamaican mother
Grace Jones	Model and actress	Born in Jamaica
Michael Lee-Chin	Billionaire business magnate and philanthropist	Born in Jamaica
Sheryl Lee Ralph	Actress and Singer, Tony Award nominee	Born in Jamaica
Lennox Lewis	Former WBA and WBC boxing champion	Jamaican parents
Bob Marley	Reggae Superstar	Born in Jamaica
Jody-Anne Maxwell	The first non USA and first black contestant to win the US National Spelling Bee	Born in Jamaica
Claude McKay	Author, poet and activist	Born in Jamaica
Orlando Patterson	Harvard sociology professor and U.S. National Book Award recipient	Born in Jamaica
Sean Paul	Grammy winning reggae musician	Born in Jamaica
General Colin Powell	Former U.S. Secretary of State	Jamaican parents
Susan Rice	US Ambassador to the United Nations	Jamaican grandparents
Patrick Robinson	President of the International Criminal Tribunal (former Yugoslavia)	Born in Jamaica
Mary Seacole	Pioneering nurse and hero of the Crimean war	Born in Jamaica
Brigadier General Horace Sewell	First Black general in the British Army	Jamaican father
Madge Sinclair	Actress and Emmy Award winner	Born in Jamaica
Kerry Washington	Award winning movie and TV actress, best known for her role in the hit tv-series *Scandal*	Jamaican mother

developing its economy such as limited resources, remoteness, susceptibility to natural disasters, vulnerability to external shocks and excessive dependence on international trade.

Economic growth is challenged by high unemployment and underemployment, a high crime rate, high level of corruption and high debt. In 2011, the island's Gross Domestic Product (GDP) was estimated at $14.7 billion. The unemployment rate was estimated at 12.7 percent and its external debt was estimated at $14.8 billion (CIA, 2011). The per capita GDP was $5,117 while GDP (PPP) was estimated at $9,100 in 2011.

The island is heavily dependent on services which comprise approximately 64 percent of the economy; industry comprises 30 percent; and agriculture six percent. Most of its foreign exchange is derived from tourism, remittances and bauxite/alumina. Remittances account for nearly 15 percent of GDP, exports of bauxite and alumina make up about 10 percent, and tourism accounts for 10 percent of GDP.

Government revenue as a percentage of GDP was estimated at 27.1 percent in 2009; total expenditures were 38 percent of GDP with a deficit of 10.9 percent (*Economic and Social Survey Jamaica*, 2011).

Imports in 2011 were estimated at $6.356 billion with the USA being the largest partner with 32.6 percent, Venezuela 15 percent, Trinidad and Tobago 14.5 percent and China 4.6 percent (2009). Exports were estimated at $1.65 billion in 2011 with the USA being largest partner with 34 percent, Canada 15.8 percent, Norway 9.4 percent, UK 6.6 percent, and Netherlands 6.1 percent (2009). As a percentage of GDP exports were 9.8 percent while imports were 36 percent.

Goods production is 23.6 percent of GDP with agriculture at 5.8 percent, mining & quarrying 1.9 percent, manufacturing 8.1 percent and construction 7.8 percent.

The Jamaican population is 52 percent urban and is comprised of the following ethnic groupings: African 90.1 percent, East Indian 1.3 percent, Chinese 0.2 percent, White 0.2 percent, Mixed 7.3 percent, other 0.1 percent. The median age of Jamaicans is 24.2 years, with females 24.7 years and males 23.7 years. (Table 2)

TABLE 2	THE DECLINE OF THE JAMAICAN DOLLAR	
YEAR	US DOLLAR	JAMAICAN DOLLARS
1971	USD$1.00	J$ 0.77
1975	USD$1.00	J$ 0.91
1980	USD$1.00	J$ 1.78
1985	USD$1.00	J$ 5.58
1990	USD$1.00	J$ 7.24
1995	USD$1.00	J$ 35.35
2000	USD$1.00	J$ 43.08
2005	USD$1.00	J$ 62.50
2010	USD$1.00	J$ 87.38
2013	USD$1.00	J$100.77

Average Annual Exchange Rates. Source: Bank of Jamaica

PROBLEMS FACING SMALL ISLANDS STATES

The risk of increasing marginalization from the global economy in the context of trade liberalization is one of the greatest challenges SIDS face. Since 1974, the specific trade-related problems of "island developing countries" have been recognized by the United Nations system, and have received considerable attention from the international community as a result of UN advocacy (UN Background Paper 2005).

According to Lino Briguglio, director of the Islands and Small States Institute at the University of Malta, writing in the *World Development Journal*, the "special disadvantages of SIDS economies are associated with their small size, insularity, remoteness and propensity to natural disasters. These factors render the economies of these states very vulnerable to forces outside their control—a condition which sometimes threatens their very economic viability. The GDP or GNP per capita of these states often conceals this reality" (Briguglio, 1995).

As Briguglio explains, "small size often implies poor natural resource endowment and low inter-industry linkages, which result in a relatively high import content in relation to GDP. This makes the small island economy highly dependent on foreign exchange earnings. It also limits import substitution possibilities, leads to a large import bill, restricts the country's ability to diversify its exports, and renders the country dependent on a very narrow range of goods and services. The ability to exploit economies of scale is also severely limited and this gives rise to "high per unit costs of production, high costs of infrastructural construction and utilization per capita, high per unit costs of training specialized manpower, and a high degree of dependence on imported technologies" (Briguglio, 1995).

Despite the limitations of being a SIDS economy, several Jamaican entrepreneurs have managed to distinguish themselves and create enterprises that have made valuable contributions to the island's economy. For example, Jamaicans have founded insurance companies, banks, IT companies, factories, stock brokerages, hotels, airlines, and many other types of businesses. They have found ways to overcome the barriers such as lack of capital, access to resources, government policies and other hindrances.

DEFINITION OF TERMS

Entrepreneur: An entrepreneur is one who has successfully established and currently manages a business for the principal purpose of innovation, profitability, and growth (Kuratko, 2009).

Entrepreneurship: A process by which individuals pursue opportunities without regard to the resources they currently control, Stevenson and Jarillo (1990). Another definition is "the process of creating something new and assuming the risks and rewards" (Robert D. Hisrich & Peters, 1998; Kinicki, 2003).

*Free Market Capitalism (*Truncated to *Capitalism* in this study*):* also called free market economy, or free enterprise economy, is the economic system that has been dominant in the Western world since the breakup of feudalism, in which most of the means of production are privately owned and production is guided and income distributed largely through the operation of markets (*Encyclopedia Britannica*). This system is based on supply and demand with little or no government control. A completely free market is an idealized form of a market economy where buyers and sellers are allowed to transact freely (i.e. buy/sell/trade) based on a mutual agreement on price without state intervention in the form of taxes, subsidies or regulation.

CARICOM: The Caribbean Community was established by Commonwealth Caribbean leaders at the Seventh Heads of Government Conference in 1972 when they transformed the Caribbean Free Trade Association (CARIFTA) into a Common Market which provides for the free movement of labor and capital, and the coordination of agricultural, industrial and foreign policies. It currently has 15 member nations: Antigua and Barbuda, The Bahamas, Barbados, Belize, Dominica, Grenada, Guyana, Haiti, Jamaica, Montserrat, St. Kitts and Nevis, St. Lucia, St. Vincent and the Grenadines, Suriname and Trinidad and Tobago.

Developing Country: According to the UN, a developing country is a country with a relatively low standard of living, undeveloped industrial base, and moderate to low Human Development Index (HDI). This index is a comparative measure of poverty, literacy, education, life expectancy, and other factors for countries worldwide. The HDI measures the average achievements in a country in two basic dimensions of human development: a long and healthy life, as measured by life expectancy at birth, and knowledge, as measured by the adult literacy rate (with two-thirds weight) and the combined primary, secondary, and tertiary gross enrollment ratio (with one-third weight).

There are significant social and economic differences between developed and developing countries. Many of the underlying causes of these differences are rooted in the long history of development of such nations and include social, cultural and economic variables, historical and political elements, international relations, and geographical factors.

Development entails a modern infrastructure (both physical and institutional), and a move away from low value-added sectors such as agriculture and natural resource extraction. Developed countries usually have economic systems based on continuous, self-sustaining economic growth and high standards of living (Educational Pathways International).

Globalization: the process of increasing the connectivity and interdependence of the world's markets and businesses. This process has speeded up dramatically in the last two decades as technological advances make it easier for people to travel, communicate, and do business internationally. Two major recent driving forces are advances in telecommunications infrastructure and the rise of the internet. In general, as economies become more connected to other economies, they have increased opportunity but also increased competition. Thus, as globalization becomes an increasingly common feature of world economics, powerful pro-globalization and anti-globalization lobbies have arisen.

The pro-globalization lobby argues that globalization brings about much increased opportunities for almost everyone, and increased competition is a good thing since it makes agents of production more efficient.

The anti-globalization group argues that certain groups of people who are deprived in terms of resources are not currently capable of functioning within the increased competitive pressure that will be brought about by allowing their economies to be more connected to the rest of the world (Investorwords. com).

Small Business: The US Small Business Administration (SBA) defines a small business concern as one that is independently owned and operated, is organized for profit, and is not dominant in its field. Depending on the industry, size standard eligibility is based on the average number of employees for the preceding twelve months or on sales volume averaged over a three-year period.

Micro, small and medium enterprise (MSME) and small and medium enterprise (SME) are terms used in the European Union (EU) and by international organizations such as the World Bank (WB), the United Nations (UN) and the World Trade Organization (WTO) to indicate small business. Individual countries or states usually set their own definitions of the size limits of these business categories.

Small Island Developing States: Small island developing states (SIDS) were recognized as a distinct group of developing countries facing specific social, economic and environmental vulnerabilities. Three geographical regions have been identified for the location of SIDS, namely, the Caribbean, the Pacific and the Atlantic, Indian Ocean, Mediterranean and South China Sea. SIDS tend to confront similar constraints in their sustainable development efforts, such as a narrow resource base depriving them of the benefits of economies of scale; small domestic markets and heavy dependence on a few external and remote markets; high costs for energy, infrastructure, transportation, communication and servicing; long distances from export markets and import resources; low and irregular international traffic volumes; little resilience to natural disasters; growing populations; high volatility of economic growth; limited opportunities for the private sector and a proportionately large reliance of their economies on their public sector; and fragile natural environments (United Nations Office of the High Representative for the Least Developed Countries, Landlocked Developing Countries and Small Island Developing States).

Socialism: The social and economic system that calls for public rather than private ownership or control of property and natural resources. According to the socialist view, individuals do not live or work in isolation but live in cooperation with one another. Furthermore, everything that people produce is in some sense a social product, and everyone who contributes to the production of a good is entitled to a share in it. Society, as a whole, therefore, should own or at least control property for the benefit of all its members.

Creative Destruction: This term was popularized by Joseph Schumpeter and was introduced in his book *Capitalism, Socialism and Democracy.* It is the disruptive force that sustains economic growth; "the fundamental impulse that sets and keeps the capitalist engine in motion comes from the new consumers, goods, the new methods of production or transportation, the new markets, the new forms of industrial organization that capitalist enterprise creates. The entrepreneur is the person introducing new combinations of products, ideas, or methods into an organization's business environment. These new combinations disrupt the equilibrium condition, forcing the organization to readjust and adapt itself to the new set of dynamics (Brouwer, 1991).

Innovation: BusinessDictionary.Com provides the following definition of innovation:

> The process by which an idea or invention is translated into a good or service for which people will pay, or something that results from this process. To be called an innovation, an idea must be replicable at an economical cost and must satisfy a specific need. Innovation involves deliberate application of information, imagination, and initiative in deriving greater or different value from resources, and encompasses all processes by which new ideas are generated and converted into useful products. In business, innovation often results from the application of a scientific or technical idea in decreasing the gap between the needs or expectations of the customers and the performance of a company's products

> A key component of innovation is risk-taking and organizations that introduce revolutionary products or technologies take on the greatest risk because they have to create new markets.

SUMMARY

Entrepreneurs can be catalysts in Jamaica's efforts to get its economy moving. Jamaican entrepreneurs lack the opportunities of entrepreneurs operating in larger, more centrally located countries. They cannot count on government largesse, as can entrepreneurs in resource rich countries. They have very limited access to venture capital, a significant source of capital available to entrepreneurs in richer countries. What capital they raise typically comes from personal savings, personal loans, and contributions from members of their extended families. Add to this the list of other problems that face developing countries and it can seem like an impossible situation.

Jamaican Entrepreneurship illuminates the accomplishments of people who have actually found a path to success. It shows what they did, how they did it and why they did it. Jamaicans have already shown they can have an impact on the world stage in areas such as sports, music, food and culture. Now it's time to make a mark on the global economy.

DR. GLEN LAMAN

PART I

BACKGROUND

CHAPTER 1

Entrepreneurship: Identifying the Characteristics of an Entrepreneur

This chapter briefly discusses what we know about entrepreneurship and provides a background with which to better understand the profiles of the Jamaican entrepreneurs.

WHO IS AN ENTREPRENEUR?

The earliest writer to recognize the role of entrepreneurship is the seventeenth century economist Richard Cantillon. In his view, the entrepreneur is someone who engages in exchanges for profit; specifically, he is someone who exercises business judgment in the face of uncertainty. This uncertainty (of future sales prices for goods on their way to final consumption) is rather carefully circumscribed, as Cantillon describes it, entrepreneurs buy at a certain price to sell again at an uncertain price, with the difference being their profit or loss (Herbert et al, 2009, p 8).

Jean-Baptiste Say (1767-1832) emphasized the role of the entrepreneur in creating value by moving resources out of less productive areas and into more productive ones with greater yield (Say, 2001). Say regarded the entrepreneur as a manager of a firm; an input in the production process. Entrepreneurs act in the static world of equilibrium, where they assess the most favorable economic opportunities. Entrepreneurs are catalysts for economic change and development (Peverelli, 2012).

John Stuart Mill used the term "entrepreneur" in his popular 1848 book, *Principles of Political Economy*, to refer to a person who assumes both the risk and the management of a business (*Concise Dictionary of Economics*).

One of the best known definitions of an entrepreneur is Joseph Schumpeter's. He held that an entrepreneur is someone who disrupts the normal way of doing things by creating a new product, process, new source of supply or new organization. Economist Israel Kirzner, widely recognized for his research on entrepreneurial economics, focused on the process of discovery in which the entrepreneur is a person who discovers previously unnoticed profit opportunities.

Entrepreneurs' personal traits have been widely discussed to explain entrepreneurship; they include creativity, innovativeness, risk taking, and proactiveness (Covin & Slevin, 1991). Kirby (2003) proposed that it is more likely that there are different types of entrepreneurs, each with a different personality type and attributes.

Some definitions stress the behavior of the entrepreneur rather than traits. For example, Drucker wrote that, "Entrepreneurs create something new, something different; they change or transmute values."

WHAT IS ENTREPRENEURSHIP?

There are many definitions of entrepreneurship. The opportunistic pursuit of economic wealth via creative initiatives of the individual operating within an uncertain environment constrained by limited tangible resources is one definition which emphasizes the judgment component of entrepreneurship (Austin et al., 2006; Mitchell et al., 2002). A quote widely attributed to Netscape founder and venture capitalist Marc Andreesen explains entrepreneurial judgment as the ability to tell the difference between a situation that's not working but persistence and iteration will ultimately prove it out, versus a situation that's not working and additional effort is a destructive waste of time and radical change is necessary (Casnocha, 2008).

Another definition focuses on one personal characteristic, charismatic leadership, and entrepreneurship is defined as "the ability to articulate a plan, a set of rules, or a broader vision, and impose it on others." According to this definition, successful entrepreneurs must be excellent communicators and be able to generate a following.

An ability to identify opportunities is a conception most attributed to economist Israel Kirzner. "Opportunities" have come to be defined as "situations in which resources can be redeployed to create value through various forms of arbitrage." Entrepreneurs are characterized as having special knowledge or insight that no one else has (Dellape, 2012).

Entrepreneurship can also be viewed as an aspect of innovation, a view championed by Schumpeter and others—innovation and invention are discussed later in this chapter. It can also be defined by personal and psychological characteristics such as imagination and creativity (Dellape, 2012).

According to Schumpeter:

> The fundamental impulse that sets and keeps the capitalist engine in motion comes from the new consumer goods, the new methods of production or transportation, the new markets, the new forms of industrial organization that capitalist enterprise creates.

THE FIRST RISK TAKERS

The first entrepreneurs, as we know them today, are reported to have been the Phoenicians, a Semitic people who lived around 1100 to 500 BCE in an area situated on the western coastal part of the Fertile Crescent and near the coastline of modern Lebanon. They had a maritime trading culture and took risks sailing in man-powered galleys to sell their wares in distant ports. Theirs was a nation of independent city states which were located on the coastline of the Mediterranean.

The Phoenicians had a monopoly on the expensive purple dye—Tyrian purple—used in royal robes and made from the mucus of murex snails. They were known in classical Greece and Rome as "traders of purple." They were merchants and traders with skills and trading practices that enhanced the quality of life in much of the Mediterranean. True entrepreneurs, they took risks, explored the unknown facing the resultant chaos on a daily basis. Phoenicia ceased to exist as an entity when the Persians took control and by 65 BCE Phoenicia had been absorbed into Syria. (Welsch, 2004).

ENTREPRENEURS THROUGH THE AGES

The Phoenician brand of entrepreneurship was trade-based and was non-aggressive. This would eventually give way to:

> …adventurers, armies and entrepreneurs who sailed the world based on military might and established trade through "uncertain environments that presented personal and financial risks. Armies brought back spoils and traded for profits for the entrepreneurs who undertook the journeys and the early venture capitalists who

financed imports of tobacco, tomatoes and rice, and other 'new' products into the economies of Europe from the New World (Welsch, 2004).

During the Middle Ages, entrepreneurs were usually the agents of the government who administered fixed price contracts and reaped any profits that could be had by parsimonious management. Increasingly, the term came to mean someone who created or took advantage of an opportunity to achieve out of the ordinary results. There was also a need for the entrepreneur to be innovative and a risk embracing individual (Welsch, 2004).

The Industrial Revolution, which took place from the 18th to 19th centuries, was a period during which predominantly agrarian, rural societies in Europe and America became industrial and urban. It was a fertile period for men with the entrepreneurial vision and disposition to take risks and capitalize on the abundant opportunities presented by this radical change in society. Prior to the Industrial Revolution, which began in Britain in the late 1700s, manufacturing was often done in people's homes, using hand tools or basic machines.

Industrialization marked a shift to powered, special-purpose machinery, factories and mass production. The iron and textile industries, along with the development of the steam engine, played central roles in the Industrial Revolution, which also saw improved systems of transportation, communication and banking (History.com).

The dynamic innovators of the 19th century include men such as John D. Rockefeller who founded Standard Oil Company which became a dominating force in America's economy. He realized that energy would be a requirement for the new economy. Andrew Carnegie borrowed money to build a steel plant in Pittsburgh and rode the expansion of the US steel industry. He is often cited as the true "rags to riches" story.

Cornelius Vanderbilt was a successful steamship operator in 1862 when he realized that the future of the transportation industry would increasingly involve the railroads. He joined the New York and Harlem railway as a director and became a railroad icon by executing an acquisition strategy by which he controlled several of the major railways including lucrative routes such as the New York to Chicago line.

The 20th century ushered in some of the most remarkable inventions which have radically transformed how we live our lives today. These inventions include radio, TV, the airplane, computers, cell phones and modern medicines, to name a few. Some of the key entrepreneurs of this period include technology giants such as Bill Gates who founded Microsoft, Steve Jobs who co-founded Apple Computer, retailing giant Sam Walton who founded Wal-Mart, and Richard Branson of Virgin Records.

INVENTION VS. INNOVATION

What is the difference between invention and innovation? An Invention is a new, useful process, machine, improvement, etc., which did not exist previously and that is recognized as the product of some unique intuition or genius, as distinguished from ordinary mechanical skill or craftsmanship (businessdictionary.com). An invention does not necessarily have economic value. An invention becomes an innovation when a target customer or market is developed:

> There are several examples of great inventions that generated little or no returns to their inventors. In 1947 some scientists at the AT&T laboratories created the first transistor in the world. The invention was obviously patented, but the organization was not able to find promptly an application for the new device. They did an outstanding job with the invention, but failed to develop the innovation. Precisely for that reason in 1952 AT&T decided to license out the transistor. For $25,000 companies like Texas Instruments, Sony and IBM acquired a technology that would produce billions of revenues in the coming years (Innovation Zen, 2011).

Xerox is a prime example of a company that missed a big opportunity. In their early years, they established themselves as technology wunderkind, anticipating the oncoming waves of high tech. But, over time, as they grew large and bureaucratic, they encountered problems in capitalizing on their intellectual capital. Just like AT&T they were very good inventors, but they lacked the ability to transform such inventions into innovations. At the famous Palo Alto Research Center (PARC) Xerox was the first company in the world to develop a personal computer (years before Apple or IBM), a graphical oriented monitor, a word processing software, a workstation, a laser printer, a local area network, a hand-held mouse, and the list goes go. Yet it profited from almost none of such breakthrough inventions (Innovation Zen, 2011).

Ultimately, Steve Jobs of Apple capitalized on PARC's vision and technology in his Macintosh computers.

Peter Drucker writes that an innovation has to be simple and focused to be successful. It should only do one thing or it confuses people and won't work. "All effective innovations are breathtakingly simple. It should focus on a specific need that is satisfied and on a specific end result that it produces" (Drucker, 1993).

Effective innovations often start small. By appealing to a small, limited market, a product or service requires little money and few people to produce and sell it. As the market grows, the company has time to fine tune its processes and stay ahead of the emerging competition. If an innovation does not aim at leadership in the beginning, it is unlikely to be innovative enough to successfully establish itself. Leadership here can mean dominating a small market niche (Drucker, 1985).

According to Drucker:
> The economy is forever going to change and is biological rather than mechanistic in nature. The innovator is the true subject of economics. Entrepreneurs that move resources from old and obsolescent to new and more productive employments are the very essence of economics and certainly of a modern economy (Forbes, 2005).

JOSEPH SCHUMPETER

Joseph A. Schumpeter was an Austrian economist who taught at Harvard, and in 1942 coined the term "creative destruction" to describe what he viewed as the engine of capitalism: how new products and processes constantly overtake existing ones. In his classic work, "*Capitalism, Socialism and Democracy*," he describes how unexpected innovations destroyed markets and gave rise to new fortunes.

The historian Thomas K. McCraw writes in his new biography of Schumpeter, *Prophet of Innovation: Joseph Schumpeter and Creative Destruction* (Belknap Press, 2010):
> Schumpeter's signature legacy is his insight that innovation in the form of creative destruction is the driving force not only of capitalism but of material progress in general. Almost all businesses, no matter how strong they seem to be at a given moment, ultimately fail and almost always because they failed to innovate.

According to G. Pascal Zachary writing in the New York Times:
> Clearly, any quick survey of technological change validates Mr. Schumpeter's essential insight. The CD destroyed the videotape (and the businesses around it). The computer obliterated the typewriter. The automobile turned the horse and buggy into an anachronism. Today, the Web is destroying many businesses even

as it gives rise to others. Though the compact disc still lives, downloadable music is threatening to make the record album history (Zachary, 2007).

National bookselling chains such as Barnes and Noble and Crown Books put many small booksellers out of business, even as e-books and web-based booksellers, such as Amazon.com, put some national chains such as Borders out of business.

Schumpeter's entrepreneur was a facilitator of innovations; a supporter of the "mechanism of change" in the capitalist economy. Indeed there can be no doubt that "Schumpeter attributed change to the creative acts associated with entrepreneurial activity" (Becker et. al. 2005, p. 110-111).

According to Schumpeter, the process of technological change in a free market consists of three parts: invention (conceiving a new idea or process), innovation (arranging the economic requirements for implementing an invention), and diffusion (whereby people observing the new discovery adopt or imitate it). These stages can be observed in the history of several famous innovations. The Xerox photocopier was invented by Chester Carlson, a patent attorney frustrated by the difficulty of copying legal documents. After several years of tedious work, Carlson and a physicist friend successfully photocopied a phrase on October 22, 1938. But industry and government were not interested in further development of the invention. In 1944, the nonprofit Battelle Corporation, dedicated to helping inventors, finally showed interest. It and the Haloid Company (later called Xerox) invested in further development. Haloid announced the successful development of a photocopier on October 22, 1948, but the first commercially available copier was not sold until 1950. After another $16 million was invested in developing the photocopier concept, the Xerox 915 became the first simple push-button plain-paper copier (Sandefur, 2008).

ENTREPRENEUR VS. SMALL BUSINESS OWNER

According to author and publisher Brian Hill, the terms "entrepreneur" and "small business manager" are sometimes used interchangeably, but an entrepreneur plays a different role than a small business manager. Not all entrepreneurs make great managers, and not all managers are cut out to be entrepreneurs.

Entrepreneurs are the dynamic forces behind the planning and launching of new business enterprises. They may be involved in all aspects of a company throughout its life span, beginning with the raw startup stage, when the venture is little more than an idea. They handle issues ranging from the company's product design to determining the most efficient production methods and even finding the company's first customers. A small-business manager is someone who operates a company that has survived the startup stage. His goal is to keep the company growing and operating efficiently. In some cases, the founder/entrepreneur may bring in a skilled small-business manager to build the company into a larger entity. He may recognize that his creative vision can take the company only so far, and having an experienced manager on board to direct day-to-day operations will allow the business to continue to grow (Hill, B).

An entrepreneur bears all the risk and uncertainties involved in running an organization whereas a manager is an employee and gets paid regardless of profitability. The manager bears none of the risks of running the business. However, the manager, in many cases, brings a level of professionalism and structure to the business.

Entrepreneurs that are most successful usually possess an unusual vision, the ability to identify what products and services customers will want or need in the future, and design products or services to meet those needs. Small business managers who operate established companies do not necessarily need this predictive ability (Hill, B).

Author and entrepreneur Luanne Teoh (2011) has compared the distinct differences in the mindset and motivations of both entrepreneurs and small business owners. The following, Table 3, illustrates the differences.

ENTREPRENEURIAL MINDSET

According to John Terry in an article entitled, *The Mind of an Entrepreneur*, the mind of an entrepreneur is a very special thing. It is the source of possibility, growth and success in business. All those things are rooted in the business owner's ability to think and dream. McGrath & MacMillan (2000) define the characteristics of an entrepreneurial mind-set in Table 4.

Entrepreneurs get things done. They are creative and they have the ability to recognize opportunities and take action. An entrepreneur views needs, problems and challenges as opportunities—hunger, for example, is an opportunity to sell food and drink.

TABLE 3	COMPARISON OF ENTREPRENEUR VS. SMALL BUSINESS OWNER	
OBJECTIVES & VIEWS	**SMALL BUSINESS OWNER**	**ENTREPRENEUR**
Primary motivation	To make a living	To make a change and impact
Personal financial goal	Regular income	Value of company
Career objective	Self-employment	Financial freedom
Financing strategy	SBA or bank loans	Investors
Business strategy	Creating more sales	Providing value
View of assets	Real estate and inventory	Employees and customers
Risk taking profile	Stability	Willing to fail
Employee compensation	Market rate or below	Will pay for top talent
Work environment	Extension of owner's home	Fast paced and growth focused
Investment profile	Main investor/owner	Investor/Involvement in different businesses
Daily actions	Day to day manager	Strategy, growth and collaboration
Work style	Long-term and enjoys repetitive tasks	Short-term and a serial innovator/inventor

Source: Luanne Teoh

TABLE 4	CHARACTERISTICS OF AN ENTREPRENEURIAL MINDSET
Passionately seeks new opportunities	
Pursues opportunities with enormous discipline	
Pursues only the best opportunities; avoids exhausting themselves and their organizations by chasing after every option	
Focuses on execution—specifically, adaptive execution	
Engages the energies of everyone in their domain by creating and sustaining networks of relationships.	

FAMILY OR PARENTAL ROLES IN IDENTITY BUILDING

One of the most prevalent factors found throughout the literature is that family or parental role models influence young adults to become self-employed (Henderson & Robertson, 1999; Scott & Twomey, 1988). This is not surprising as entrepreneurs often come from families with a self-employed parent (Collins & Moore, 1970). Having entrepreneurial family members is only one characteristic that has been researched. Studies have also shown that personality, ethnicity, marital status, educational level, size of family, residence location, work status, experience, age, gender, socio-economic status, and religion influence the decision to become an entrepreneur (Bernstein, 2011).

Murnieks and Mosakowski argue that entrepreneurial roles and entrepreneurial identities serve as powerful entities that propel entrepreneurial actions. "According to Burke and others, identities motivate behavior (Burke, 1991a; Burke & Reitzes, 1981; Erez & Earley, 1993; Foote, 1951; Marcussen & Large, 2003; McCall & Simmons, 1978). McCall and Simmons (1978) suggest that identities are perhaps the primary sources of motivation for human behavior. Identity control theory (Burke, 1991) argues that identities are powerful motivators because they fulfill the human need for self verification (Swann, Pelham & Krull, 1989), which then contributes to a sense of efficacy (Erez & Earley 1993)" (Murnieks and Mosakowski, 2007).

LOCUS OF CONTROL

Locus of control is the extent to which people believe they have power over events in their lives. A person with an *internal locus of control* believes that he or she can influence events and their outcomes, while someone with an *external locus of control* blames outside forces for everything (*Encyclopedia of Psychology*).

Locus of control is a frequently cited personal trait associated with entrepreneurial potential; it pertains to an individual's expectancy that the outcome of any particular situation is controlled by chance (external) or one's own behavior (internal) at any given time (Rotter & Mulry, 1965). An individual's internal or external tendency has been proven to have a strong correlation to achievement motivation. Individuals who possess an external locus of control may show little interest in taking steps towards increasing their skills if they believe the situational outcome is dependent on chance as opposed to personal skills and behaviors. (Rotter & Mulry, 1965). An individual who believes his or her actions produce an intended outcome:

> . . . is more likely to take social action to better his life conditions, is more likely to attend to, and to learn and remember information that will affect his future goals, and is generally more concerned with his ability, particularly his failures (Rotter and Mulry, 1965, p. 598).

LEVEL OF EDUCATION

The Global Entrepreneurship Monitor (GEM) project is an annual assessment of the entrepreneurial activity, aspirations and attitudes of individuals across a wide range of countries from all over the globe. Its surveys indicate that entrepreneurial perception levels tended to be higher in participants with a post-secondary education (Acs, Arenius, Hay, & Minniti,

2004; Autio, 2005; Minniti, et al., 2006). Individuals with a high level of education are more likely to engage in entrepreneurship. An individual with more work experience, a higher level of education, more knowledge of the market and business practice is more likely to be able to identify an opportunity for starting a new business (Wit & Van Winden, 1989).

Studies show a direct, positive relationship between level of education and entrepreneurial performance (Brush & Hisrich, 1991). Dolinsky, Caputo, Pasumarty, and Quazi (1993) found level of education to be positively correlated to the likelihood of self-employment pursuits (Dolinsky et al., 1993). Since entrepreneurial activity spurs economic growth, interest in entrepreneurial education has increased significantly over the past decade. Therefore, it is not surprising that the field of entrepreneurial education has grown in direct proportion to the growth rates of entrepreneurial activity over the past decade (Moutray, 2006). Currently, research comparing general education to entrepreneurial education is sparse at best (Solomon, 2007; Vesper & McMullan, 1988; Vesper & Gartner, 1997).

Education plays an important role in the process of economic wealth as it increases the supply of highly educated entrepreneurs in the economy and it improves the effectiveness of potential entrepreneurs by enhancing their interpersonal, management and business skills (Scott, et al., 1998).

On the other hand, there are long lists of successful entrepreneurs who had very little education and yet rose to the pinnacle of their respective industries. In the USA, Steve Jobs, Bill Gates, Mark Zuckerberg and Michael Dell are just a few of the well known entrepreneurs who dropped out of college to start businesses.

The British business magnate and founder of the Virgin Group, Sir Richard Branson, struggled in school due to his dyslexia and decided to leave school at age 16. However, his father Edward Branson wanted him to follow in his footsteps and become an attorney. He drove to the boarding school and was successful in dissuading Richard from leaving. But his mother was not happy with this. She told his father to drive back to the school immediately and inform Richard that it was OK to leave school (Branson, 2010).

INNOVATIVENESS

According to Drucker, entrepreneurs innovate. "Innovation is the specific instrument of entrepreneurships. It is the act that endows resources with the new capacity to create wealth. Innovation, indeed, creates a resource. There is no such thing as a resource in nature until man finds a use for something and thus endows it with economic value" (Drucker, 1985).

Innovation can be defined as the "introduction of a new product, process, technology, system, technique, resources, or capability to the firm or its markets." (Coven and Miles, (1990). And innovation can be divided into three categories: product innovation, process innovation and organizational innovation (Vokola, 2000).

Drucker contrasts the small business owner who opens a delicatessen with McDonald's. The delicatessen owner is simply doing what many others have done and did not create "new satisfaction nor new consumer demand." When McDonald's opened, they did not invent anything new. But by applying management concepts and management techniques asking, 'What is "value" to the customer?', standardizing the "product," designing process and tools, and by basing training on the analysis of the work to be done and then setting the standards it required, McDonald's both drastically upgraded the yield from resources, and created a new market and a new customer. This is entrepreneurship" (Drucker, 2006).

According to Drucker:

> Successful entrepreneurs do not wait until 'the muse kisses them' and gives them a 'bright idea': they go to work. They do not look for the 'biggie,' the innovation that will 'revolutionize industry,' create a 'billion-dollar business' or 'make one rich overnight.' Those entrepreneurs who start out with the idea that they'll make it big— and in a hurry—can be guaranteed failure. They are almost bound to do the wrong things. An innovation that looks very big may turn out to be nothing but technical virtuosity; and innovation with modest intellectual pretensions, a McDonald's, for instance, may turn into gigantic, highly profitable businesses (Drucker, 1993).

PROPENSITY TO TAKE RISKS

It is generally accepted that entrepreneurs assume moderate, calculated risks and do not have a greater propensity for risk taking than managers or even the general population (Brockhaus, 1980); Gartner, 1985; Pinillus, 2003). There are larger differences between entrepreneurs whose primary goal is venture growth versus those whose focus is on producing family income (Stewart & Roth, 2001). These risky tendencies may be observed because entrepreneurs are "overconfident and prone to oversimplify from limited characteristics or observations" (L. W. Busenitz & Barney, 1997). Baron (1998) echoes this assertion "that entrepreneurs often underestimate risks and overestimate the likelihood of success."

It may be that entrepreneurs have such a strong belief in their ability to influence business goals that their perceived possibility of failure is fairly low. Thus, the entrepreneurs perceived level of risk is correspondingly lower than a non-entrepreneurial personality (Brockhaus & Horwitz, 1986).

According to Ted Sun in the book, *Survival Tactics: the Top 11 Behaviors of Successful Entrepreneurs*:

> Studies have shown that risk perceptions differ by age, achievement and environment. Gender, on the other hand, has no significant impact on risk-taking or risk-avoiding behaviors. Depending on the stage of life or the environment people can choose to take on more risk. For example in an environment with a high need for achievement, people are significantly willing to take more risk. Higher levels of education have also been attributed to willingness for taking risks. Other studies have shown that age and seniority is inversely related to risk-taking (Sun, 2007).

Entrepreneurs face a number of risks in pursuit of success; they include financial risk, career risk, family and social risk and psychic risk. Financial risk may include personal savings and the possibility of default on loans. Career risk is a major concern for those who have a job or career that they have to give up. Family and social risk is created when an entrepreneur has to spend a lot of time and energy on the venture to the detriment of family and friends. Psychic risk may be the greatest risk to the well being of the entrepreneur as it can be very difficult to recover from a financial catastrophe (Kuratko & Lodgetts, 2009).

It is often argued that the risks entrepreneurs engage in are largely *calculated* risks. In other words, entrepreneurs do their homework before launching an initiative. While entrepreneurs may not be crazy risk takers, what distinguishes them from most business people is that they are not inherently risk-averse. Risk-averse people demand zero risk—but zero risk doesn't exist. Entrepreneurs realize this.

NEED FOR ACHIEVEMENT

Psychologist David McClelland (1961, 1953) is credited with developing the Achievement Motivation Theory. He found that entrepreneurs' highest need is for achievement, a desire to prove themselves through the accomplishments of tasks, rather than by influencing their environment or building a network of friends (Cromie, 1987; Brockhaus, 1982). According to McClelland, people exhibiting a need for achievement (N-Ach) have four main behavioral traits: taking responsibility for finding solutions to problems, taking calculated risks, setting goals for achievement, and desiring concrete feedback on performance (Johnson, 1990).

In a longitudinal analysis of the need for achievement in scores of college freshmen,

McClelland (1965) concluded that a high need for achievement is a predictor of entrepreneurship and is based on influences of childhood and adult training and experiences. He posited that needs are learned and therefore culturally, not biologically determined; and some cultures produced more entrepreneurs because of the socialization process that creates a high need for achievement (Okhomina, 2010). A number of studies suggest that need for achievement is higher in company founders, compared to managers (Begley & Boyd, 1987; Miner, Smith & Bracker, 1989).

According to Sir Arthur Lewis, the St Lucian Economics Nobel Laureate:
> Business men are not alone in feeling a need for achievement; they share this with successful people in every other walk of life: with artists, musicians, generals, professors, politicians, cricketers, comedians -- people who succeed in their professions are usually driven by this need for achievement. They need this drive to keep them going when all the others have stopped. For example, to succeed you must be willing to work hard, while the rest of your companions are at play.... There is no doubt that achievers have a special type of personality. This drive for achievement is not identical with brain power. Many people with excellent brains achieve nothing, while men with moderate brains can be highly successful if they have the drive to achieve (Lewis, 1973).

COGNITION

Entrepreneurs are said to be able to imagine a different future. They envision or discover new products or services. They perceive or recognize opportunities. They assess risk and figure out how to profit from it. They identify possible new combinations of resources. Common to all of these is the individual's use of their perceptual and reasoning skills, what we call cognition, a term borrowed from the psychologists' lexicon (Katz et al., 2003).

Many people may identify an opportunity but it's the entrepreneur who takes action by using the cognitive properties necessary to exploit it (Shane & Venkataraman, 2000).

According to Baron & Ward (2004), research suggests that entrepreneurs generally have arrangement cognitions—thoughts and mental frameworks concerning the resources, relationships, and assets needed to engage in entrepreneurial activity; willingness cognitions-thoughts and mental frameworks that support commitment to starting a new venture; and ability cognitions—thoughts and mental frameworks concerning the skills, knowledge and capacities needed to create a new venture. Recent findings (Mitchell et al., 2002) suggest that entrepreneurs who are high in certain aspects of all three dimensions make better choices in hypothetical business situations than non entrepreneurs—that is, they show evidence of having better developed and richer cognitive scripts for such situations (Baron & Ward, 2004).

GENETIC FACTORS

Genetic factors may play a role in who becomes an entrepreneur and who does not. Nicolaou et al., (2008) studied 609 monozygotic and 657 dizygotic (same sex) twins to indicate whether genetic disposition plays a part in determining who becomes an entrepreneur and who does not. Findings were reasonably high supporting heritability for entrepreneurship with little consequence of family setting and background (Nicolaou et al., 2008).

One study looked at different measures of entrepreneurial activity and found that between 37 and 42 percent of the differences between people in their tendency to have started businesses; been self-employed; been owner operators of businesses; and engaged in the start-up process, is accounted for by genetic factors (Shane, 2008).

CULTURE

Culture, as the underlying system of values peculiar to a specific group or society, shapes the development of certain personality traits and motivates individuals in a society to engage in behaviors that may not be evident in other societies (Mueller & Thomas, 2001). Cross cultural studies conducted by Hofstede have shown that approximately 50 percent of the differences in work-related attitudes are explained by culture (Hofstede, 1980).

In Jamaica, the Chinese are overrepresented in business and entrepreneurship. And, they have a reputation for industriousness. In the past, young Chinese boys were sent to China to learn the culture before being sent back to Jamaica. This ensured that the Chinese cultural traditions were maintained. The Chinese owned most of the small groceries found in Jamaican towns and villages and many attribute the experience of working in them as a preparation for other business pursuits. Geert Hofstede conducted cross cultural studies and found that culture explained approximately 50 percent of the differences in work-related attitudes (Hofstede, 1980).

In researching his popular book, *Outliers*, Gladwell found that success is not merely a function of individual merit and that it was important to look beyond the individual to his or her culture, family background, values, and even often overlooked factors such as birth date and luck (Gladwell, 2008). According to Gladwell, to understand success the focus should be on where the individual is from, rather than who he or she is:

> What I came to realize in writing Outliers, though, is that we've been far too focused on the individual—on describing the characteristics and habits and personality traits of those who get furthest ahead in the world. And that's the problem, because in order to understand the outlier I think you have to look around them—at their culture and community and family and generation. We've been looking at tall trees, and I think we should have been looking at the forest (Gladwell.com).

Cultural differences exist at multiple levels such as regional, ethnic, and organizational levels, but their influence is more readily recognizable at the national level and therefore it is appropriate for researchers to use the word culture when referring to national culture (Hofstede, 199).

According to a study by Mueller & Thomas, culture:

> …may condition potential for entrepreneurship, generating differences across national and regional boundaries. One tentative conclusion is that a "supportive" national culture will, ceteris paribus, increase the entrepreneurial potential of a country. This suggests that in addition to support from political, social, and business leaders, there needs to be a supportive culture to cultivate the mind and character of the potential entrepreneur. To be motivated to act, potential entrepreneurs must perceive themselves as capable and psychologically equipped to face the challenges of a global, competitive marketplace (Mueller & Thomas, 2001).

Non-conformity

Entrepreneurs are known for thinking "outside the box," going against the crowd and being non-conformists. According to Cummins & Kelly

(2010), right hemisphere dominant entrepreneurs tend to question accepted approaches and explanations. In this sense they are non-conforming. This is the same right hemisphere ability that leads them to do something that may involve a risk or be innovative. An approach to curriculum and the delivery of a curriculum that prescribes one way of thinking and bases assessment on being confined to this can work against the way the entrepreneurial mind thinks. Their findings show overwhelming evidence that entrepreneurs questioned and challenged accepted views at school and preferred to consider options than to be given one way to do something. It is possible that this person can often be seen as a "trouble maker" in the class and either removed by those in authority or left to drift out of the system (Cummins & Kelly, 2010):

> The differences in approaches to and ways in how people learn have been comprehensively studied for decades. From these investigations, the concept of individualized "learning styles" emerged during the 1970s and gained increased popularity in recent years. It differs from ability in that one learning style is not presumed to be better than another (Messick, 1994). Right and left hemispheric dominance (also known as lateralization) is one of the most fundamental categories of learning preferences. It is based on the theory that each of the cerebral hemispheres "works" in different and complementary ways. While both hemispheres are involved in learning, different preferences in learning are associated with the dominance of one hemisphere over another: The Left Hemisphere is associated with 'part-to-whole' thinking. Information is processed 'logically' and 'sequentially'. It focuses on detail. The Right Hemisphere is associated with 'whole-to-part' thinking. Information is processed 'holistically' or 'globally' (Cummins & Kelly, 2010).

Table 5 compares left and right hemisphere thinking tendencies.

TABLE 5 LEFT AND RIGHT HEMISPHERE TENDENCIES	
LEFT HEMISPHERE	**RIGHT HEMISPHERE**
FOCUSED ATTENTION	GENERALIZED ATTENTION
SEQUENTIAL THINKING	RANDOM THINKING
PREDICTABILITY	POSSIBILITY
DETAILS	BIG PICTURE
CONFORMING	NON-CONFORMING
REFLECTIVE	IMPULSIVE
LOGICAL	INTUITIVE
ABSTRACT	CONTEXTUALIZED

Source: Entrebraineur: Investigating Entrepreneurial Learning

The consummate non-conformist and "out of the box" thinker was Apple's founder Steve Jobs. He dropped out of college after only one semester. He took courses in subjects such as calligraphy. At one time, "he walked barefooted, ate a diet of mostly fruit, and practiced Buddhism." But he also brought to the masses the computer mouse, the graphic user interface, Apple computers, the iMac, iPhone, iPod, and the iPad.

Steve Jobs admits he gave trouble in school. He told an interviewer, "I was pretty bored in school and turned into a little terror…. We basically destroyed our teacher. We would let snakes loose in the classroom and explode bombs…I was thrown out of school a few times" (Sheff, 1985). As an innovator, he epitomized the "think different" and "To the crazy ones" philosophy that Apple computer popularized in its advertising campaigns. Thanks to his different way of thinking, he changed the ways in which we use computers, listen to music and communicate.

SOCIAL CAPITAL

Social capital can be defined as the many resources available to us through our personal and business networks. These resources include information, ideas, leads, business opportunities, financial capital, power, emotional support, goodwill, trust and cooperation. Without well-managed and well-built networks, however, these resources remain hidden. Even natural talent, intelligence, education, effort and luck are not individual attributes at all; they are developed shaped and expressed by and through relationships with others (Baker, 2000).

According to Ivan Misner social capital is:

> …in fact, very similar to its monetary sibling. It, too, is accumulated by an individual or a business and used, or is available for use, in the production of wealth. Put more simply, it's the accumulation of resources developed through personal and professional networks. These resources include ideas, knowledge, information, opportunities, contacts and, of course, referrals (Misner, 2004).

Social capital is built by design, not chance. According to Wayne Baker, author of *Achieving Success through Social Capital* , "Studies show that lucky people increase their chances of being in the right place at the right time by building a 'spider web structure' of relationships that catch information." Furthermore, according to Baker, "Success is social; all the ingredients of success that we customarily think of as individual—talent, intelligence, education, effort and luck—are intertwined with networks."

ENTREPRENEURS AND ECONOMIC DEVELOPMENT

According to Welsch, evidence continues to accumulate that the national level of entrepreneurial activity has a significant association with subsequent levels of economic growth…Literature cites that innovation is a critical driver of economic growth and means to develop and maintain prosperity (Welsch, 2004). And throughout the world, small entrepreneurial firms are viewed as dynamic and innovative enterprises that contribute to economic well-being, and entrepreneurship is perceived as an engine of economic and social development (Acs & Audretsch, 2005).

When history and culture in more than 40 countries over the last two decades are examined, some hypotheses emerge (Welsch, 2004). They are as follows.

- Entrepreneurship flourishes in communities where resources are mobile.

- Entrepreneurship is greater when successful members of a community reinvest excess capital in the projects of other community members.

- Entrepreneurship flourishes when the success of other community members is celebrated rather than derided.

- Entrepreneurship is greater in communities that see change as positive rather than negative.

According to Schumpeter's model of economic development, a perfectly competitive economy is in stationary equilibrium and there is no profit, no interest rates, no savings and no involuntary unemployment. The "circular flow" of this equilibrium repeats itself year after year and produces the same products over and over. Economic development only occurs when there is "spontaneous and discontinuous change in the circular flow." This disturbance of the equilibrium forever alters and displaces the previous equilibrium state. Innovations are what cause development since they produce new combinations which disrupt the stationary equilibrium state.

Innovations are produced by entrepreneurs who introduce a new product, a new method of production or the opening of a new market or a new source for raw materials or the new organization of an industry. These innovations are the:

> ...fundamental impulse that sets and keeps the capitalist engine in motion" and they come from the "new consumers, goods, the new methods of production or transportation, the new markets, the new forms of industrial organization that capitalist enterprise creates (Drucker, 1942).

The opening up of new markets, foreign or domestic, and the organizational development from the craft shop and factory...illustrate the same process of industrial mutation that incessantly revolutionizes the economic structure *from within*, incessantly destroying the old one, incessantly creating a new one. This process of Creative Destruction is the essential fact about capitalism (Drucker, 1942).

CHAPTER 2

The Historic and Socio-Political Climate in Jamaica

Christopher Columbus landed in Jamaica on his second voyage to the New World in 1494 and annexed the island on behalf of the Spanish monarchy. At the time, the island was populated by Taino Indian natives whom the Spanish enslaved and proceeded to exterminate. In the early years of the 16th century, the practice of importing slaves from West Africa to work in Jamaica began.

The British captured the island from the Spanish in 1655 and established a plantation economy based on sugar, cocoa, and coffee. Under the British plantation system, the island became the major producer and leading exporter of sugar in the world (Sugar Industry Authority of Jamaica, 2000). The British continued the Spanish practice of importing slaves from Africa to work on the plantations.

The Jews were among the first ethnic groups to settle in Jamaica, arriving in the early sixteenth century. Many came from Spain and Portugal where they fled the Spanish Inquisition, and although small in number they still have significant influence in Jamaica in business and commerce.

THE SPANISH OCCUPATION OF JAMAICA

The West Indian islands at the time of Columbus "were occupied by two distinct races of Indians. The most warlike of these, known as the Caribs, were not found in Jamaica…which was occupied by a more gentle race" (Gardner, 1873). The Indians of Jamaica were known as the Tainos. The Caribs and the Tainos both spoke a language known as Arawakan and for this reason they are sometimes referred to as Arawaks (Sherlock & Bennett, 1998).

Francisco de Garay was a companion to Columbus on his second voyage to the New World and was governor of Jamaica from 1514 to 1523. He was described as a "cruel, avaricious and vain man" who on reaching Jamaica introduced that system of slavery that had already reduced the Indians on Hayti and Cuba from millions to thousands, and which resulted there, as in Jamaica, in their utter extermination" (Gardner, 1873).

The Spanish never did much to develop the paradise they had discovered. They had plans to build a city in Seville de Nueva but had to abandon them for causes undetermined. According to Gardner, "the enforced abandonment of Seville led, with other causes to the comparative neglect of this beautiful island." They eventually built a settlement in St Jago de la Vega, now known as Spanish Town—on the other side of the island—which became the seat of government. Sugar plantations were established in several places, cotton was cultivated, also the vine from which good claret was made. The cattle introduced to the island flourished and numbers were exported to Cuba for sale. But, "never during the whole period of Spanish occupation had it been a prosperous colony. Its trade was at all times very insignificant" (Gardner, 1873).

THE BRITISH COLONY

Before sugar became king, the island provided most of the necessities of life for the British. But as sugar became the focus, other industries and products were not developed. For example, with almost no effort salt could have been obtained from natural salt ponds that existed on the island. Gardner laments:

> The earliest settlers seemed to have been far more alive than those of later days to the importance of preserving the numerous articles of food with which the island and the seas surrounding it abounded and moreover they did not at first discover the adaptation of the soil for the production of sugar. Perhaps had they even done so they would not have expended all their energies in the production of this single staple to the almost utter neglect of the other gifts of a gracious Providence so abundantly scattered on every hand. This was the folly of a later age. To preserve for use such food as it was not necessary or desirable to consume at once, salt was requisite. This article is now imported; the first settlers produced it themselves... Yet articles of food were largely imported...for sugar cultivation had then become the leading idea with men of substance...But that salt beef and pork, salt fish and mackerel should be then as now imported largely, can only be regarded in the light of a contribution to the history of human folly.

> It is idle to mourn the events of the irrevocable past but it is impossible to overlook the fact that if sugar had not become the chief staple of this magnificent island it would in all probability have become the home of hundreds of thousands of Englishmen

and men of English ancestry who in farming occupations and the cultivation of what are now called minor products would have founded a colony almost if not quite equal to those on the northern continent. The glorious mountain districts would gradually have been penetrated and in such climates as that of the Pedros, the highlands of Manchester, Clarendon, St Elizabeth, and the corresponding elevations of the north, the English settlers would have found a healthy pleasant and with a few needful precautions and regular habits an English colony would then have flourished (Gardner, 1873, 84).

This was not to be, "colonists gave place to sugar planters, sugar planters required slaves and gradually the island became a mighty aggregation of cane fields in which Negroes toiled and white men were the taskmasters" (Gardner, 1873).

Labor was cheap and the Jamaican soil was good. "...the sugars of Jamaica were worth five shillings a hundred weight more than those of Barbados, so greatly had the soil improved the plants" imported from Barbados.

ECONOMICS AND SLAVERY

Eric Williams in his book, *Capitalism and Slavery* contends that slavery in the Caribbean had been too narrowly identified with blacks and it was basically an economic and not a racial phenomenon as..."unfree labor in the New World was brown, white, black and yellow; Catholic, Protestant and pagan. And the first instance of slave trading and slave labor in the New World involved, racially, not the Negro but the Indian" (Williams, 1944).

According to Tortello:

> The cultivation of sugar was intricately intertwined with the system of slavery. This connection has set the course of the nation's demographics since the 18th century when slaves vastly outnumbered any other population group. The descendants of these slaves comprise the majority of Jamaica's population (Tortello, 2004).

Plantation Jamaica was:

> ...a garrison society, committed to the production of one major commodity, sugar, for export to the protected market in Britain as an integral part of the mercantile system. It was dedicated also to maintaining White superiority by a closed system of representative government and by maintaining and protecting the system of slavery and making money from sugar. It was incapable of change...the African-Jamaicans somehow found within themselves the obstinate strength to reject, and to continue to reject, slavery. They did so by marronage, sabotage and sporadic outbursts of violence as well as by acquiring the language, skills and knowledge of their masters (Sherlock & Bennett, 1998).

The mortality rate during slavery was very high. Children under four often died of epidemic disease and ignorance. Some mothers preferred to see their own children dead rather than be obliged to witness their daily punishment. Recently arrived slaves had one of the highest mortality rates. Records from the Worthy Park Estate showed that of 181 slaves bought, over a quarter had died after a year and a half. Environmental diseases, smallpox, fevers, the lack of the will to live soon struck them down. Add to this the tendency of some planters to overwork the slaves during the period of seasoning and so cause their death (Sherlock & Bennett, 1998, p.230).

In July 1833, a Bill to abolish slavery throughout the British Empire passed in the House of Commons, followed by the House of Lords on 1st August. The Act of Emancipation ended slavery in Jamaica and the Commonwealth Caribbean. The former slaves became "apprenticed laborers"—no longer slaves but not free citizens either. Full freedom was granted in 1838. Slave owners in Jamaica received £6,616,927 from the British Government as compensation for their loss and inconvenience. The emancipated people received no compensation, no guidance, no training to enable them to rearrange their lives independent of the oppressive slave plantation system (Sherlock & Bennett, P. 230 1998).

The abolition campaign in England was started by the Society of Friends, a religious group known as the Quakers. A central belief of theirs is the priesthood of all believers. They pleaded the case against slavery in a petition to Parliament in 1784. Others churches and individuals later joined the cause including such notables as Granville Sharp and Member of Parliament, William Wilberforce. William Allen, the scientist, was one of the first to stop eating sugar in protest. Although women had no vote and little political influence, they organized boycotts against buying sugar produced on plantations that used enslaved people.

Several factors contributed to the success of the bill to end slavery. The British economy was moving from sugar to cotton as the main product, fueled by the industrial revolution. Major slave revolts across the Caribbean—including the 1832 slave rebellion led by Jamaican National Hero Samuel "Sam" Sharpe—shocked the British government, terrified plantation owners, and made them see that the costs and dangers of maintaining slavery were too high. The once powerful West India Lobby lost political strength in the parliamentary reforms of 1832. The chorus demanding freedom for slaves had become almost universal and was supported by a coalition of non-conformist churches as well as evangelicals in the Church of England (*The Abolition Project*).

INDENTURED SERVANTS

When slavery was abolished in 1838, the planters turned to indentured servants from China, India, Germany and other places to provide the labor force for the sugar plantations. Upon completion of their service, many of these indentured servants moved into other areas of work.

In 1845, the first Indians arrived in Jamaica to work as indentured servants on the sugar plantations that had been abandoned by the African-Jamaicans after the abolition of slavery. The first laborers came from Northern India, but others arrived later from Uttar Pradesh, Bihar, the Central Provinces, Punjab and the North West Frontiers.

In 1854, the first Chinese migrants arrived as indentured laborers. Most were Hakka Chinese, a group of Han Chinese that is known for migrations to countries all over the world. They arrived from Hong Kong and from the Guangdong Province (formerly Canton) in southeast China. In the early years of the twentieth century, migrants from Palestine and Lebanon settled in Jamaica, fleeing political and religious persecution in their home countries and in search of a better way of life (embassyofjamaica.org).

KING SUGAR

By the year 1700 Jamaica was awash with sugar plantations:

> Each estate was its own small world, complete with an entire labor force of field workers and skilled artisans, a hospital, water supply, cattle, mules and horses as well as its own fuel source. Each plantation fueled the wheels of British mercantilism. Sugar, molasses and rum were exported to England for sale and ships were financed to return to Africa and collect more slaves in exchange for trinkets and transport them to the West Indies as a labor source. This became known as The Triangular Trade. Money was not left in England's colonies, the financing came from Mother England, and to Mother England the profits returned.

> To a large extent, Jamaican customs and culture were fashioned by sugar.

> According to John Hearne (1965), for two hundred years sugar was the only reason behind Jamaica's existence as a centre for human habitation (as quoted in Sherlock and Bennett, 2001, p. 157). For centuries, sugar was Jamaica's most important crop.

Jamaica was once considered the 'jewel' in Britain's crown. In 1805, the island's peak of sugar production, it produced 101,600 tonnes of sugar. It was the world's leading individual sugar producer (Tortello, 2004).

Jamaica's economy in the Depression years was still dominated by the production and refining of sugar cane for export. The island's economic crisis was, first and foremost, a sugar crisis. Increased availability of cheap refined sugar on global markets and a widespread switch to beet sugar to help meet European demand made Caribbean sugar production commercially unprofitable for much of the pre-war decade. Imperial preference backed by British subsidy of Jamaican sugar prices kept the industry afloat, while Canada played a crucial role as a reserved market for British West Indian sugar. Facing declining profit margins, private plantation owners and larger foreign-owned commercial concerns cut production costs to the bone (Thomas, 2008).

According to Professor Norman Girvan, former director of the Sir Arthur Lewis Institute of Social and Economic Studies at the University of the West Indies:

> In the 17th and 18th centuries the sugar colonies of the Caribbean were among the richest places on earth, more highly valued than the North American colonies. The profits enriched capitalists in Britain, France and Holland; and stimulated shipbuilding and other industries supplying the Triangular Trade. Very little was invested in economic diversification, infrastructure, industrial development and educating the population. Hence after slavery was abolished and the plantations became unprofitable, the sugar colonies went into decline (Girvan, 2012).

In 1938 Jamaica and other Caribbean islands experienced riots and civil unrest. Jamaica's unrest was centered on the Frome sugar factory. Lord Moyne was sent from England to conduct an inquiry into the islands' long-term future. He identified extreme poverty as one cause of the disturbances:

Endemic urban unemployment, the settler oligarchy's hold on prime agricultural land, and failure to diversify crop production and so break the dominance of the sugar plantation in the rural economy, were all identified as structural economic problems requiring urgent redress (Thomas, 2008).

BANANAS

Despite the banana's popularity in the tropics, it remained virtually unknown in the USA. One of the first to sell the fruit outside the tropics was a sea captain from Cape Cod, Lorenzo Baker who came across the fruit in

Jamaica on an unscheduled stop in Port Antonio, Jamaica and took some to New Jersey in 1870. He sold the fruit at a substantial profit and began shipping them back on a regular basis. He and a partner would eventually form the Boston Fruit Company. This company would later merge with another to form the United Fruit Company which dominated the trade in bananas (Koeppel, 2008, 52).

In the 1880s banana replaced sugar as the main export and more remunerative crop. Sugar prices had come under pressure as production of beet sugar increased worldwide. Sugar is very labor intensive while banana is not. Also the capital requirements were much lower for bananas—no factory infrastructure was required. This shift resulted in a drop in agricultural employment which normally is a good thing as it indicates increased employment in manufacture and other higher paying sectors—but this was not the case in Jamaica. Sugar's share of exports fell from 45 percent in 1870 to eight percent in 1910 while the share of bananas went from one percent to 52 percent (Eisner, 1961).

In the latter half of the 20th century, the Jamaican economy was dominated by mineral extraction, metal refinement and tourism. In fact, the development of the sugar sector was neglected to the point where it lost its international competitiveness. Jamaica exports sugar within the quotas provided by the EU and the USA, and the country's own production does not meet its own consumption needs, so that imports of sugar have taken an upward turn over the same period (Laaksonen, 2007).

THE WEST INDIES FEDERATION

The West Indies Federation was established in 1958 and comprised the ten territories of: Antigua and Barbuda, Barbados, Dominica, Grenada, Jamaica, Montserrat, the then St Kitts-Nevis-Anguilla, Saint Lucia, St Vincent and Trinidad and Tobago. The Federation was established by the British Caribbean Federation Act of 1956 with the aim of establishing a political union among its members.

The Federal government was headed by an executive governor-general, appointed by Britain and included a prime minister, elected from among and by the members of the House of Representatives, a Cabinet, comprising the prime minister and ten other elected members chosen by him. It also had a Council of Senate, a House of Representatives and a Senate.

The Federation, however, faced several problems. These included: (i) the governance and administrative structures imposed by the British; (ii) disagreements among the territories over policies, particularly with respect to taxation and central planning; unwillingness on the part of most territorial governments to give up power to the federal government; and (iii) the location of the federal capital.

The decisive development, which led to the demise of the Federation, was the withdrawal of Jamaica—the largest member—after conducting a national referendum in 1961 on its continued participation in the arrangement. The results of the referendum showed majority support in favor of withdrawing from the Federation. This was to lead to a movement within Jamaica for national independence from Britain. It also led to the now famous statement of Dr. Eric Williams, the then premier of Trinidad and Tobago that, "one from ten leaves nought," referring to the withdrawal of Jamaica and signifying and justifying his decision to withdraw Trinidad and Tobago from the federal arrangement a short while later (CARICOM, 2011)

INDEPENDENCE

After a rebellion in Morant Bay in 1865, in which 439 Black Jamaicans were killed directly by soldiers, and 354 more were arrested and later executed, the Governor of the island, fearing further violence, appealed to the National Assembly to surrender their government in favor of making the island a pure crown colony in which the entire legislature was nominated by the British Crown. In 1884, a semi-representational system was introduced but was frequently criticized as all authority rested with the governor (Black, 1958).

By 1938, protest action by labor groups demanding better wages and improved working conditions paved the way for the rise of national leaders such as Sir Alexander Bustamante and Norman Washington Manley, and the formation of political parties. Criticisms of the Crown Colony government grew louder (JIS).

In 1944, all men and women over twenty-one years were allowed to vote for the first time in Jamaica's history, thanks to universal adult suffrage. Britain substituted the crown colony system with a bicameral Parliament, comprising a House of Representatives and a Legislative Council.

On August 6, 1962, Jamaica was granted full independence from Britain. The island experienced several years of economic growth, initially, but has since struggled to find its economic footing in an increasingly complex world.

According to native son and Harvard sociologist, Orlando Patterson:

Jamaica is a test case of all that's best and worst about democratic regimes in less developed countries. It shares with most of the other Caribbean islands of the British Commonwealth a deeply rooted commitment to personal freedom and democratic governance. Voter participation rates here put the United States to shame. What's more, unlike Japan and many other modern democracies, it has repeatedly passed the ultimate test of any thoroughly institutionalized democracy: it has had several changes of government since independence in 1962, the two dominant parties each having ruled and been thrown out of office by the voters about the same number of times. Supporting this democracy are a free and vigilant press, a sophisticated tradition of social and political discourse, and a vibrant civil society. The country also has a complex and highly developed popular culture and intellectual tradition... The bad news is that Jamaica's attempts at economic development have largely failed. (Patterson, 2001).

THE 1970s - DEMOCRATIC SOCIALISM

Jamaica was hurt in the oil shock of the 1970s and its fiscal problems were compounded by the socialist policies of Prime Minister Michael Manley. Manley's government misspent foreign loans, discouraged entrepreneurship, and annoyed the United States by flirting with Fidel Castro (Cassel, 2001).

Two years after being elected prime minister on a mandate of social change, Michael Manley made his most ambitious move to ensure equal opportunities for Jamaicans by announcing in November 1974 that democratic socialism would be the country's new political philosophy. At a People's National Party (PNP) rally in Trench Town, Kingston, Manley said: "The capitalist system is the system that brought slavery to Jamaica. Under capitalism, we supported 300 years of colonialism and no way shall capitalism continue in Jamaica. Socialism is running Jamaica now!" (*Gleaner*, June 20, 2005).

Manley's vision was one of "equality and justice" and to that end he enacted sweeping social reforms that earned him the love of the people. The foreign-owned electricity, telephone, bus and other companies were nationalized. Secondary education was made free and accessible, and a partial land reform policy was enacted.

According to Arnold Bertram, a historian and former parliamentarian, writing in the *Jamaica Gleaner*:

> The Jamaica which Michael Manley inherited had nearly doubled its per capita income in the previous decade, with direct private foreign investment reaching an all-time high as the economy grew at an average of six percent between 1967 and 1972. The problem, as he perceived it, was more so one of equity than production, and consistent with this analysis it was social reconstruction of society to which he primarily committed himself. This commitment was reflected in the range of social legislation and interventions which dominated his entire administration (Bertram, 2006).

The economy deteriorated and international reserves dwindled during Manley's first term forcing the government to approach the IMF for assistance with balance-of-payments support. Strapped with an ailing economy, the Jamaican Government agreed to an IMF stabilization program a few months before the 1976 election. Manley initially rejected the IMF terms, saying "we are not for sale."

In the December 1976 election Manley was re-elected in a landslide, winning 47 of the 60 seats in the parliament. But after Manley's refusal to adhere to the terms of the IMF, "the economy was strangled by sanctions while a media campaign sent a wave of fear among potential tourists. Lay-offs increased, interest rates skyrocketed and everything from soap to canned fish was in desperately short supply." According to Abbie Bakan, University of Toronto social sciences professor and author of a book on Jamaican politics:

> ...this was the limit of social democratic reform. Manley would soon prove an unreliable ally of the poor and the working class—and there would not be sufficient independent organization among the mass of the Jamaican working class to steer their own course when he started to retreat (Bakan, 2007).

Manley abandoned democratic socialism, embraced the market and announced the "People's Plan" for new economic and political reform in 1977. By May of that year, Jamaica had accepted an IMF "standby agreement" of £38 million to ease the balance of payments crisis. The IMF re-established a line of credit—with massive strings attached:

> The loan was conditional on an attack on the standard of living of the population. The poorest were hit the hardest, with a dramatic cut in public spending as the leading edge of the program. At the end of the eight years of Manley's democratic socialism, the average income in Jamaica was 25 percent lower and the cost of living 320 percent higher (Bakan, 2007).

THE 1980s

Edward Seaga's Jamaica Labour Party defeated Michael Manley's government in the 1980 elections—the same year Ronald Reagan won the election in the US. Seaga would be the first foreign leader to visit Reagan after his inauguration. The IMF agreement continued under Seaga but many unprecedented hardships resulted from the adjustments that were imposed by the IMF as a condition for any disbursement of funds.

According to an article entitled, *In the Clutches of the IMF,* published on January 13, 2013 in the *Jamaica Observer*:

> In the case of the average consumer, a plank of the structural adjustment program was a sharp reduction in the public sector of 30,000 workers. The decision by the Government of the day to pursue this strategy further cemented the social antagonism of the previous period and led to a national strike spearheaded by the unions. Additionally, the liberalization of the product markets was seen as the death knell of the small farmer, especially in sugar and bananas.

The article goes to point out that the irony of this period is that, in conjunction with preferential duties by the American Government (the Caribbean Basin Initiative), progress was made in generating new jobs and there was also improvement in the growth figures, but this was accompanied by an increase in the debt to GDP ratio.

Seaga would lose the 1989 elections because:

> ...the stridency of the Seaga Administration in implementing the structural adjustment program—even despite his reluctance to devalue the currency on one occasion—made the Administration appear unsympathetic to the concerns of the poor. It is in this context that the change in Administration in 1989 is sometimes interpreted. ("In the clutches of the IMF," *Jamaica Observer*, January 13, 2013).

THE 1990s

According to Norman Girvan, the 1990s was a lost decade as far economic growth is concerned. The *Economic and Social Survey* for 1998 shows that real income per person in that year was six percent below the 1990 level. The decline of manufacturing, weak export performance and growing dependence on remittances from abroad are other signs of lack of dynamism in the economy during the 1990s. Recent problems in the health, education and security sectors and a marked upsurge in violent crime and other social pathologies attest to the deterioration in human and social capital during the decade (Girvan, 1999).

FINANCIAL SECTOR MELTDOWN

In the 1990s, Jamaica's financial sector experienced a serious melt-down or banking crisis from which the island is still recovering. According to Laeven & Valencia in a:

> ...systemic banking crisis, a country's corporate and financial sectors experience a large number of defaults and financial institutions and corporations face great difficulties repaying contracts on time. As a result, non-performing loans increase sharply and all or most of the aggregate banking system capital is exhausted. This situation may be accompanied by depressed asset prices (such as equity and real estate prices) on the heels of run-ups before the crisis, sharp increases in real interest rates, and a slowdown or reversal in capital flows. In some cases, the crisis is triggered by depositor runs on banks, though in most cases it is a general realization that systemically important financial institutions are in distress (Laeven & Valencia, 2008).

The economic environment in Jamaica in the 1990s was characterized by high inflation, high interest rates plus a declining dollar. For example, in 1990 the lending interest rate was 25 percent but by 1995 it had risen to 50 percent. The Inflation rate was an astounding 35 percent in 1994. The Jamaican dollar dropped against the US dollar from 7:1 in 1990 to 37:1 in 1995.

According to Dr. Neville Swaby, acting vice-dean, College of Business and Management, and executive director, UTECH/JIM School of Advanced Management, the fundamental causes of the Jamaican banking crisis were:

(a) financial sector governance;

(b) government macroeconomic policies;

(c) bank regulation and supervision;

(d) the domestic entrepreneurs; and

(e) management of financial institutions.

From 1993, the commercial banks began to suffer the consequences of high liquid asset reserves and excessively high interest-rate structures. The cash-reserve ratio (CRR) ranged from 22 percent to 25 percent, and liquid reserve ratio (LRR) ranged from 47 percent to 50 percent. The lending rates of commercial banks were excessively high, ranging from 61.3 percent per annum in 1993 to a low in 1997 of 44.22 percent per annum (Swaby, 2011).

Many of the island's financial institutions were experiencing "declining profitability, illiquidity and a reduction in asset quality as loan repayments began to lag and the real estate market, upon which the quality of many loans was dependent, stagnated" (Wint, 1997). Fear and rumors of an imminent banking collapse gripped the island. In order to restore calm to the sector, the government created the Financial Sector Adjustment Company (FINSAC) Limited, to resolve the problems.

FINSAC provided assistance to five banks, five life insurance companies, two building societies, and nine merchant banks. Government recapitalized 21 troubled institutions via non-tradable government guaranteed bonds. By June 30, 2000 the outstanding recapitalization bonds were estimated to account for 44 percent of Jamaica's GDP (Laeven & Valencia, 2008).

Wilberne Persaud, a former head of the Department of Economics at The University of the West Indies, Mona and a member for all six years of the operational life of the FINSAC, lays most of the blame for the meltdown on the indigenous financial institutions in his book, *Jamaica Meltdown: Indigenous Financial Sector Crash 1996*. According to Persaud, in the lead-up to the crash, there was a blind, unwarranted optimism evident in the behavior of Jamaica's indigenous financial sector institutions. In a search for profits and rapid capital gain, the groups attempted to grow too quickly in a period of both rising interest rates and high inflation. They invested other people's money, predominantly in commercial real estate.

The crash affected the local indigenous institutions while the foreign-owned banks continued with business as usual. The overseas institutions were constrained by foreign supervision and good banking practice while it appears that many of the local institutions that crashed had embarked on unsupervised and risky practices (Persaud, 2006).

An opposing explanation of the meltdown is provided by Dr. Paul Chen-Young in his book, *The Entrepreneurial Journey in Jamaica, when Politics Derail*, which argues that the collapse was mostly due to the government's monetary and macroeconomic policy. He is supported in a foreword by former Prime Minister Edward Seaga, who states that the government reacted to the gross distortions that existed in the financial system by significantly reducing the money supply in 1996 from 33.2 percent to 10.7 percent which created chaos in the financial system and the crash followed (Sangster, 2007).

One banker who suffered in the meltdown supports the view that the government policies led to the crash. He makes the following points. First, in the political climate of the time that preceded the crash, there was pressure on the local financial intuitions to support the government's initiatives at diversification of operations. Second, there was encouragement to engage in non-traditional core business. The banks were encouraged to move from merely holding government paper as securities and to invest in non-core real-life businesses. Third, the government itself engaged in these practices (Sangster, 2007).

In October 2008, a commission of enquiry was appointed to probe the collapse of the financial sector in the 1990s and the resulting treatment of people whose debts were taken over by the government-owned FINSAC. While the hearings have been concluded, no report has yet been published.

JAMAICA AND THE IMF

Jamaica first became involved with the International Monetary Fund (IMF) in 1977, according to Michael Witter, senior research fellow at the Sir Arthur Lewis Institute of Social and Economic Studies at the University of the West Indies:

> Seven of the 12 agreements with the IMF were cancelled because Jamaica failed some performance tests. Of the five that were completed, two required special waivers of performance tests by the IMF. The critics of the IMF among us believe that the conditions of the loans were too harsh for Jamaica to meet. The defenders of the IMF among us believe that governments' mismanagement of the agreements caused us to fail so many, and not to benefit much from those we managed to complete (Witter, 2012).

Whatever the reason, the economy has failed to generate much traction since working with the IMF. As Witter explains:

> In all the loan agreements, the IMF has called for reducing the government's Budget deficit. Inevitably, this means increasing taxes and reducing non-debt expenditure on social services and economic development projects. Allied to this is the sale of public enterprises in order to raise revenue, as well as to reduce the role of the State in the economy. The momentum of these agreements has shifted the focus of the Jamaican State away from social and economic development to repayment of debt and providing security against antisocial behavior by large sections of the population who feel disenfranchised and excluded.

> The IMF always asks for exchange-rate flexibility, which means reducing the value of the Jamaican dollar. That always drives up the costs of imports, and hence all

DR. GLEN LAMAN

costs, but never stimulates Jamaica's traditional exports. Devaluations may make non-traditional exports more attractive to foreigners, but we have too few of those to make any significant difference to our balance of payments. Over the course of these agreements, the IMF led the campaign to liberalize the Jamaican economy, arguing that the free play of market forces would promote the growth of the economy. The record of extremely low growth—less than one percent per year—is evidence that these projections were uniformly optimistic (Witter, 2012).

Michael Manley questioned the appropriateness and effectiveness of the IMF "medicine" for Third World countries such as Jamaica in his book, *Up the down Escalator: Development and the International Economy; a Jamaican Case Study:*

> To what extent are IMF adjustment strategies helpful in Third World context? And to what extent should they be subject to change? Jamaica's experience stands as eloquent testimony to the role of the IMF in maintaining the status quo internationally while furthering the cause of the free enterprise system, in general, and Western capitalism in particular...The Third World dilemma does not consist of underutilized capability but underdevelopment with regards to the broad social needs of the group.

> It does not escape attention that the major beneficiaries of the opening up of the economy are the big producers of the developed countries whose goods immediately begin to flood the local market...there is the assumption that only private sector expenditure, management and planning can solve the economic problems of a particular country...but Third World private sectors are by no means shining examples of entrepreneurial imagination, managerial skill, and technological innovativeness (Manley, 1987).

In May 2013, the IMF approved a long awaited and highly anticipated Extended Fund Facility agreement with Jamaica. But some voices expressed caution in the months leading up to the agreement. According to Delroy Warmington, writing in the *Jamaica Observer:*

> It will help Jamaica regain access to the capital market, but this will only be a Band-Aid solution. Obviously, a chasm has opened up between the IMF and Jamaica. No doubt the Government has been profligate. Wasteful spending is prevalent throughout. There is nothing in the anticipated agreement that addresses the real problem of the Jamaican economy, which is growth. And austerity will only diminish domestic demand even though this could be only temporary.... Regardless of what the IMF proposes, the focus should be on growing the economy. A robust economy can solve any debt or deficit problem (Warmington, 2013).

REMITTANCES

Jamaica has one of the highest rates of remittances in the Latin American and Caribbean region ranking 5th according to the World Bank. In 2011, more than US$2 billion were sent to the island by Jamaicans overseas. This represented approximately 14 percent of GDP and is the top contributor to the island's foreign exchange (Bank of Jamaica).

> According to Jamaican economist, Dennis Morrison:
> ...the rise in remittances has been dramatic over the past decade, with this source of foreign-exchange inflows outstripping all export sectors. In 2008, remittances amounted to US$2.3 billion, up from US$661 million in 1997, or nearly four times. Over the period, some US$16.5 billion came from this source, and if we go back to 1982, the figure rises to US$20.2 billion (Morrison, 2009).

This rate of remittances is maintained by a high rate of migration of tertiary graduates. At 85 percent it is the second highest rate in the world. The top destination for emigrants is the United States followed by the United Kingdom, Canada, The Cayman Islands, The Bahamas and Antigua and Barbuda.

TOURISM

Jamaica is one of the top five tourism-generating destinations in the Caribbean, after the Dominican Republic, Puerto Rico, The Bahamas and Cuba (Wood, 2006). Tourism contributed some US$2 billion (J$170 billion) to the economy in 2010 and is the second biggest earner of foreign exchange for the island (Jackson, 2012).

Visitor arrivals by air and sea hit a record 3.07 million in 2011, an increase of 8.4 percent over 2010 and an all time record for the island. US, Canadian and European visitors, account for the three largest groups of tourists to the island (Jackson, 2012). The Falmouth cruise facility, which opened in March 2011, accounted for much of the visitor growth, with 1.12 million arrivals, up 25 percent from 909,619 arrivals in 2010. Nearly half of all cruise ship visitors to Jamaica docked at the Falmouth Pier, and the port has made Jamaica the Caribbean's fastest-growing cruise destination according to statistics from the Jamaica Tourist Board.

Visitors from the United States of America declined during the period, down 1.4 percent to 1,225,565, while Canadian visitor totals increased by 16.5

percent to 379,000 arrivals. Tourist arrivals from the Europe and the United Kingdom were down 7.2 percent versus 2010, to 253,049.

The average room capacity in 2011 grew by 3.2 percent in 2011, moving from 18,759 rooms in 2010 to 19,369 rooms in 2011. Total room nights sold of 4,275,303 increased by 3.1 percent in 2011 compared to 4,145,603 room nights sold in 2010. Hotel room occupancy was at the same level as in 2010 at 60.5 percent. The number of stopovers that intended to stay in hotel accommodations increased from 1,286,366 in 2010 to 1,314,135, an increase of approximately 2.2 percent in 2011.

BAUXITE

Bauxite was first produced commercially in Jamaica in 1952 by Reynolds Metals Ltd. In only six years, Jamaica became the largest producer of bauxite in the world. It retained this position until 1971, when it was surpassed by Australia. In the late 1980s, Jamaica ranked third in worldwide production behind Australia and Guinea and accounted for roughly 13 percent of world output of bauxite and seven percent of alumina.

Bauxite mining is carried out by open-pit methods, so no miners work underground. The topsoil is cleared from a few acres and the underlying bauxite is removed with huge mechanical shovels. A single deposit 50 acres in extent may yield over five million tons before it is exhausted and the land restored. Some of the mining companies export the bauxite itself. They dry the ore in rotating ovens and load it onto ships at the north coast ports of Discovery Bay and Ocho Rios to be taken to their alumina factories in the United States. In alumina factories, bauxite is processed first into alumina, and then into aluminum by electrolysis.

During the first half of the 1980s, Jamaican bauxite production declined drastically as half of the six North American operators ceased production or left the island completely, and world prices for bauxite entered a prolonged depression because of oversupply. The departure of foreign companies encouraged the government to buy into the bauxite industry, and by 1986 the government-run Clarendon Aluminum Plant was the most successful producer on the island.

Although generally beneficial for the economy—exports of bauxite and alumina make up about 10 percent of GDP—Jamaica's bauxite industry must import large amounts of caustic soda and heavy machinery to mine and export the ore, making the industry highly import intensive. Likewise, the mining of the ore has raised environmental concerns over bauxite by-products discharged in highly visible red lakes.

MICRO SMALL AND MEDIUM ENTERPRISES (MSME)

The Jamaican Ministry of Industry, Investments and Commerce defined the MSME sector as follows.

- Micro enterprises—one to three employees and / or annual sales turnover of < J$10m.

- Small enterprises—between four to 10 employees and /or an annual turnover of more than J$10,000,000 but less than J$40m.

- Medium enterprises—between 11 to 50 employees and or an annual sales turnover that falls between J$40m and J$150m.

The sole-trader category comprises the majority of the micro and small sector players with approximately 37.6 percent of the employed labor force, averaging approximately 411,600 persons in the year 2010. Males accounted for 65.3 percent and females 34.7 percent of this sole trader-employed labor force (PIOJ).

GLOBALIZATION

Jamaica was the subject of a full length documentary *Life and Debt* which illustrated the devastating impact globalization can have on a Third World country by contributing to the erosion of local agriculture and industry (Holden, 2001). As a result of globalization, Jamaica has had to eliminate trade restrictions and allow cheap imports free access to the local market.

One movie scene depicts how government subsidized powdered milk from America decimated the Jamaican fresh milk industry. Subsidized Idaho potatoes have similarly impacted Jamaican potato farmers. Another scene touches on the fate of the Jamaican banana industry where US complaints to the World Trade Organization (WTO) have deemed the preferential prices to the European market long enjoyed by the Caribbean islands to be in violation of WTO rules.

According to a WTO press release announcing a settlement on the long-running banana dispute between Latin American banana producing nations, the USA and the European Union, "the banana issue is one of the longest running disputes in the post-WWII multilateral trading system. It has generated considerable debate and litigation among the widest range of the entire WTO membership. And, it has resulted in multiple legal rulings by dispute panels, the Appellate Body and special arbitrators. All this attention has focused on the treatment the EU gives to the import of bananas from the African, Caribbean and Pacific (ACP) countries in preference to bananas from Latin America (WTO Press Release, 2009).

In April 1999, the WTO granted the USA authorization to impose sanctions up to an amount of US\$191.4 million per year on EU products entering the USA market. The latest agreement essentially removes the preferential treatment Europe provided their former colonies. In Jamaica's case, wages and production costs are much higher than those of USA companies operating in Latin American countries.

The benefits of globalization are well known. Countries can specialize in producing goods where they have a competitive advantage and import other goods at a cheaper price than they could produce them. It promotes lower prices for consumers, a wider choice of goods, access to export markets and competition in the global marketplace.

However, developing economies, like Jamaica, struggle to compete in the global market and claim most of the benefits are going to the developed countries. And developed countries, while pushing for free trade, maintain large subsidies to their agricultural sectors, for example.

"We have been reminded of the spread of the consequences of the process of globalization in a world that has become increasingly cold and heartless," with those words Former Prime Minister of Jamaica, the Hon. P.J. Patterson, in his closing address at the summit of the Group of 15 (G-15) in Jamaica in 1999, captured the sentiment of many a developing country struggling to cope with the impact of globalization on their economy (Associated Press, 1999).

CARICOM

The Caribbean Community (CARICOM) was established in August, 1973 to foster regional integration among Caribbean states. Its objectives are to foster economic cooperation through the Caribbean Common Market;

co-ordination of foreign policy among the independent Member States and common services and cooperation in functional matters such as health, education and culture, communications and industrial relations.

Jamaica's experience with CARICOM, the 15 member Caribbean common market, has not been good and the purported benefits of a single market of Caribbean states have not been realized:

> Complaints in Jamaica about CARICOM are primarily code for Trinidad and Tobago and that country's big trade surplus with Kingston. Last year, for instance, more than 80 percent of Jamaica's US$1.1 billion in imports from its CARICOM partners was from Trinidad and Tobago. The island exported a mere US$68 million to the region. Jamaican businesses complain that "Trinidad and Tobago provides energy subsidies to its manufacturers, affording them an unfair competitive advantage. They say, too, that Port-of-Spain maintains non-tariff barriers against Jamaican products (*Jamaica Observer*, 2012).

According to Edward Seaga, former prime minister of Jamaica:

> It became apparent that CARICOM, as an integrated organization, would fail to produce coherent integrated policies, especially a single market and economy. The Caribbean Single Market and Economy (CSME), the CARICOM standard bearer, had no agreed single currency nor could it support one although this was essential to lubricate regional transactions. It was evident that the differing productivity levels of different countries would increase exports in a few states while showing decrease in most others. A reality check, in this case, because the data was readily available, would have foretold that the CSME would be a grand design of conflicting performance in which Jamaica, disappointingly, would become the supermarket, not the factory (Seaga, 2012).

Amid an escalating trade war between Jamaica and Trinidad and Tobago, a frustrated former Jamaica commerce minister suggested what was once unthinkable: that his country consider leaving the Caribbean Community (CARICOM) regional trade bloc. "We should not support the notion of CARICOM forever; it must be CARICOM for as long as it satisfies Jamaica," Karl Samuda said during a recent budget debate. Jamaica's leaders have said the country is unlikely to leave CARICOM anytime soon, but the debate illustrates the larger challenge facing the regional bloc almost four decades after Caribbean leaders re-created the EU-like integration movement to allow for the free movement of goods, services and skilled labor across the geographically fragmented region (Luton, 2012).

CHAPTER 3

The Jamaican Diaspora and Doing Business in Jamaica

OVERVIEW

Jamaicans followed available employment opportunities in the region in the late 19th and early 20th centuries. Many moved to Central America to work on major construction projects such as the trans-Isthmian railway and the Panama Canal. Others moved to Cuba to provide labor for expanding sugar production there (Glennie & Chappell, 2010).

When the United States of America and the United Kingdom needed labor during World Wars I and II, both countries recruited workers from Jamaica and other Caribbean colonies. For instance, some estimates suggest that more than 10,000 Jamaicans—a mix of skilled and unskilled laborers—were recruited for the British West Indies Regiment as part of a strategy to draw in soldiers from the colonies (Glennie & Chappell, 2010).

Post-World War II reconstruction in the United Kingdom also required labor, much of which came from Jamaica and Barbados. Large numbers of skilled, semiskilled, and unskilled workers were recruited for hospital services, while others gained employment in industry and transport. The 1961 census in Great Britain recorded some 200,000 West Indians in England, of which half were from Jamaica (Glennie & Chappell, 2010).

However, in the 1960s, changing migration policies in traditional receiving countries altered the direction of Jamaican emigration. Restrictive immigration laws in the United Kingdom coincided with the passage of legislation in the United States of America and Canada that made education and skills more important determinants than nationality and race. From the late 1960s onwards, the United States became the chief destination for skilled migrants from Jamaica and the rest of the Caribbean (Glennie & Chappell, 2010).

Over the last several decades, no fewer than 1.3 million Jamaicans went legally to settle in countries such as the USA, UK, Canada and other countries which explain why it is often said that "as many Jamaicans live abroad as the 2.7 million who remain...." From 1971 through 1980, some 276,200 Jamaicans left the island, 142,000 for the USA. In the mid-1990s, there were 350,000 Jamaican-born people in the USA. Some estimate that the island lost perhaps as much as 40 percent of its middle class during this period.

The highest migration of nearly 300,000 occurred in the 1960s, and in the '70s, '80s and '90s, the outflow continued at just over 220,000 per decade. Being aggressively upwardly mobile and of working age, the migrant Jamaicans have been able to realize the economic means that allow them to remit funds home on a regular basis (Morrison, 2009).

According to Portes and Rumbaut in the book *Immigrant America*, there were 554,897 Jamaican-born people living in the USA in 2000. This represented 61 percent of the approximately 911,000 Americans of Jamaican ancestry. Many Jamaicans are second and third generations and descend from even older generations as there have been Jamaicans in the USA since the early twentieth century. The regional composition is as follows: 59 percent live in the northeast, mainly in New York; 4.8 percent in the Midwest; 30.6 percent in the southern United States, particularly South Florida; and 5.6 percent on the west. The New York metropolitan area and South Florida have the largest number of Jamaican immigrants in the United States (Portes & Rumbaut, 2006).

THE BRAIN DRAIN

According to Glennie & Chappell;

> Although many destination countries have limited labor migration, particularly in the context of the global economic downturn, migration remains important in Jamaican society. Despite its political stability, Jamaica is a poor country dependent on services, tourism, and remittances, with high unemployment generally—estimated at 14.5 percent in 2009—and limited employment opportunities for its most skilled citizens (Glennie & Chappell, 2010).

Some 20 percent of Jamaica's specialist nurses and eight percent of its registered nurses leave the island annually in pursuit of greener pastures overseas. This is according to senior UWI lecturer, Keith Nurse's policy paper entitled, "Diaspora, Migration and Development in the Caribbean." Additional information from the Ministry of Education suggests that approximately 2,000 teachers left the country between 2000 and 2002 (*Gleaner*, "Brain drain hurting Jamaica." December 11, 2007).

A study done by the Planning Institute of Jamaica and Dr. Pauline Knight concluded that over 82 percent of Jamaicans with tertiary level education that were living and working in the United States in the 1990s were trained in Jamaica. This brain-drain robs the country of much needed skilled and academic labor required for nation building (*Gleaner*, December 11, 2007).

GLOBAL ENTREPRENEURSHIP MONITOR (GEM)

The Global Entrepreneurship Monitor (GEM) is the largest ongoing study of entrepreneurial dynamics in the world. Started in 1989 as a partnership between the London Business School and Babson College, the first study covered 10 countries; since then nearly 100 'National Teams' from every corner of the globe have participated in the project, which continues to grow annually. The primary objective of GEM is to capture data on the attitudes, aspirations and activities of individuals to determine their entrepreneurial behavior. Jamaica joined the GEM project in 2005 and conducts two surveys: the National Experts Survey (NES) and the Adult Population Survey (APS).

One of the most important measures of entrepreneurship constructed and applied by GEM is the Total Early Stage Activity (TEA). The TEA is the proportion of the working age population who are either nascent entrepreneurs or new business owners-managers. The TEA rates of

TABLE 6	PRIMARY DESTINATIONS OF JAMAICAN EMIGRANTS		
Official Flow Data on Primary Destinations of Jamaican Emigrants by Decade, 1970s to 2000s			
Decade	Total number of migrants	United States	Canada	United Kingdom
1970s	327,779	256,984	56,964	13,831
1980s	239,207	201,177	33,973	4,057
1990s	212,892	170,291	39,443	3,158
2000-2006	135,493	117,205	15,374	2,914
Total	915,371	745,657	145,754	23,960
% of Total	100	82.4	15	2.6

Source: Thomas-Hope 2004 (updated to 2006).
Compiled from data in the Economic and Social Survey of Jamaica,
the Planning Institute of Jamaica, volumes for years 1970-2008.

ll countries participating in GEM showed that the average TEA for factor-driven countries (13.4%) was less than that in innovation-driven economies (14.1%) but twice as much in efficiency-driven states (6.9%) (*GEM 2011 Global Report*, p.12). Jamaica is considered a factor driven economy—characterized by extractive industries and subsistence agricultural undertakings, relying heavily on natural resources and labor.

According to the GEM Jamaica Report for 2011:

> Entrepreneurship as a career path is highly recognized and applauded in Jamaica. Eighty-one (81%) percent of working-age Jamaicans agreed with the statement that most people in the country consider starting a business as a desirable career choice. The average for all factor-driven countries is 77%, efficiency-driven countries—70%, and innovation-driven economies—57%. Indeed, much status is accorded to successful Jamaican entrepreneurs as 83% in the 18-64 age group supported the statement that in their country, successful entrepreneurs receive high status. Only 69% of persons in innovation-driven and efficiency-driven economies agreed with the aforesaid statement. Moreover, about 76% of all working-age Jamaicans agreed with the statement that they often see stories in the media about successful new businesses. The average for all factor-driven countries is only 58%, efficiency-driven—60%, and innovation-driven, 58% (GEM Jamaica 2011 Report).

Jamaica is categorized among the factor–driven economies. Characteristics of these economies include the utilization of labor and other factors to create economic value-added. The income levels of the APS sample are reflective of these characteristics. The majority (approximately 60% of respondents), falls within the lowest income category of J$0.0—J$211,639, the equivalent of US$0.0—US$2,404.00 per annum. Additionally, 18 percent of incomes is within the low income bracket of J$211,640—$411,639 (approximately US$4,625) annually. If nearly 80 percent of respondents earn less than US$4,625 per year, this has implications for consumer purchasing power and the ability to accumulate funds to start a business (*GEM 2011 Jamaica Report*).

With regard to the types of industries in which entrepreneurs were involved, the 'Retail Trade, Hotels & Restaurants' continued to be the industry of choice for entrepreneurs both at the early-stage (57.5%) and established business (EB) (48%) levels. This was followed by agriculture, forestry and fishing industries, with 18.8 percent for TEAs and 30.6 percent for EBs. However, unlike the retail trade where the TEA exceeds the EBs it is the opposite in agriculture, where there is greater participation of EBs

DR. GLEN LAMAN

in this sector and its related industries. Entrepreneurial participation in the other industries lagged way behind these two types. It is interesting to note that there were more established businesses involved in agriculture-related industries as opposed to early-stage businesses denoting some level of growth in the sector (GEM 2011 Jamaica Report).

GEM evaluates innovation from the perspective of the market and industry. This measure represents the extent an entrepreneur's product or service is new to some or all customers and where few or no other businesses offer the same product or service (Kelley, Singer and Herrington, 2012). The GEM 2011 global data indicated that innovativeness increases as economic development rises and that innovativeness is highest among the innovation-driven economies. Most Jamaican consumers (66%) did not consider their products or services new or unfamiliar, implying that the level of innovation in the country was low (GEM 2011 Jamaica Report).

DOING BUSINESS IN JAMAICA

According to the World Bank Report, *Doing Business 2013*, Jamaica ranked 90th out of 183 countries in its overall "Ease of Doing Business." This was a drop of five positions from the previous survey. Jamaica is headed the wrong way in several categories on this survey. For example, Jamaica ranks 123rd in the "Getting Electricity" category, a drop of 13 positions in the ranking from 2012. It ranks 129th in "Enforcing Contracts" and 105th and 104th in "Registering Property" and "Getting Credit" respectively.

It is clear that you have to surmount a variety of bureaucratic and legal hurdles to do business in Jamaica. Kimala Bennett, a young entrepreneur who wanted to register a video production business, was so frustrated by the convoluted process in Jamaica that she wrote a book to help others navigate the maze of permits and approvals. It is titled *Starting a Business in Jamaica* (Bennett, 2009).

THE ROAD AHEAD FOR JAMAICA

A growth inducement strategy document by the Planning Institute of Jamaica (PIOJ) recaps the Jamaican economy as follows:

> The Jamaican economy has been in a chronic state of near stagnation since the 1970s. During that time, there have been fits and starts, but no demonstrated capacity of the economy to sustain forward movement. The deadweight of that history now hangs heavily over the present. The process of awakening and recovery from this

state of inertia is a difficult one that will take time. It requires a systematic approach to designing and implementing integrated policy solutions aimed to modernize and transform the economy so as to meet the challenges of operating in a dynamic, competitive world where the country has lost ground relative to others that it led or equaled some 50 years ago. It also requires determined and forceful leadership (PIOJ, 2012).

With a high structural unemployment rate, many Jamaicans are forced to turn to "entrepreneurial activities" to survive. According to GEM economic growth is not driven by these "necessity" entrepreneurs, who decrease in number as the economy develops. The key to fostering growth is to support "opportunity" entrepreneurs, who launch new enterprises in response to market needs.

Universities in Jamaica have incorporated entrepreneurship programs into their curriculum. The University of Technology (UTECH) has established the Joan Duncan School of Entrepreneurship, Ethics & Leadership which offers a bachelor's degree in entrepreneurship. The UWI offers a bachelor's degree in entrepreneurship management studies. Also at UWI is the Vincent HoSang Entrepreneurship Programme which seeks to foster entrepreneurship among students.

Northern Caribbean University offers Bachelor of Science degrees with a major in entrepreneurship and an MBA in entrepreneurship marketing. The Morris Entrepreneurship Centre is also available to assist existing micro, small and medium size businesses (MSME) with access to professional services at a reasonable cost.

The Jamaica Business Development Corporation (JBDC) is another important resource available to new businesses. It provides business and technical support services across the spectrum, from guiding business startups to a wide range of consultancy advice for established businesses. Advisors and consultants who have experienced real-life business management are available to assist. The Incubator & Resource Centre (IRC) was established in 2008 to advance the productivity of MSMEs through: 1) access to production space in incubators for three specific sectors targeted by the Government of Jamaica: Fashion and Food and Craft; and 2) use of conference facilities, available to all sectors. The IRC also houses the Technical Services Unit which has responsibility for assisting clients in developing products that meet competitive international standards.

In 2011, the Branson Centre of Entrepreneurship—Caribbean was opened in Montego Bay, Jamaica by Sir Richard Branson, the English business magnate and founder of the Virgin Group of companies. The centre is a hub for aspiring entrepreneurs. Its mission is to offer practical business skills, access to coaches to offer guidance, mentors to share their experiences, professional services to build strong businesses, exposure to networks, finance and investment opportunities (Bransoncentre.org). The *Jamaica Observer* has also been encouraging entrepreneurship through its Entrepreneur of the Year program which recognizes local success stories.

PART II

Success Profiles of 15 Jamaican Entrepreneurs Who Defied the Odds

CHAPTER 4

Michael Lee-Chin, OJ

Michael Lee-Chin is a self-made billionaire and founder of Portland Holdings Inc. who went from night club bouncer to being on the cover of the Forbes' billionaire edition. He has also been listed as the seventh richest Black person in the world. He is regarded as a visionary entrepreneur whose philosophy of "doing well and doing good" has resulted in phenomenal success and inspiring philanthropic initiatives.

Michael Lee-Chin was born in Port Antonio, Jamaica in 1951. Port Antonio is the capital of the parish of Portland on the northeast coast of the island. The parish is a leading producer of bananas, coconuts, breadfruits, coffee, mangoes and ackee which are grown for export as well as local consumption.

According to the article, "Michael Lee-Chin Renaissance Man," he was raised by his teenage-orphan mother, Hyacinth, who worked three jobs to support them, including one as a bookkeeper at a high-end hotel. When Lee-Chin was seven, Hyacinth married Vincent Chen, who had had a son of his own before fathering seven children with Hyacinth (Stephenson, 2011). Lee-Chin's parents are both of mixed Chinese and Black heritage.

RESPONSIBILITY AT AN EARLY AGE

Lee-Chin described his childhood environment to Ian Portsmouth in this way:

> Back then, it was a town of about 8,000 people. It's a seaside town, very rural. Everybody knew everyone, so as a child, we were very safe. We could roam around as we pleased. For fun, we'd take slingshots we'd made ourselves and shoot birds. Or

we'd make yo-yos from discarded bus windows, which were made of Plexiglas. We were very, very creative and self-sufficient.

My parents were budding entrepreneurs. They ran a very small dry-goods store. At the age of 12, I had to take over the shop after school for three hours while my dad went out to sell Singer sewing machines. I had to do things like make change, cut cloth and close down the store, all by myself. So I had to shoulder responsibilities very early (Portsmouth, October 11, 2011).

EDUCATION

Lee-Chin recalls that from his class of 120 students in primary school, he was one of only two to go on to high school when he was awarded a "free place" tuition scholarship based on the Common Entrance Exam that all Jamaican students took between the ages of 11 and12. He went on to complete high school after which he worked and was able to save some money for college.

In 1970, Lee-Chin went to Canada to study civil engineering at McMaster University in Hamilton, Ontario. He was awarded a one year scholarship which paid for his second year of studies. When he realized he would not have sufficient funds to pay for his third year, he appealed to Hugh Shearer, Jamaica's prime minister at the time, for help from the government, even making a trip to Jamaica to make the request in person. His request was approved.

PORTLAND HOLDINGS INC.

After college, Lee-Chin decided to explore career opportunities within the mutual fund industry. At the age of 26, he became a financial advisor and worked two years at the Investors Group, in the Hamilton, Ontario office. His next job saw a promotion to regional manager.

In 1983, at the age of 32, he borrowed money to purchase shares of Mackenzie Financial stock. It was a company he understood; he had been selling their products. The stock appreciated seven-fold in four years and Lee-Chin used the profits to make his first acquisition, a small Ontario-based investment firm called AIC Limited for $200,000. Within 20 years, this 1987 acquisition grew from less than $1 million to, at one point, having more than $15 billion in assets under management and servicing over one million Canadians. AIC Limited was to become the first in a series of acquisitions for Lee-Chin, the Chairman of Portland Holdings, Inc.

BERKSHIRE

Lee-Chin created an additional financial firm with multiple divisions, known as Berkshire. It consisted of an investment planning arm, a securities dealership and an insurance operation. This company grew to manage over Can$12 billion in assets. Both of these companies were sold. In 2007, Manulife acquired Berkshire from Portland Holdings in exchange for shares. In 2009, Lee-Chin sold AIC Limited to Manulife for an unknown amount.

NATIONAL COMMERCIAL BANK

When Jamaica experienced financial turbulence in the late 1990s, he stepped in and acquired 75 percent of the National Commercial Bank of Jamaica (NCB) from the Jamaican Government for J$6 billion (US$127 million). Since becoming part of the Portland group, NCB profits have increased to approximately US$100 million from US$6 million. Today, NCB is Jamaica's largest bank with 45 branches, 2,400 employees, and offices in The Cayman Islands and the United Kingdom. National Commercial Bank was awarded the Latin Finance 2007 Bank of the Year Award (Portlandholdings. com, retrieved December 20, 2012).

OTHER JAMAICAN INVESTMENTS

Lee-Chin created a global money transfer company called Senvia Money Services in 2003. He also followed with buying out AIC Financial Group Limited, located in Trinidad and Tobago. In 2006, he bought an 85 percent stake in the United General Insurance Company, the largest auto insurer in Jamaica, and renamed the firm Advantage General Insurance Company. Around the same time, he bought a major stake in the CVM Communications Group, comprised of radio and television stations and newspapers.

COLUMBUS COMMUNICATIONS

In 2005, Portland partnered with the Risley Group to form Columbus Communications Ltd.—a Barbadian corporation that holds controlling interest in a number of telecommunications providers in the Caribbean including Cable Bahamas Ltd., Caribbean Crossing Ltd., Columbus Communications Jamaica Limited (operating under the name Flow America), Fibralink Jamaica Limited, and Columbus Communications Trinidad Limited (operating under the name Flow Trinidad).

Columbus is a diversified telecommunications company whose core operating business is providing cable television services, high speed internet access, digital telephone and internet infrastructure services (retail) and, the development of an undersea fiber optic cable network as well as the sale and lease of the telecom capacity provide by the network (wholesale). It operates in 21 countries throughout the Caribbean and Latin America (Portlandholdings. com).

TOURISM AND HEALTH CARE

In the tourism sector, Lee-Chin has guided Portland through a number of acquisitions in Jamaica. These include the Trident Villas and Spa in Jamaica, Reggae Beach and Blue Lagoon. The first Portland acquisition in the health care industry sector was in July 2006, when Medical Associates Limited, a privately held hospital in Kingston, Jamaica, joined the Portland group.

OTHER PORTLAND HOLDINGS

Portland Holdings Inc. also runs a private equity fund focused on investing in the Caribbean region. Clients include Overseas Private Investment Corporation (OPIC), a division of the US government; European Investment Bank (EIB); and Verizon Pension Fund and Export Development Canada (EDC).

Portland Holdings Inc. today owns a collection of diversified businesses, operating in sectors that include financial services, telecommunications, tourism, media and health care.

PROSPERITAS CUM CARITATE –
"NOT ONLY DO WELL, BUT ALSO DO GOOD"

Over the years, Lee-Chin's vision for sustainable growth for Portland Holdings Inc. has been anchored in two principles. First, Portland will invest in businesses that are economically substantial and provide exceptional products and services in the marketplace. And, equally important, these businesses must also seek to improve the social well-being of the communities in which they operate. Lee-Chin formally established as the Portland mantra —"prosperitas cum caritate"—which in Latin speaks to his goal that businesses must "not only do well, but also do good" – that is the measure of success (Portlandholdings.com, retrieved December 20, 2012).

THE MICHAEL LEE-CHIN CRYSTAL

In 2007, the Royal Ontario Museum (ROM) opened its new extension designed by Daniel Libeskind with Bregman+Hamann. It is called the Michael

Lee-Chin Crystal in honour of Lee-Chin who donated $30 million to the museum. The Crystal comprises five interlocking, self-supporting prismatic structures that interface with but are not attached to the original historic ROM buildings.

THE MICHAEL LEE-CHIN FAMILY INSTITUTE
FOR CORPORATE CITIZENSHIP

The AIC Institute for Corporate Citizenship, a respected research centre for corporate citizenship at the University of Toronto's Rotman School of Management was renamed the Michael Lee-Chin Family Institute for Corporate Citizenship (Lee-Chin Institute). The name was changed to honour the continuing involvement of founding donor Michael Lee-Chin and his family, following the sale of AIC's Canadian retail investment business. The Lee-Chin Institute's purpose is to help current and future business leaders integrate corporate citizenship into business strategy and practices.

HONOURS

In 2008, Lee-Chin received one of Jamaica's highest national honours—The Order of Jamaica, for his significant contributions to business and philanthropy. He was named Ernst & Young Entrepreneur of the Year *in the services category* in 1996.

He has been profiled in *Forbes, Fortune, Canadian Business, Black Enterprise,* and *National Post* magazines. The July 5, 2004 issue of *TIME* magazine named Michael Lee-Chin one of "Canada's Heroes"—and one of "the country's most intriguing and inspiring citizens."

In 2007, Lee-Chin received an honourary Juris Doctor degree from the University of Toronto in celebration of his visionary leadership and philanthropic initiatives. He also holds honourary Doctor of Laws degrees from McMaster University (2003), Northern Caribbean University (2007), Sir Wilfrid Laurier University (2008), University of the West Indies (2008), and York University (2009).

Lee-Chin is a divorced father of five children.

DISCUSSION

Lee-Chin's profile was compiled from published sources. He is reported to have said his success is a statistical probability. Born to a teenage orphan mother in colonial Jamaica, he was fortunate to win a scholarship that enabled him to get a high school education.

His early training in his parents' store no doubt boosted his self-efficacy. Self-efficacy may be defined as a person's belief in his or her ability to succeed in a particular situation. Stanford University psychologist Albert Bandura described these beliefs as determinants of how people think, behave, and feel (1994). This is often related to a person's family or parental influence.

As discussed earlier, one of the most prevalent factors found throughout the literature is that family or parental role models influence young adults to become self-employed (Henderson & Robertson, 1999; Scott & Twomey, 1988). This is not surprising as entrepreneurs often come from families with a self-employed parent (Collins & Moore, 1970).

Lee-Chin demonstrated out-of-the-box thinking when he appealed to the Jamaican prime minister for help with his tuition—not many students would have thought of doing that. Entrepreneurs often have to think outside the box to solve problems. They also have to take risks. Lee-Chin took calculated risks borrowing $500,000 to buy stock in McKenzie Financial whose upward trajectory he predicted correctly and which provided the funds to make his first acquisition. It was not just a wild gamble—he knew and understood the company and had been selling its products to his customers.

Bold moves have been a staple of Lee-Chin's success. These often involved going against the herd and being a non-conformist; entrepreneurial traits discussed earlier in this book. In 1999, while the telecom and dotcom booms were driving valuations into the stratosphere, Lee-Chin remained invested in cash-flow-generating businesses that no one wanted to buy. A major newspaper predicted a drop in his fund price as clients cashed in to chase the boom. He was expected to sell further depressing prices. He did just the opposite, he borrowed $50 million and bought more McKenzie stock at a discount and quickly made $100 million for himself and $400 million for his clients on the deal.

Vincent Chang, OD

Vincent Chang rose from very humble beginnings to create one of the most recognized brands in Jamaica—Tastee Limited. He transformed the Jamaican snack which consists of a meat filling surrounded by a flaky crust from an occasional snack to an important element in the island's cuisine and he built a fast food empire that satisfies consumers in Jamaica and other Caribbean islands.

Vincent Chang was born in China on December 1, 1938. His father, Percy Chang, was born in Jamaica but had been sent back to China by his family, as was common at that time, to learn the culture. His father met and married his mother, Onn Len Tai, in Hong Kong where they had four children: Vincent, Herbert, Peter and David.

AN EARLY TRAGEDY

Chang's father had made arrangements to take his family to Jamaica but three days before the ship was to sail, he died in a tragic accident. The plans had already been made and so they embarked on the long journey to Jamaica. Chang was accompanied on the voyage by his mother and brother, Peter. Two brothers stayed behind; Herbert was later sent to Canada and David to Jamaica. Chang was 13 years of age when he disembarked from a Blue Funnel line cargo ship in Kingston harbor.

GROWING UP THE HARD WAY

Chang's early life in Jamaica was not an easy one. Separated from his family, he worked for his keep in the Chinese grocery shops wherever he stayed. He was first sent to live with his aunt, Maisey, who had a shop in Smithville, Clarendon, and then to his grandfather who had a shop in

Frankfield, Clarendon. After about a year in Clarendon, he was back to living with Aunt Maisey who had now moved to Kingston, the capital, and was now living on East Avenue near Spanish Town Road in a neighborhood known as Greenwich Farm. He attended the Chinese Public School on North Street under the guidance of legendary headmistress Joy Moo-Young. After leaving the Chinese school, he took night classes at St George's extension school while working in the shop by day.

THE CHINEY SHOP

The 1943 census of Jamaica showed 12,394 Chinese residing on the island; these were divided into three categories by the census, namely "China-born" (2,818), "local-born" (4,061), and "Chinese coloured" (5,515), the latter referring to multiracial people of mixed African and Chinese descent.

A recent documentary film, *The Chiney Shop*, by Jeannette Kong, explores the impact the Chinese grocery stores, such as the ones Chang worked in while growing up, had on Jamaica. From the 1930s to the early 1970s, the ubiquitous Chinese-owned groceries were located on many busy street corners from downtown Kingston to remote towns in every parish. The Chinese usually lived above or behind the shops and consequently, the only time most people saw them was when they were behind a shop counter and it appeared that "they had no feet."

According to Jeannette Kong, the Chinese dominated the grocery business in Jamaica during this period. Many of these shops were like convenience stores, dollars stores and grocery stores all rolled into one. The Chinese who owned these shops across the island formed a close knit community and all knew each other as some had come from the same villages in China.

According to Tony Wong who grew up in a "Chiney Shop," the first Chinese had landed on the island in 1854 as indentured servants working on plantations. They eventually moved up the economic ladder by opening tiny stores, which would sometimes grow into substantial chains. Before this, food would be purchased in local markets, or outposts run by plantations…these ubiquitous businesses had an impact small and large on all aspects of Jamaican society. Author Malcolm Gladwell discusses the sequence of events that led to his own success in his bestselling book, *Outliers*. His grandmother couldn't afford to send his mother to school. So she borrowed the money from the local

Chinese-Jamaican shopkeeper. That loan set off the fateful chain of events that sent his mother to England where he was born. Years later, he would become an influential writer (Wong, 2012).

Many successful Jamaicans of Chinese descent credit the early experiences working in these Chinese groceries as providing "business smarts" that was fundamental to their success. Among them are billionaire business magnate Michael Lee-Chin who made his fortune in the Canadian mutual fund industry (Wong, 2012).

A LOVE FOR BAKING

When he was 20 years of age, Chang got a job in the production department at Hannah Town Bakery (HTB) and was introduced to baking. He discovered that he was good at baking and developed a love for pastry. To improve his skills, Chang enrolled in a course at the American Institute of Baking in Chicago, Illinois in 1964. The following year he took a course that specialized in cakes and pastries at the William Hood Dunwoody Industrial Institute in Minneapolis, Minnesota.

Shortly after returning to Jamaica, he accepted a position with the National Continental Bakery as a production supervisor. As luck would have it, he just happened to meet Valerie Lue Shing one day while visiting some friends. It was love at first sight; Chang pursued her vigorously and they were married in 1966.

CREATING THE TASTEE PATTY

There was only one problem with his new job. Chang worked the night shift and his new wife was home alone at nights. Valerie complained about this arrangement. And so when a small snack shop at Union Square, near Cross Roads in Kingston was placed on the market, Chang saw an opportunity to be independent and put an end to the night shift.

Unable to get a bank loan, Chang was able to borrow approximately US$3,000 from friends to buy the snack shop. The shop specialized in meat loaf and also sold buns, biscuits, coco-bread, patties and beverages. He added pastries to the lineup. He changed the name of the shop to "Tastee" a variation of the word "Tasty" which he had seen used while studying in the USA.

Initially, he sold about 20 to 30 patties per day. Now, the patty is to Jamaicans what hamburgers are to Americans. Meat loaf was the better selling item, at the time. Gradually, he improved the patty crust making it flakier and also experimented with the meat filling, the spices, the size and shape. He would take home patties each day and get feedback from Valerie and family. Sales of patties improved and Chang began to notice that the other items were hardly selling.

One day he made the significant decision that would dramatically change his life and the Jamaican patty—he dropped all other products and focused entirely on selling patties and drinks.

FAMILY TO THE RESCUE

Business was soon going well for Chang. He rented more space. After two years in business, patty sales were over 1,000 per day. Suddenly, an illness sidelined him for several months. The business was in jeopardy, but Valerie sprang into action. She took command of operations and rallied family members and staff to keep the business humming until Chang's health was restored.

EXPANSION IN PROGRESS

In 1971, Chang built a new facility at 25a Half-Way-Tree Road in Kingston. This became the main factory and housed the corporate offices as well as a Tastee restaurant. This time around, he was able to get a loan from a commercial bank to finance construction. Patties were selling so fast that the old method of making the pies by hand on an assembly line could not keep up with demand. But there was no such thing as a patty machine. There was however, an apple turnover machine manufactured by Colburn which he ordered and modified to process patties. This enabled him to take production to new levels. With two new industrial ovens over 6,000 patties could be produced in an hour.

A CHANGE IN THE ECONOMIC CLIMATE

By 1973, Tastee had expanded with three additional outlets. Patties were now being distributed by independent wholesalers and distributors. Schools were beginning to show an interest in Tastee products. But all was not smooth sailing. The political winds had changed with the election of Michael Manley's People's National Party (PNP) in 1972. Manley had decided to experiment with democratic socialism and aligned himself with Cuba's Fidel Castro. This did not sit well with the United States of America which threw its support behind the opposition Jamaica Labour Party (JLP), headed by Edward Seaga. Political violence erupted.

The Jamaican economy fell into a tailspin and shortages and other problems ensued. The government started acquiring companies and capitalism fell out of favor. An exodus of the wealthy and entrepreneurial class began. Many fled to the USA and Canada. Chang stayed put. His downtown restaurant had to be closed due to violence. It was a time of turmoil and uncertainty.

BACK TO THE BUSINESS OF GROWTH

A change of government in 1980 and an improving business climate allowed Tastee to resume its upward trajectory. The business added several new restaurants. His expansion now extended to areas outside of Kingston such as Spanish Town and Portmore. The menu was also expanded to include items such as chicken and vegetable patties as well as other items.

Today, the Tastee Empire also includes franchisees that operate restaurants selling Tastee products under license from the company. Tastee products were always popular among high school students and they have been able to leverage that by providing management and operations to several school canteens and cafeterias under the Tastee logo. A second factory was opened in Montego Bay to help meet demand.

Chang says he has been encouraged to enter the UK market but he has shied away from doing so because he would not be able to provide the proper level of attention from so far away. Tastee is, however, actively exporting to other Caribbean islands such as The Cayman Islands, Antigua and Barbuda, Barbados, Grenada, St Vincent and the Grenadines and Trinidad & Tobago.

IN SEARCH OF TALENT

The general public is most familiar with Chang's philanthropy through the Tastee Talent Search Competition which was started in 1979. It has become Jamaica's longest running and most successful talent show. Over the years it has unearthed talented performers such as Yellowman, Beenie Man, Paul Blake, Papa San, Nadine Sutherland, Miss Tiny and Henry 'Yrneh' Brown. Chang also provides scholarships to students studying medicine, law and nursing. Drug Addiction Prevention Alert and many other worthy causes are beneficiaries of his largesse.

A GENEROUS AND HUMBLE MAN

Despite his tremendous success, Chang's humility and unassuming nature are evident to all who meet him. All who know him speak of his kindness and generosity. His success, however, has been tempered by two great tragedies in his life—his father's untimely death when he was just a boy and his son Warren being severely brain damaged from a swimming pool accident when he was just 11 months old. Sadly, Warren passed away after some 30 plus years in a heart-rending condition.

A SUCCESS STORY

Chang is a true Jamaican success story. Hard work mixed with a dose of training, determination and a love of baking has paid off handsomely. He has reduced his involvement in day-to-day matters but his business is in good hands. Vincent and Valerie's children are playing vital roles in the business with daughter Simone guarding the secret recipes with responsibility for quality control. Daughter Lisa heads up the finance department while son Robert has provided project management.

In 1995, Chang's philanthropic efforts were recognized by the Jamaican Government when he was awarded the Order of Distinction (OD). Over the years he has received numerous awards including the *Jamaica Observer* Business Leader Award in 2002; Observer Lifetime Achievement Award in 1998; and Ernst & Young Caribbean Entrepreneur for Distribution and Retail in 2003.

DISCUSSION

Vincent Chang has made his mark on the Jamaican business scene and today he is revered as an exemplary capitalist and business leader. While his parents did not have a business, he, nevertheless, had the experience of the proverbial "Chiney shop." In fact, he had a more varied experience than most since he moved around to different shops while growing up.

According to his wife, Valerie, it was her complaining about his working at night that prompted him to start his own business. He was able to buy an existing small snack shop with funds borrowed through his network of friends and family.

Chang's entrepreneurial genius led him to innovate and create a Jamaican patty like no other that captivated the taste of the Jamaican consumer. His kitchen became a laboratory in which he experimented with various variations of fillings and crusts until he found the winning recipe. Next, he had the vision to concentrate all his efforts on this one product and develop the outlets by which he would make them available to the maximum number of customers.

Although most entrepreneurs assume calculated risks, Chang says he never felt he was taking a risk but rather following the natural progression of his business, whether it was by expanding the number of locations, franchising, targeting schools and other institutions or exporting product to other islands.

One of the lessons of Chang's success is that opportunities are often to be found by merely looking at things differently. When he stated his business, patties were already quite commonplace and everybody made them using their own recipe. There was no obvious opportunity in making a different patty but he set about doing so with a passion. He disrupted the existing equilibrium in the Jamaican patty business by introducing his own version of the meat filling and pie crust that soon replaced most of the competing products. He did not invent the Jamaican patty but he improved it and sales took off.

CHAPTER 6

Rita Humphries-Lewin, CD

Rita Humphries-Lewin is the first woman in Jamaica to become a stockbroker. She did this in the 1960s. She is the founder and chairman of the Barita Group of Companies, which includes Barita Investments Ltd, Barita Portfolio Management Limited, the Barita Unit Trusts Management Company Ltd, and BPM Financial.

Rita Humphries-Lewin is the fifth of seven children—five girls and two boys—born to Edmund and Roselyn Humphries in St. Andrew, Jamaica. Edmund was originally from the parish of St James while Roselyn was a McLaren from St Andrew. She considers her family "real country people" as they lived in Barbican which at that time had a lot of open land and few residents.

A CAREFREE CHILDHOOD

She recalls her childhood as being "fun, carefree, being able to roam about the bushes with a horse and buggy" along with her siblings and three cousins who later moved in with her family. Although they walked to church every Sunday morning, they had, unlike so many at that time, electricity, running water, a telephone, and eventually a TV when that came to the island in 1963.

GOOD AT MATHEMATICS

Humphries-Lewin attended Immaculate Conception High School in Kingston where she was successful with her General Certificate of Education "O Level" examinations but did not continue on to the advanced or "A Levels" and college because she was "so confused" about what she wanted to do with her life and school was not fun but just "boring." Her one love in school was mathematics where she excelled with distinctions in every major examination. Though she loved math and numbers, she knew she did not like the fields of banking, accounting, or insurance. She took a commercial course and after moving around from odd job to odd job she settled with the Kaiser Bauxite Company in Mandeville.

SEARCHING FOR HER PASSION

After three years at Kaiser, and making what was considered a "bundle of money," she still had not found her passion so she returned to Kingston to seek employment with the Caribbean Cement Company—the only company offering a comparable salary to Kaiser. She failed to find employment there but after a few weeks someone from the Cement Company called her to say that the company's brokerage firm in Canada would be establishing a subsidiary in Jamaica and was looking for Jamaicans to be trained in Canada for the local positions.

She was excited at the prospect of traveling and jumped at the opportunity. She laughed as she recounts her mother's worry about her being recruited to go to Canada—it was well known at the time that young women were being recruited and shipped there for prostitution. Her mother not only insisted that she buy a return airline ticket but she also demanded to see it.

ANNETT AND COMPANY LIMITED

After training as a secretary in Canada, she returned to Jamaica to work for Annett and Company, the Canadian stock brokerage subsidiary. While in Canada, she had become fascinated with the stock market and began to sense that she had found her niche which matched her strength in math and her dream of being involved in "high finance." With encouragement from a stockbroker, Rita began taking Canadian securities courses via correspondence courses, and in no time became a qualified stockbroker. She worked with the Canadian agency for 10 years, mainly as a trader and analyst.

THE JAMAICA STOCK EXCHANGE

During the early 1960s, there was no official stock market in Jamaica— all trading was done over-the-counter at the Bank of Jamaica. According to Humphries-Lewin, it was not until 1969, with help from Finance Minister Edward Seaga, that the Jamaica Stock Exchange (JSE) was set up with only four members. Humphries-Lewin laments that there were actually more companies listed on the JSE in those early days than there are today. Investments were flowing into Jamaica during the early years after independence.

IT WAS A MAN'S WORLD

In 1969, when the Canadian company pulled out of Jamaica, Humphries-Lewin was made a director of a new company called Investment Brokers Ltd. She travelled a lot to Canada to learn as much as she possibly could because being the only woman in the business was not easy. She discovered that this prejudice was not specific to Jamaica but even in countries like England where the stock market was well established. She recalls that there were times when men would come in and when she asked if she could help them, they would point to her male junior for assistance. She credits these situations as helping her to "develop determination."

THE JAMAICA INDUSTRIAL DEVELOPMENT CORPORATION

Humphries-Lewin was helping a lot of big businesses to make money as a broker but she always wanted to help small businesses have the same success so she did not hesitate when asked by P.J. Patterson to head the Jamaica Industrial Development Corporation (JIDC) Small Business Division, a consulting firm for small business. During her tenure at the JIDC the economic situation in Jamaica was deteriorating rapidly, "things were going from bad to worse daily," imports were banned and even basic food items were hard to come by. It was a discouraging time and people resorted to the black market. She decided to leave JIDC after three years, having had her fill of government bureaucracy.

BARITA INVESTMENTS LIMITED

Through her work with the JIDC and with encouragement from former associates, Humphries-Lewin decided to start her own business. In 1977, with $10,000 of her own savings, she founded Barita Investments—ironically starting with ten male clients. The name Barita comes from a combination using letters from her name and her sister's.

Barita Investments had the opportunity to do work for some of the biggest firms in Jamaica. It was the broker responsible for the take-over of the Caribbean Cement Company by the Jamaican Government and was also the broker for Life of Jamaica, Mutual Life, Dyoll Insurance, National Commercial Bank and Seprod Limited, to name a few.

The Barita Group of Companies includes Barita Investments, Barita Unit Trusts, and a Cambio dealership. The group offers a wide range of financial products and services including being a primary dealer for the Bank of Jamaica, trading in commercial paper, a capital growth fund, trading in United States securities, trading in bank deposits, producing daily and weekly market updates, and even providing the internationally famous Standard & Poor's rating agency based in New York with statistics for its monthly and annual publications.

OTHER PEOPLE'S MONEY

According to Humphries-Lewin, "when you are responsible for other people's money, it's not yours to play with—don't go there." She explained that Barita Investments operates on the Canadian Model which emphasizes getting rich slowly. As a result, they did not suffer like the Americans in the Great Recession of 2008.

RISK AVERSION

She describes herself as risk averse and she claims never to have lost any money. Her company has always been profitable although some years were less profitable than they had projected. She admits that she once bought Argentina notes when everyone else was running away from it and she made money on it. But she used the company's money not the clients'.

WORKING WITH MEN

Humphries-Lewin explains that her overall experience working with men has actually been quite good. She recalls being the only the woman on the trading floor and doing quite well. Although the clients preferred to deal with men, while in the office she got along fabulously with men and they always treated her as "one of the boys." Humphries-Lewin's husband, Karl Lewin, is Managing Director of Barita Unit Trusts.

JAMAICA STOCK EXCHANGE

Barita Investments is one of the smaller players in the Jamaican securities market. It was listed on the JSE in January 2010 after an initial public (IPO) offering in which it raised $450 million. Some 445,001,824 ordinary shares were listed at $2.50 per unit, and trade under the symbol BIL. For the year ended September 30, 2012, the company's net profit increased by 16 percent to approximately $255 million.

The company attributes the performance to increased operating revenues across income streams for the period. For the reporting year, Barita's fees and commissions totaled $94.5 million, reflecting a significant increase of 62 percent compared to the $58.5 million it recorded last year. Foreign-exchange trading and translation gains also more than tripled to $46.6 million over the $12 million it reported in the previous year. Net interest showed a marginal one percent movement to $453 million from $448.6 million in the previous year. For the year, the company's bottom line was also boosted from increased dividend income, which grew to $8 million, up from $6.8 million. The company also said the improvement in net profit translated into earnings per share of $0.57 in comparison to $0.49 for the same period last year (*Jamaica Gleaner*, "Barita profits increase by 16%." December 12, 2012).

OTHER ROLES

From 1998 to 2000, Humphries-Lewin was the chairman of the JSE where she spearheaded the establishment of the Jamaica Central Securities Depository in 1998 and the development of electronic trading on the stock exchange in 2000. She also served as the chairman of The Development Bank of Jamaica participating in Jamaica's "Highway 2000" project and the "Harmony Cove" project in Trelawny.

THE BARITA EDUCATION FOUNDATION

In 2004, Humphries-Lewin founded the Barita Education Foundation to help improve the literacy and numeracy of children in early-childhood institutions across the island. A major thrust of the foundation is to teach the basic school teachers. The company has a staff of trained teachers who go into the inner city communities and schools where they teach the teachers.

AWARDS

In 1999, Humphries-Lewin was awarded the Order of Distinction, Commander Class, by the Government of Jamaica for her contributions to the development of the island's financial industry.

DISCUSSION

Rita Humphries-Lewin was able to capitalize on the post-independence boom in the Jamaican economy when many foreign companies left the island thereby opening up opportunities for locals to fill. Single and without any familial responsibilities, she was an ideal candidate to start a securities firm when others chose to avoid taking such a risk.

Humphries-Lewin went against the herd at school. While her classmates were heading off to university, she was searching for her passion. The fact that many entrepreneurs are non-conformist was discussed earlier. The existing educational system and traditional schools do not work well for many potential entrepreneurs. According to Cummins & Kelly (2010), the approach to curriculum and the delivery of a curriculum that prescribes one way of thinking and bases assessment on being confined to this can work against the way the entrepreneurial mind thinks.

Humphries-Lewin is one of several entrepreneurs in this study who spoke of having difficulties in the traditional school environment. Although she was good at mathematics she found classes boring and did not pursue advanced education until she discovered the securities industry and pursued the necessary certifications.

CHAPTER 7

Lowell Hawthorne, OD

Lowell Hawthorne is CEO of the Golden Krust Caribbean Bakery and Grill, one of the largest Jamaican-owned businesses operating in the United States of America. It is also one of the top 100 Black-owned businesses in the USA. The company produces and distributes Jamaican patties, jerk chicken, Jamaican breads, spiced buns, desserts and spices in a state of the art manufacturing plant in the Bronx, New York. Products are sold in 120 franchise restaurants. They are also available in wholesale clubs, supermarkets, schools, airports, and prisons. In 2011, Golden Krust sales topped US$100 million.

The story of Golden Krust is the story of the power of family—the Hawthorne family and their 11 siblings—and their rise from rural Jamaica to international success.

Lowell Hawthorne was born in the small village of Border, near Lawrence Tavern in rural St Andrew, Jamaica in 1961. He is the sixth of 11 children. His father came from the nearby village of Paisley while his mother grew up in Windsor Castle in the parish of St Mary. His parents, Ephraim and Mavis, operated a small bakery in the village. His father often worked in the USA as a migrant farm worker to help augment the family income and this would take him away from home for several months at a time. His mother had the task of keeping the family functioning while his father was away.

LEARNING TO WORK FROM AN EARLY AGE

Hawthorne recalls that his parents were, "two extraordinary parents, spiritual leaders, confidants and advisors who instilled in us values of hard work, determination and Christian principles." His Grandfather had been an overseer for a local church and his father was a part-time minister.

Hawthorne's grandfather wanted his father to become a tailor but his father loved baking and felt he was destined to be a baker. His father established Hawthorne's Bakery in 1949 when he and his Mavis moved to Border to start a family. The name of the business was later changed to Hawthorne & Sons Bakery. The bakery soon became a source of pride for the small rural community.

Hawthorne and his siblings worked in the bakery where all mixing and kneading was done by hand—there was no electricity in the village at that time. He recalls being at his "papa's side, as I measured and mixed and perfected the Easter dough" for the production of Jamaican Easter buns (Hawthorne, 2012). Family life was centered on the bakery and Hawthorne and his siblings learnt early "that getting the product right and marketing it successfully required cooperation, reliability and going the extra mile."

As children, they had duties before school each day. Family activity started at four o'clock every morning. The bakery had to be started, water had to be fetched from the local spring and stored in drums for the bakery and for laundry as there was no running water in the village. Clothes were washed by hand. There was bread to be delivered to the various small shops in the village by the children on foot and there were animals to tend.

VENTURING INTO BUSINESS AT AN EARLY AGE

Lowell's first business venture occurred when as a child he raised chickens, pigs, rabbits and goats he bought with his savings. He sold chickens to his mother who would resell them to the public. According to Lowell, these and other examples helped him to begin "thinking in multiples and seeing the possibilities of seeds becoming forests and eggs become flocks of chickens."

Hawthorne learnt how to drive using a delivery van his father bought for the bakery. He made deliveries to distant towns and parishes for the bakery as a teenager. He loved driving and one of his earliest ambitions was to become a minibus driver. At the age of 16, Hawthorne sold some of his livestock and used the proceeds to purchase a VW minivan which he operated as a minibus between Border and the capital city of Kingston in his spare time and on weekends. He loved being a minibus driver and the sense of freedom it brought him. His main goal at that time was to own a coveted Toyota Coaster minibus which cost J$250,000 and was nicknamed "the quarter million."

COMING TO AMERICA

In 1981, at the age of 20, Hawthorne boarded a flight to New York where his sister Lauris was already living. She had filed the necessary immigration papers for him to get a visa. He was somewhat reluctant to leave what he had behind. But at that time, many Jamaicans, including his siblings, were leaving the island for better opportunities as the island's economy had stuttered through most of the 1970s.

GETTING AN EDUCATION

When Hawthorne graduated from high school in Jamaica going to college was out of the question, "I was forced to conclude that having passed only three GCE "O" level subjects, entering any of Jamaica's universities or teacher's colleges was next to impossible" (Hawthorne, 2012). But America offered many more options for those seeking a college education.

Lowell's first job in the USA was with the New York Police Department (NYPD) as a stock handler. It wasn't glamorous work but his punctuality, discipline, respectfulness and work habits made him an exemplary employee. He enrolled at the Bronx Community College and later studied accounting at Baruch College of the City University of New York. He was able to do this by starting his work day earlier and thus was able to leave early for classes with the permission of his supervisors.

Obtaining the associate degree in accounting allowed Hawthorne to get a much better job as a pension's accountant with the Police Department. He also studied tax preparation and developed a part-time business preparing tax returns. He was able to get a fair amount of work from police officers in the department. He took on a partner and eventually his client list numbered over 600.

JAMAICAN SPICED BUNS IN NEW YORK

By 1989 most of his siblings had migrated to the US and the family bakery in Jamaica was succumbing to competition and imports. Hawthorne had married and had bought a house. His father was now a regular visitor to New York at Easter and had begun baking Jamaican spiced buns in his daughter's basement. Informally, the family was able to sell several hundred of the Jamaican treat each year.

One afternoon Hawthorne held a family gathering over a meal. It was there that his father floated the idea of starting a Jamaican bakery in New York. The decision was made to accept the challenge and produce bakery products for the Jamaican community in New York, much as they had done in Jamaica. The initial plan was "informal and only moderately ambitious." According to Lowell, "family unity and support gave me the motivation and confidence to step out into the world of business and prepared me for the challenges of being an entrepreneur."

RAISING START-UP CAPITAL

The first challenge was to obtain the necessary funds to start the business. He went first to a commercial bank and then to the Small Business Administration. Both rejected his applications for a loan. Undaunted, Hawthorne and his sister Lauris put their houses up as collateral; other family members tapped into their savings and altogether they raised $107,000 in capital to get things started.

GOING ALL-IN

Next Hawthorne had to make the momentous decision of quitting his job with the NYPD that had been the basis of his family's security. "It was not an easy decision for me. I had a wife, four children and other responsibilities as well," recalls Lowell. He was giving up a job with prospects of long-term income security. Plus, many of his colleagues at work thought it was a bad idea to give up his job to start a bakery business. Other family members also quit jobs to fill the key jobs in the business.

GOLDEN KRUST CARIBBEAN BAKERY & GRILL

They soon identified a location for the business on Gun Hill Road in the Bronx, NY and proceeded to navigate the "cobweb of city codes" to get permits for the business. They acquired the necessary baking equipment and the first items came out the oven to celebratory cheers. The whole family pitched in and did whatever was necessary for opening day. They baked "hard dough" bread, spice bun, bulla, coco bread and other Jamaican treats. The baking of patties was not part of their skill set so they purchased product from a wholesaler who had a tried and true product.

Before long there were several stores with the Golden Krust logo, some the result of partnerships, scattered over the Bronx, Brooklyn and even New Jersey.

CHALLENGES AND OPPORTUNITY

There were many bumps and challenges along the road including a shakedown by Mafia garbage contractors which had them fearing for their lives if they did not pay exorbitant fees. One year while vacationing in Negril, Jamaica, Hawthorne received a phone call that their supplier of patties had decided to terminate their supply. Patties at that time represented some 40 percent of revenue. After the initial panic, Hawthorne called his father for advice. His father's calm response was, "don't leave, some things work together for good."

It was now clear that Golden Krust had to figure out how to make patties. Luckily, now they were in a position to get bank financing. Experimenting with patty recipes began in earnest. One sticking point was the making of a suitable crust. They finally found a British supplier of pie making equipment who could not only provide production machines but expertise in making the pie crust. Next they imported a patty chef from Jamaica to develop the right recipe for the filling of the meat patty.

It wasn't long before customers were coming from all over for the taste of authentic Jamaican patties. The Golden Krust brand started growing by leaps and bounds and mostly by word of mouth. Soon they were producing patties around the clock and barely able to meet demand. They went looking for space to construct a dedicated production facility. As luck would have it, they found and were able to acquire a former hot dog factory that was already USDA approved.

BECOMING A FRANCHISOR

By 1995 it was evident that the business had staying power. The flagship store was experiencing strong growth and people were asking how they could participate in its success. The decision was made to pursue franchising. An experienced franchising attorney was retained and the process initiated.

Becoming a franchisor is not for the faint of heart. It involves working with and nurturing people of varied personalities to become successful using your business concept. If they do not succeed they could sue you. On the other hand it can provide a business with more growth and profits using fewer employees and less capital than it could otherwise.

Eight years after opening for business, Golden Krust was granted a franchise license. To get to that point, operations had to be streamlined and documented. Stores had to be redesigned for consistency. Manuals had to be developed and printed. They also realized that they did not own the "Golden Krust" name; several other businesses operated under the name "Golden Krust." Before franchising could proceed they had to own the name and they were able to do this by buying out the other companies using the name.

Ed Dinger writing about the company in the *International Directory of Company Histories* explains the success of one franchisor:

> In 1997 the first handful of franchised operations began to open. An early success story was Jamaican-born Hillary D. Hurbs, an acquaintance of Hawthorne. She already had experience at the Pepsi-Cola Company and with a consulting firm before deciding to become a Golden Krust franchisee and going to work for herself. Most Golden Krust outlets were small affairs, some as small as 600 square feet, located in enclaves of West Indian immigrants. But Hurbs's restaurant was 4,350 square feet in size and capable of seating 74. It was located in lower Manhattan on Chambers Street, much closer to Wall Street than to the Bronx or Brooklyn. She also would provide catering to nearby City Hall, as well as the mayor's residence at Gracie Mansion (Dinger, 2005).

With a business background, Hurbs was an unusual Golden Krust franchisee. A large number of other women launched Golden Krust restaurants, but many of them were nurses. It was an understandable connection on a number of levels. Many West Indians worked in hospitals, leading Golden Krust to locate many of its units close by. As a result, a lot of registered nurses became regular customers, and some took an interest in going into business for themselves. Moreover, many nurses developed strong leadership skills and brought other attributes to the table. In a *New York Times* profile of the company, Jeffrey E. Kolton, a lawyer specializing in franchising, explained why nurses made ideal candidates: "Good franchisees are people who want to follow systems. Nurses take pride in their work, are good at following orders and manuals, and they're customer service oriented" (Dinger, 2005).

MUNICIPAL AND STATE CONTRACTS

In the 1990s, Golden Krust pursued municipal and state contracts. It won contracts to supply food to the prison at New York's Rikers Island and the New York City public school system. Inmates at the Rikers Island prison were served Jamaican patties, consuming more than 50,000 each month. In 1995 New York City schoolchildren would start eating the patties as part of the school lunch program. Later city hospitals, Mount Vernon, New York-Schools, Rockland County jails, and supermarkets in some 30 states also would be added as customers.

EXPANDING THE CUSTOMER BASE

By mid-1999 the Golden Krust chain was 35 units strong, 24 of which were franchise stores. The company also had a new 60,000-square-foot Bronx plant, funded by $1.2 million in city-backed business development loans. The chain was now moving well beyond its base of Caribbean customers and appealing to the general public. In an effort to reach everyone, the chain modified its menu to meet the tastes of a neighborhood. For instance, it offered soy protein patty fillings for vegetarians and halal patties for Muslims. In the Chambers Street store, customers could find cold cuts as well as curried goat. Golden Krust's success did not go unnoticed. In 1999 Ernst & Young named the company its Entrepreneur of the Year in New York City (Hawthorne, 2012).

GROWTH IN THE 2000s

According to Dinger (2005) "Golden Krust continued to make strides in the new century. It entered the Philadelphia market, where it hoped to open more than 20 stores within five years. The first Philadelphia outlet would also introduce the chain's jerk chicken dish and be the first to use the Golden Krust Caribbean Bakery & Grill name. The management of the company to this point had been dominated by members of the Hawthorne family, but in early 2003 Golden Krust hired experienced outside management help to take the business to the next level. Brought in were a vice-president of franchising; director of research, development, and training; director of marketing and public relations; and a director of franchise sales and development.

The immediate goal was to better promote the Golden Krust brand and grow the franchise operation. The chain was also improving its advertising program with the signing of a spokesperson, Tiki Barber, star football player with the New York Giants.

The next big step was a seven-year agreement with Pepsi USA. Pepsi would install soda fountains in all of the Golden Krust stores, help the chain redesign its menu boards, provide assistance in marketing, and also help in analyzing demographics for use in selecting new store locations. The chain was also in line to receive rebates based on the volume of Pepsi products it sold. Several months later Golden Krust, in conjunction with Pepsi, introduced combo meals to drive sales for both parties. To support the program, the company launched a major advertising campaign, making full use of Tiki Barber in all media, including radio, television, newspapers, billboards, and buses" (Dinger, 2005).

JAMAICAN INGREDIENTS

The company sources many of its raw materials from Jamaica including produce and spices such as yams, calaloo, ackees, thyme, peppers and escallion. It is the number one seller of Jamaican sodas and Jamaican juice drinks in the USA. Hawthorne meets with Jamaican producers frequently to ensure ample supplies of products needed by Golden Krust to maintain the authentic Jamaican flavors. This has provided an export market for the island's farmers and earns valuable foreign exchange for the island.

Today, the company under Hawthorne's leadership as president and CEO has over 120 franchisees operating in several states. Many of his family members hold key positions in the company. It is now a major force in the quick service restaurant (QSR) category. The company invests in real estate and leases space to franchisees in addition to manufacturing foodstuff. The Golden Krust Empire is strong and growing and projections are that sales will exceed $500 million by 2020.

COMMITTED TO GIVING BACK

Hawthorne has won numerous awards including the Honourary Doctor of Letters degree from Medgar Evers College for contributions to the community. He has received an Order of Distinction from the Government of Jamaica. He won the *Jamaica Observer's* Business Leader Award for 2010; and was the North American *Gleaner's* Man of the Year in 2007.

The Hawthorne family is committed to giving back and in 2005 the Mavis & Ephraim Hawthorne Foundation was established in honour of their parents to support educational and social service programs in Jamaica and the USA.

Golden Krust has adopted two Jamaican schools—Norman Hawthorne Basic School and Paisley All-Age School—and regularly donates to the fight against cancer.

DISCUSSION

Lowell Hawthorne's rise from humble beginnings in his rural Jamaican village without running water or electricity to franchising success in the USA is an inspiration to countless Jamaicans. He presides over the largest manufacturer, distributor and franchiser of Caribbean-based products in the USA. Golden Krust Caribbean Bakery and Grill came along at the right time to cater to the influx of Jamaican immigrants who had located in the New York metro area. Thousands have been employed as a result of his company and he has been able to give back to his native Jamaica by importing Jamaican produce and products for his restaurants. The family's foundation named for his parents contributes to education and other projects in the USA and Jamaica.

Hawthorne, like many of the entrepreneurs in this study, grew up in a family that had a business while he was growing up. It was here he developed his work ethic as the family would rise early before dawn each day to get the bakery started and each child had duties to perform before heading off to school. His raising of livestock and selling at a profit as a boy were early indications of an entrepreneurial streak. Even as an employee with the NYPD he sought out additional opportunities such as tax preparation to augment his income.

Hawthorne, as well as other entrepreneurs in this study, recalled that they had difficulty in school. This may be related to the fact that many entrepreneurs are non-conformist in their thinking and the way they solve problems. A recent study of entrepreneurs found right-brain dominance was the norm among the sample of entrepreneurs studied, in contrast to the 'left brain' abstract-type thinking favored by the education system (Cummins & Kelly, 2010). Dr. Kelly is reported to have said: "We need a bias in the education system towards those who can create jobs. Teachers must recognize the existence of right brain and left brain learners in class."

Hawthorne understands that entrepreneurs have to take risks. He took calculated risks to start the Golden Krust enterprise when he mortgaged his house in order to raise start-up capital and even gave up his job. He was joined by other family members who also provided cash and he was bolstered by the baking expertise of his father.

One definition of an entrepreneur is:

> ...a person who creates something different with value (added) by devoting time and effort, assuming the financial, psychological and social risks in an action-oriented perspective and receiving the resulting rewards (and punishments) of monetary and personal satisfaction (Solomon & Winslow, 1988, p. 164).

Hawthorne certainly fits this description. He realized that Jamaican immigrants in New York longed for a taste of Jamaica and although there were existing Jamaican bakeries, they focused mainly on the wholesale trade. He saw opportunity in the retail sector.

One lesson from Hawthorne's success is the benefit of a large cohesive family unit or some sort of social network that provides social capital. His large family was a source of capital, know-how, encouragement and support to get Golden Krust off the ground. Also as the first employees were family members, this reignited a synergy that they had when working together in their parents' bakery in Jamaica as children.

According to Wayne Baker, author of *Achieving Success through Social Capital*, "Studies show that lucky people increase their chances of being in the right place at the right time by building a 'spider web structure' of relationships that catch information." Furthermore, according to Baker, "Success is social; all the ingredients of success that we customarily think of as individual—talent, intelligence, education, effort and luck—are intertwined with networks." A large family provides a readymade network.

CHAPTER 8

Dr. Paul Chen-Young

Dr. Paul Chen-Young is a pioneer in Jamaican banking, and in the development of its capital market. In 1975, he started his first company on a shoestring budget and went on to establish a conglomerate of companies that provided a range of financial services: the Eagle Financial Network (EFN), with Eagle Merchant Bank (EMB) as the flagship company. This network was unmatched in Jamaica at the time and was a veritable "one stop shopping center" of financial services for customers.

When Jamaica's financial sector collapsed in the late 1990s, the Eagle Financial Network was acquired and liquidated by FINSAC.

Dr. Paul Chen-Young was born in Kingston, Jamaica in 1938. His father, Albert, was an immigrant from Shenzhen in Southern China, who came to Jamaica as a teenager in the 1920s and learned the retail grocery business by working with his uncle. Albert married Iris King, a Jamaican, and set up his own mom and pop grocery store in Smithville, Clarendon, a rural village that had no paved roads, running water nor electricity.

THERE WAS ALWAYS WORK

Chen-Young and his siblings attended the Smithville Elementary School. He remembers that from an early age "there was always work" and they always had to find something to do in the shop, "whether it was sweeping the floor, cutting paper for wrapping codfish, flour, rice, cornmeal, sugar and bread, or dealing with customers." In those days there was no television and the only radio in the village was owned by the school's headmaster.

A PROMISING STUDENT

For his high school education, Chen-Young was sent to Clarendon College—primarily through the efforts of his mother—at an early age. In order to attend, he lived with his grand-uncle who had a grocery store about a mile from the school. He was a boarder at the school for a short while. After passing the Senior Cambridge Exams, he graduated high school at age 15. As his parents could not afford it, he realized he needed to save some money if he was going to achieve his goal of a university education. He worked at a variety of jobs after high school including payroll clerk at New Yarmouth Estate, a clerk at Monymusk Sugar Estate, tagging farm machinery at Reynolds Jamaica Mines in St Ann, and as a night chemist at Alcan's Alumina plant.

THE COLLEGE YEARS

Chen-Young was admitted to Howard University, the historically Black college in Washington, D.C., at the age of 19 in 1957. It was one of the least expensive schools and one that was attractive to Jamaican Students. At various times during his college career, he worked on campus, as a taxi driver or sold shoes, cosmetics and clothing to pay his expenses. Despite having to work, Chen-Young found time to be active in student activities and served as president of the Economic Society and Student Council.

After his first year he was awarded a tuition scholarship by the university. In his second year, he was elected to Phi Beta Kappa the most prestigious National Honor Society in the USA. He graduated Magna Cum Laude with a BA in Economics in 1961. Chen-Young went on to study economics at the University of Pittsburgh where he met his late wife, Michele Pauyo, a student from Haiti, who was studying for her MA in economics, "She was a lovely person, very supportive and influential in shaping my future career as an economist," Chen-Young recalls. He earned MA and PhD degrees from Pittsburgh and conducted research at the Central Planning Unit of Jamaica for his thesis, "An Economic Evaluation of the Tax Incentive Program in Jamaica" (University of Pittsburgh, 1966)

THE WORLD BANK

After receiving his doctorate in 1966, Chen-Young joined the prestigious Young Professional Program (YPP) at the World Bank in Washington, D.C., where his work included projects for the Africa Department. At the World Bank he, "learned discipline and exposure to the world of finance and the highest levels of professionalism." It was here that he honed his writing capability by learning how to take notes in economic committee meetings and producing minutes. He also learned how governments operated and dealt with macroeconomic issues by going on missions to countries like Malawi and East Pakistan.

THE JAMAICA DEVELOPMENT BANK

When an opportunity to return home was presented two years later, he accepted a position as deputy general manager of the Jamaica Development Finance Corporation. This provided valuable experience in management, financial analysis and forecasting, plus he was quickly thrust into greater responsibility because the general manager only worked on a part-time basis. He spearheaded the effort to transform the corporation into the Jamaica Development Bank. What gave him the greatest sense of accomplishment was "being able to assemble Jamaicans to form a strong management team that made the transformation possible." Despite his good record, a government appointee was given the top job.

INTRODUCTION TO RISK TAKING

Chen-Young accepted a job in the private sector as managing director of Lai Corporation Limited, a real estate development company. The package that included a free house was too good to refuse as by then he had children to consider. The corporation was in financial distress and this forced him to be very creative in using whatever assets were available to generate cash flow to meet payroll and other expenses. This involved taking risks and Chen-Young thinks this is where an appetite for risk-taking entered his blood and stayed throughout his career.

In 1973, he was selected as general manager of the newly formed Workers' Savings and Loans Bank. It was here that he decided that he needed to be his own boss when he became frustrated by difficulties with the board.

PAUL CHEN-YOUNG & ASSOCIATES

In 1975, he ventured out on his own and established Paul Chen-Young and Associates to provide consulting services and conduct economic research. It produced a monthly magazine that analyzed economic trends as well as commentary by Chen-Young. It also provided consultation to governments of both political parties.

CARIBBEAN LEASE FINANCE CORPORATION

His next business venture was the Caribbean Lease Finance Corporation which he founded in order to add another source of income to the consulting business. Financing was provided by a local bank plus deposits made by customers. It made money by facilitating companies in selling and then leasing back their used equipment which was already depreciated under tax law. This allowed companies to have more cash for investment.

PAUL CHEN-YOUNG AND COMPANY LIMITED

In 1977, although inexperienced in trading stocks, Chen-Young started a stock brokerage company, Paul Chen-Young and Company Limited. The main source of business for the company was buying and selling shares listed on the stock exchange and trading in government securities on behalf of its clients. The company initially used the same staff of four that ran the consulting business and the leasing corporation. This company has been profitable since inception and is the second oldest stock brokerage in Jamaica.

THE EAGLE MERCHANT BANK

The idea for starting his own bank came to him in a "sleepless period" one night during the positive economic climate of the early 1980s. He decided to open a merchant bank since relatively little capital was required. It was also easier from a regulatory standpoint and lower statutory reserves had to be maintained with the Bank of Jamaica. A merchant bank could not be advertised or promoted as a "bank" but could do mostly everything else that a normal bank does. He chose the name Eagle Merchant Bank and it would become the flagship company of the Eagle Financial Network.

The Eagle Merchant Bank was capitalized with J$1 million dollars (about US$250,000). It was the first Jamaican bank created without any foreign or government support. Much of this capital came from equity in a building on Barbados Avenue that he had constructed and leased to the National Planning Agency. He had acquired the land when property values fell during the 1970s and was able to get a construction loan to build office space for leasing. Private shareholders provided the balance of the capital, but as the major shareholder, he had majority control. He recalls that early board meetings were held on a ping-pong table in his office until they could afford office space. The bank was started with only four employees.

FOCUS ON INNOVATIVE PRODUCTS

The Eagle Merchant Bank negotiated lines of credit with other banks such as Citibank, Workers' Bank and National Commercial Bank. It aggressively solicited fixed-deposits by offering higher interest rates and monthly interest payments that were attractive to pensioners and an innovative product—a bond featuring high tax free interest, flexible deposits and high growth with free life insurance to regular depositors under age 62 who regularly reinvested the interest.

Chen-Young looked for opportunities in areas largely ignored by commercial banks. One such area was lease financing in which he had developed some expertise when he started the Caribbean Lease Finance Corporation. Eagle was the first banking entity to develop the lease financing business. He provided financing for "trucks in the sugar industry, cars in tourism, construction equipment and machinery for industry, and financing for insurance premiums."

The Eagle Merchant Bank was well received by the public and was profitable from the outset. At the end of its first year of operation in 1983 it had "assets of J$28 million, deposits of J$16 million and loans of J$13 million." By the end of 1996, just prior to the government takeover, "the capital base of the bank had increased to J$488 million."

BUILDING THE EAGLE FINANCIAL NETWORK

The next step in constructing the Eagle Financial Network was acquiring an interest in Crown Life Insurance Ltd, a subsidiary of the Crown Life Insurance Company of Canada in 1984. The new company was called Crown-Eagle Life Insurance Company. Chen-Young explains that he did not start out with the goal of creating a financial network, rather the goal emerged as he saw "complementarities and cross fertilization of businesses as a sound business model since the captive customer base could be used for marketing a range of financial services."

EAGLE TRADE SERVICES

In 1985, Eagle Trade Services was formed. This did not require any additional staff or capital of its own as the Eagle Merchant Bank provided factoring financing to businesses looking to improve their cash flow. Later the same year, he purchased Mortgage Guaranty Insurance Company of Jamaica. This was paid for by the issuance of more shares in the Merchant Bank which increased the capital base without having to inject new cash. This would become the Eagle General Insurance Company when the range of insurance coverage provided was expanded beyond mortgages.

EAGLE INSURANCE BROKERS AND EAGLE UNIT TRUST

In 1987, Eagle acquired the Atlas Insurance Brokers and renamed it Eagle Insurance Brokers. This allowed him to expand into the insurance brokerage business.

The Eagle Unit Trust was formed as a subsidiary of the Merchant Bank in 1988. It was the first privately created unit trust in Jamaica. It provided tax free returns and was similar to a mutual fund.

THE EAGLE COMMERCIAL BANK

The Eagle Commercial Bank was created in 1988 as a subsidiary of the Merchant Bank. This proved to be "the pearl of the Eagle group" as it was the most profitable company. It was policy that the commercial bank would handle the accounts of all Eagle companies. The commercial bank expanded to eight branches across the island and proved popular with customers as it was the first commercial bank in Jamaica to offer interest on current accounts with low balances.

The Eagle Commercial Bank was the first indigenous bank to be established in Jamaica without any support from either the government or foreign institutions. According to Chen-Young, the bank's excellent reputation "was a well deserved one. It had the lowest bad-debt ratio of all commercial banks…by 1997 its net worth was J$510 million with assets of J$2 billion."

CROWN-EAGLE LIFE INSURANCE

By 1988, Chen-Young had exercised his option and acquired controlling interest in Crown-Eagle Life Insurance. The life insurance business is very capital intensive and Chen-Young did not anticipate the massive amount of cash it would eventually require. Crown-Eagle would eventually be the main reason the Eagle Financial Network failed.

THE EAGLE PERMANENT BUILDING SOCIETY

In 1989, Eagle expanded further by creating from scratch the Eagle Permanent Building Society to meet the growing need for mortgage financing. Initial capital was just J$1 million but by fiscal year 1995 its net worth had increased to J$200 million.

120

INTERNATIONAL EXPANSION

Eagle also expanded overseas with the opening of an office in Miami, Florida in 1991 and The Cayman Islands in 1992. In doing so it became the first Jamaican and Caribbean owned bank to set up operations in the United States of America. In the same year, Eagle Holdings (Cayman) Ltd., was established and would mobilize close to US$100 million by 1996. Eagle would go on to become the first Caribbean Financial Institution to own a USA-based brokerage or investment bank when it acquired First Equity Corporation of Florida in 1994.

SHAKING UP AN INDUSTRY

Eagle's success sparked interest in the merchant banking business. Many new competitors entered the arena; established commercial banks created subsidiaries and government enacted more stringent limitations. "Commercial banks lobbied for closing the disparity in the reserve requirements despite the fact that merchant banks did not have the benefit of interest-free checking accounts like the commercial banks."

At its peak, Eagle was "the most exciting financial group of companies in Jamaica in terms of the diversity of talent and its ability to pull together talented Jamaicans to start new entities from scratch." All the companies in the network complimented each other—except for Crown Eagle Life Insurance whose capital requirements were completely different.

THE EAGLE VISION

Eagle's vision was that they could be the leaders in the Jamaican financial sector and contribute to nation-building by applying intellect, knowledge, experience and sound management practices. According to Chen-Young, "it was exciting to be a part of Eagle. Our people were motivated, dedicated and totally committed to our goals. That's what made us an extraordinary group of companies."

NON-FINANCIAL COMPANIES

Eagle also diversified outside of financial services industry and acquired controlling interest in Martin's Travel Service. It became the first Jamaican financial entity to arrange financing for Jamaican-based hotels in the tourism industry. Eagle Merchant Bank took the lead in arranging and participating in financing for several new hotels in Jamaica including Sandals Ocho Rios and Ciboney.

HOLIDAY INN, MONTEGO BAY

In 1994, Crown Eagle Life purchased the Holiday Inn, Montego Bay, a property the government had been trying to divest without success as part of its privatization policy. A refurbishment and upgrading program was undertaken resulting in it becoming the second largest hotel property in Jamaica and the first ever Holiday Inn all-inclusive hotel in the world.

INFORMATION TECHNOLOGY

Eagle Information Services (EIS) was the technology unit of the Eagle Network, created to improve IT capabilities and provide a competitive edge through information technology. Eagle created the largest information technology company in the Caribbean when it acquired WTG-APTEC and merged it with EIS.

A GOOD CORPORATE CITIZEN

Eagle was supportive of many worthwhile causes with particular emphasis on education and the arts. It provided scholarships and bursaries for students at high schools, technical colleges, universities and the Edna Manley School for the Visual and Performing Arts. It was one of the pioneers in the "homework hotline" call-in program. Chen-Young and Eagle both acquired impressive collections of Jamaican art.

The Eagle Foundation for Enterprise was started in 1991, "to encourage innovative business education and to contribute to the formulation of public policy." The foundation's directors included Professor Rex Nettleford and Dr. Velma Pollard of the University of the West Indies.

Eagle provided longstanding support for dance and commissioned a highly acclaimed work, *Gerrehbenta*, by the National Dance Theatre Company. It was a principal sponsor of the annual Jamaica Cultural Development Commission's Festival and funded various artistic and charitable efforts in the community.

THE COLLAPSE OF THE EAGLE FINANCIAL NETWORK

The economic environment in Jamaica in the 1990s was characterized by high inflation, high interest rates plus a declining dollar. For example, in 1990 the lending interest rate was 25 percent but by 1995 it had risen to 50 percent. The Inflation rate was a whopping 35 percent in 1994. The Jamaican dollar dropped against the US dollar from 7:1 in 1990 to 37:1 in 1995.

Many of the island's financial institutions were experiencing "declining profitability, illiquidity and a reduction in asset quality as loan repayments began to lag and the real estate market, upon which the quality of many loans was dependent, stagnated" (Wint, 1997).

This environment created pressure on the indigenous financial services sector, and by 1996, it had become apparent that the island's insurance companies were on the verge of insolvency. Most were overexposed to the real estate sector. As it happened, the insurance companies were linked to the commercial and merchant banks—Life of Jamaica owned Century National Bank, for example—and so rumors of an imminent banking collapse filled the airwaves. Indeed, one bank, Century National, was closed and investors were denied access to their accounts. In order to restore calm to the sector, the government created FINSAC Limited, to resolve the problems.

Crown-Eagle Life Insurance was one of the insurance companies affected by the crisis. According to Chen-Young, the other Eagle companies were all viable and profitable companies, but:

> The Crown-Eagle investment was a mistake as its funding requirements are totally different from other financial entities—the more business, the greater the capital requirements. We also made the mistake—like other entities in the life insurance industry that experienced problems--of using high cost short term borrowings to make long term loans and investments. One of the reasons for doing so was that commitments had to be funded and there was also the possible upset from currency devaluations.

Chen-Young and members of his board participated in talks with the Ministry of Finance to discuss a restructuring of the Eagle Network and left with assurances of a bailout plan. To his chagrin, there would be no bailout.

Chen-Young is still reeling from the shock of losing the financial empire he had created and what he sees as betrayal by two of his senior directors who reportedly met privately with the Ministry of Finance to urge the demise of the Eagle Financial Network. He was also distressed by what he terms:

> …vindictiveness by the government in seeking to destroy me both in Jamaica and overseas by a baseless lawsuit brought by FINSAC against me in 1997 after I sold the Eagle companies for $1 and thought that the Eagle chapter was closed.

A BLOW AGAINST ENTREPRENEURSHIP

Asked his opinion of the FINSAC bailout program, Chen-Young asserts that:

> ...it did the exact opposite of what it was supposed to do. For example, all Eagle Companies were viable except for Crown-Eagle Life Insurance. We would have today a very strong financial group. National Commercial Bank (NCB) was treated differently as their bad assets were removed. Eagle's assets were not. Today, most financial outfits in Jamaica are owned by foreign companies. There was no vision and no understanding employed in the FINSAC process—it destroyed Jamaican entrepreneurs and has been disastrous for entrepreneurship.

AWARDS AND RECOGNITION

Chen-Young received numerous awards throughout his career. They include: The "Innovator for 1990" and "Business Achiever of the 1980s" awards from the *Financial Gleaner*; "Entrepreneur of the Decade" from Investor's Choice Magazine; an award for the "Company that best displayed the Human Face of Business" award by the Jamaica Chamber of Commerce in recognition of the outstanding contribution to Jamaica in the areas of Business, Education, Arts, Health and Sports.

He was the first Howard University graduate from the English-speaking Caribbean and Latin America to receive the second highest award granted by the university for "Distinguished Postgraduate Achievement in the field of Business"—Howard University's 1993 Alumni Achievement Award. And, he was awarded a "Special honour for contribution in the field of Finance and Banking" by the American Universities Graduates Association of Jamaica.

A CAUTIONARY TALE

Chen-Young brought excellent academic qualifications and business experience to bear on the creation of the Eagle Financial Network. He had an appetite for risk-taking and was a creative problem solver, an innovator and a visionary. And he was dedicated to nation building. His real genius was being able to bring talented Jamaicans together with enthusiasm and commitment for a common purpose. But the business environment can shift very quickly in a developing economy such as Jamaica's. Chen-Young's advice: "exercise care and develop a vision being mindful of the potential pitfalls."

Chen-Young says he no longer misses the hectic pace of the business world and is comforted by the love of his family and close friends.

DISCUSSION

On December 31, 2012 an elderly couple was found hanging in their home in the Jamaican city of Mandeville. A suicide note linked their deaths to Jamaica's financial sector meltdown of the 1990s. They were entrepreneurs who owned and operated two businesses. Apparently, they were saddled with enormous outstanding loan balances as a result of the economic crisis in which interest rates on loans exploded sending outstanding loan balances into the stratosphere (Reynolds, 2013). And so the fallout from Jamaica's economic meltdown of the 1990s continued almost two decades later.

According to comments on the back cover of Wilberne Persaud's book, *Jamaica Meltdown: Indigenous Financial Sector Crash 1996*:

> ...a fully emancipated, indigenous financial sector combined with and fuelling release of the people's creative energies could have produced true economic development. Instead it was pushed into a tailspin and crashed. Rather than progress, retarded development ensued. The Jamaican economy and people now faced the tremendous cost of rebuilding confidence—paying down non-productive debt precisely when education, technology, and health initiatives for the intensified global economy warranted highest priority. (Persaud, 2006).

Chen-Young's experience demonstrates how entrepreneurs can be impacted by the macro environment. Devaluations, high interest rates, government policy and other vagaries can derail success in an instant.

Despite the demise of the Eagle Financial Network, there are many entrepreneurial lessons that can be gleaned from it. In its heyday, Chen-Young's network created jobs for hundreds of people in the over 12 businesses he started. It also helped spark the growth in tourism by providing financing for several hotel projects. There were many other contributions to Jamaica such as scholarships and bursaries plus donations to various projects.

Chen-Young's entrepreneurial mind saw an opportunity to enter the banking industry by starting a merchant bank when he realized that the financial requirements were easier than for starting commercial banks. Eventually, when he had amassed sufficient capital, he opened the Eagle Commercial Bank. His many innovations stimulated interest in the Jamaican financial industry when he scored a number of firsts. His entrepreneurial mindset was evidenced by the number of companies he went on to create even venturing into the US market as the first Caribbean financial institution to do so.

With an excellent education and experience, Chen-Young was able to tap into a tremendous amount of social capital. He therefore had access to some of the most talented Jamaicans from whom he recruited personnel to start new ventures.

CHAPTER 9

Lois Lake Sherwood, JP

Lois Sherwood is a leading Jamaican painter who has won numerous awards and is recognized internationally. While her first love is art, she is also an astute businesswoman who has achieved remarkable success due to her dogged determination and tenacity. She is chairman of Restaurant Associates Limited which operates the Burger King and Popeyes restaurants in Jamaica. She is also chairman of Island Homes Limited a real estate development and sales company. And she is the managing director of Sherbourne Limited, a justice of the peace and the honourary consul for the Republic of Lithuania.

Lois Sherwood was born one of twin girls on February 12, 1932 in Kingston, Jamaica. Her father, Cecil Carby was born in Port Royal; his family name was originally McCarby. He worked as a mechanical engineer for the government in the Public Works Department. Her mother was Yvette Robin-Carby, a dressmaker born in Kingston to Haitian parents. She had one brother, Wayne. The family lived on Kensington Crescent near Cross Roads in Kingston.

A PERIOD OF LABOR UNREST IN THE COLONIES

Sherwood was born around the time that Alexander Bustamante returned to Jamaica and became a leader in the struggle against colonial rule. At that time, widespread poverty, discontent with low wages, unemployment and deplorable living conditions were extant in Jamaica and other Caribbean islands. These conditions led to a series of spontaneous, uncoordinated strikes and demonstrations across the Caribbean (Hart, 2002). In Jamaica, they culminated in the 1938 labor rebellion in which Bustamante emerged as a voice for the workers. Bustamante and his cousin, Norman Manley, would go on to form the two major political parties that agitated for independence from Britain.

The sustained and unprecedented militancy of the laboring classes unleashed events that transformed the political history of Jamaica, with major implications for the wider Caribbean. The 1938 labor riots spurred two momentous processes. First, the riots gave birth to Jamaica's modern nationalist movement, with the emergence of notable leaders, development of party politics, and a mature trade unionism. Second, labor's militancy in 1938 convinced the British Colonial Office to end colonial rule and initiate major reforms. In the aftermath of the unrest, the British made significant concessions to the strikers and, equally important, initiated constitutional reforms that ended colonialism (Gray, 2009).

When Sherwood was born, ordinary Jamaicans could not vote. Before Universal Adult Suffrage, implemented in 1944, the right to vote was determined by the amount of wealth or property a man held—women did not have the right to vote. Universal Adult Suffrage extended voting rights to all adults irrespective of race, sex, or social class (Buddan, 2004).

EDUCATION AND TRAINING

Sherwood recalls her family as being a very creative one. Her mother designed the clothing she sewed for sale and her father made all the furniture in their house. She and her twin sister were different personalities—they are fraternal twins. As a child she was not interested in school, reading books or exams, but her sister was. She attended St. Andrew's High School for Girls and was goalkeeper on the 1951 field hockey team that won the Issa Cup.

When she expressed her desire to be an artist, her father remarked that he didn't know any artists who earned enough money to pay rent. But Sherwood was very determined and convinced her mother to send her to art school in Haiti where she had an aunt who was willing to help her. She enrolled in Centre d'Art in Port-au-prince at age 16. Her father knew nothing about the plan until she had already arrived in Haiti.

As a young woman, she entered and won the *Star* newspaper's Miss Pin-up beauty contest in the early 1950s. Her prize was a trip to Haiti where she was featured in a parade through the city streets.

FIRST JOB AND FIRST VENTURE

After completing art school, Sherwood returned to Jamaica and started hunting for a job. After seeing an ad for a telephone operator, she went to the Gleaner Company to see what exactly a telephone operator did. She sat with an operator and observed her until she understood what exactly was involved. The next morning she showed up for the job interview at the Issa Brothers & Company. She was offered the job from a field of 23 candidates. She enjoyed interacting with people and received high praises for her customer service. When someone was unavailable she offered to call back the caller and let them know when they became available—that had not been done before.

Sherwood married Rodwell Lake in 1953. She did not plan to be an entrepreneur but when she realized her husband was unhappy in his job, she looked for a creative solution. She told him to resign. His reply, "Are you crazy! What are we going to do?" She told him they were going to open a furniture store. His response: "With what money?" Sherwood recalls he was speechless when she produced money she had saved. He could not understand where she got the money. She explained that when they had pooled their money for living expenses she would always save most of the money allocated for food.

Sherwood had also been quietly buying up antique furniture cheaply from departing expatriates. In 1966, she and Rodwell opened a store called, "Mahogany House" on Orange Street in downtown Kingston. According to Sherwood, it was the island's first antique store. Sherwood took her antiques to local craftsmen and had them duplicate the pieces which she then sold as "period reproductions" in her other store, also on Orange Street, known as Grace Furniture.

It was a good business selling mahogany furniture such as chairs, side tables, chest of drawers, and Victorian bed posts. Jamaican mahogany is a tropical hardwood that was used in making a variety of items such as houses, furniture and even ships throughout the 18th, 19th and 20th centuries. Someone in the 19th century wrote that, "mahogany in Jamaica was like gold in the reign of Solomon" (Ebenist, 2002).

REAL ESTATE DEVELOPMENT

Sherwood recalls that she realized, "people need a place to live, furniture for their houses and food to eat. I decided to focus on providing these three things." She started several land development projects across the island. She would buy land, install roads and a water system, subdivide it into lots and sell them to prospective home buyers.

When she first approached a bank for a loan to purchase land, they told her she was the first woman to ever ask them for a loan and were skeptical. She laid out in detail how they would get their money back and pointed to her success in the furniture business. She left with an approved loan.

ISLAND HOMES LIMITED

Sherwood's early forays into land development have been parlayed into a real estate company known as Island Homes Limited. It handles commercial and residential real estate sales and development as well as property management and rentals.

Her early real estate projects included Grace Development Limited in Hope Bay, Montego Hills Limited in Montego Bay, and Leighton Estates Ltd in the parish of Portland. Most of the land she bought was formerly owned by colonialists who were leaving the island and eager to sell after Jamaica gained independence from England. Sherwood was the first to offer land on hire-purchase terms. She simply applied the same principle she had used for selling furniture to the sale of land.

A SECOND MARRIAGE

Sherwood met her second husband, Kenneth Sherwood, an American of Jamaican parents, and a cousin to her first husband. He was an entrepreneur and prominent businessman in New York's Harlem. He was fascinated by Sherwood and pursued her relentlessly; he proposed often, promising to do "anything, just as long as I can be with you." And so they were married and became business partners.

BURGER KING

While attending a function in Kingston, Sherwood and Kenneth overheard someone saying that Burger King was looking to expand into the Caribbean. Kenneth made some enquires and they submitted an application. It was rejected. But they had not heard the last of Lois Sherwood who did not believe in taking no for an answer.

At the time, Burger King's parent company, Pillsbury, operated a flour mill in Jamaica. Sherwood arranged for a meeting with its executives to discuss the Burger King Franchise application. They reiterated the reasons for the rejection. Sherwood then said, "Can I speak now?" And she pulled up the research she had done on how much money the company was making in Jamaica. She said, "Look how much you're taking out of our little economy. What are you doing to develop people on the island?" One executive reached to turn off the voice recorder. She told him to leave it on as she was not yet finished. She then proceeded to rattle off the names of all the company executives and how much they were being paid while the islanders got little. She presented her own analysis of how they planned to operate the franchise, if approved. She asked them to reconsider the application and they did.

The Burger King Corporation is a Florida corporation that franchises and operates fast food hamburger restaurants, principally under the Burger King brand. It is the world's second largest fast food hamburger restaurant, or FFHR, chain as measured by the total number of restaurants. As of December 31, 2011, the company owned or franchised a total of 12,512 restaurants in 81 countries and U.S. territories, of which 1,295 restaurants were Company restaurants and 11,217 were owned by franchisees. Of these restaurants, 5,012, or 40 percent are located outside the USA and Canada and account for over 33 percent of revenue.

The Burger King restaurants feature flame-grilled hamburgers, chicken and other specialty sandwiches, french fries, soft drinks and other affordably-priced food items. With more than 50 years of operating history, the company has developed a scalable and cost-efficient quick service hamburger restaurant model that offers customers fast food at affordable prices.

Burger King generates revenues from two sources: retail sales at Company restaurants; and franchise revenues, consisting primarily of royalties based on a percentage of sales reported by franchise restaurants and franchise fees paid by franchisees as well as property income derived from properties leased or subleased to franchisees. Approximately 90% of current restaurants are franchised.

RESTAURANT ASSOCIATES LIMITED

Restaurant Associates Limited was incorporated in March, 1983 with Kenneth as chairman and CEO and Lois as vice president. Burger King approved their franchise application in 1984 when they became convinced of Kenneth and Lois's ability to run a successful operation.

Sherwood decided to locate their first store in the resort town of Ocho Rios after realizing that not many people in Kingston were familiar with hamburgers. She felt that tourists visiting Ocho Rios would patronize the restaurant and locals would soon follow suit. She was right. The store was soon reporting the best sales in the Caribbean. This time, Sherwood had no problem getting the necessary loans as the bankers told her, "you have shown us time and time again, we'd be fools not to back you."

The second Burger King restaurant was located in the Half-Way-Tree area of Kingston. At first everyone was against the location: For one thing, it was on a one-way street. The Burger King representatives rejected it and told her to find another location. But Sherwood was adamant the store would be located in the spot she had selected and took them on a tour of the immediate area and pointed to the many schools within walking distance of the location. She also explained that she understood the consumer and many students would be having a meal before they went home from school as their parents worked and had little time for cooking. Burger King relented and the store was built. When the restaurant opened, even Lois was pleasantly surprised at the long lines around the block waiting to be served. It quickly surpassed the other store in sales.

ECONOMIC IMPACT

That Burger King was opening restaurants in Jamaica was welcome news in the 1980s. It was a media event. Articles and advertising welcoming and extolling the virtues of the company were abundant. Government and business leaders alike spoke of the expected impact on the local economy; Minister of Tourism Hugh Hart saw it as a boon to tourism with many benefits:

> …the most obvious being to provide Jamaicans and visitors alike with fast food outlets offering relatively inexpensive fare of internationally proven standards. They will certainly enhance the amenities available in the tourism industry, since most of our visitors are from North America (*Gleaner*, 1985).

Burger King's focus on education and training was another feature that resonated in Jamaica. By the time the restaurants opened several Jamaicans had been sent to Burger King University in Miami, Florida for training. The company also promised to lend considerable support to Jamaica's primary youth-training and development program—the HEART Trust—by employing about 50 HEART trainees in each of its restaurants.

Burger King's presence in Jamaica was expected to have considerable impact on the Jamaican economy, in areas such as agriculture, tourism and employment:

> A strong stimulus was expected in Agriculture by Burger King's demands on the industry for high quality food supplies. Already, contracts have been signed with the Christiana Potato Growers Association for Irish Potatoes and with a number of small farmers for a wide variety of vegetables, as well as the other ingredients of their varied menu. A preliminary arrangement has been made with the Midlands group and others for a steady supply of beef and discussions on chicken supplies are being held with Caribbean Broilers. This is to ensure total Jamaicanization of supplies. As additional new Burger King Restaurants open across the island demand, supply and production will increase thereby helping to create more employment in the sector. (*Gleaner*, 1985).

Today, Restaurant Associates operates some 26 Burger King restaurants across the island and two Popeye's restaurants. Over 1,000 people are employed by the company.

THE ARTISTIC ENTREPRENEUR

Sherwood's original ambition was to be an artist. She has achieved that and more. In addition to being an astute and clever entrepreneur, she has excelled in the art world and has been the recipient of numerous awards for her work as an artist and her outstanding contributions to Jamaica. She has exhibited in the USA, Poland and Lithuania. In 2004, one of her paintings entitled *Earth Rhythm* was presented by the Jamaican Government as a gift to the Association of Caribbean States for display in the secretariat's offices in Port of Spain, Trinidad and Tobago.

She has won numerous awards for her art including, an award of excellence from the Consular Corps of Jamaica; Bronze, Silver and Gold medals at the Festival of Fine Art.

Sherwood is committed to maintaining a balance between her art and her business persona. She leaves her business office at a fixed time each day to visit her studio where she puts in a number of hours each day. She freely admits that her artistic side provides her the most satisfaction and pleasure although it is not nearly as profitable as the business side.

THE RODWELL LAKE MEMORIAL SCHOLARSHIPS

In 2001, Sherwood established the Burger King Scholarship program in memory of her first husband, Rodwell Lake. It provides scholarships and grants to students at the secondary and tertiary education levels.

At the annual awards ceremony held at the Pegasus Hotel in New Kingston in August, 2012, over 20 students received scholarships or awards from the program. Some were off to college with their awards while others received grants to purchase books. Awards for high school graduates are based on the results of the Caribbean Advance Proficiency Examination (CAPE) taken by Jamaican high school students each year. Book grants are based on the Grade Six Achievement Test students take to gain admission to high school (Spaulding, 2012).

The signature scholarships, named after Lois Lake-Sherwood, and Rodwell Lake, father of the company's vice-chairman are awarded to past students from their alma maters; St Andrew High School for Girls and St George's College respectively (*Jamaica Observer*, 2011). Not all awards are based on academic ability as two students received the Lois Sherwood Arts Scholarship for studies at the Edna Manley College of the Visual and Performing Arts. One student received an award for athletics.

BURGER KING NATIONAL SCHOOLS' DEBATE COMPETITION

Restaurant Associates is the major sponsor of the Burger King National Schools' Debate Competition among the island's high schools. Each year some 128 high schools vie for the coveted trophy. Sherwood has been known to attend and present the victors with the trophy.

LIFE CHALLENGES AND OBSTACLES

Sherwood believes in never taking no for an answer and in the motto "never give up." And her life has presented many challenges and obstacles to test her resolve. Her first husband Rodwell Lake suffered a heart attack at the age of 36. He died a few years later at age 44 in 1974. She suffered another tragic loss when her second husband, Kenneth Sherwood was killed in a dispute with a household employee in 1989.

One day, while Sherwood was alone in her first business, the antique store, a robber held a gun to her head. Luckily, a local policeman just happened to be passing by. He interrupted the robbery and arrested the suspect. As a result, Sherwood decided to relocate the store to 20 Hope Road, a location which today houses some of her current businesses. She has been held at gunpoint a total of four times including once in her land development office and twice in her Burger King office. She has remained undeterred and grateful.

A BALANCED LIFE

In 1987, Sherwood was appointed as a Justice of the Peace in Jamaica and in 2002 she was appointed Honourary Consul of the Republic of Lithuania. She had come to the attention of the Lithuanian Government through her art and was asked to represent them after she conducted an art exhibit in the capital, Vilnius.

Her children have been involved in her businesses and also pursue their own interests: Richard Lake is a contractor who runs the day to day operations of Restaurant Associates as vice chairman and president of the company while her other son, Michael is an architect. Her daughter, Ann Ventura, is an artist and the owner of Sanaa Studios where Sherwood also teaches on occasion.

Sherwood truly believes that "art does the most fantastic things for your brain." She practices yoga, loves music and of course, art.

ONE OF JAMAICA'S FIVE MOST POWERFUL WOMEN

In 2005, Sherwood was mentioned as one of Jamaica's most powerful women in a *Jamaica Observer* column entitled, *Jamaica's Five Most Powerful women*. The section on Sherwood reads as follows:

Lois Lake Sherwood is Managing Director, Restaurant Associates Ltd, operators of Burger King and Popeye's. Petite and sophisticated, Lois Lake Sherwood is an accomplished and successful visual artist, but although that makes her essential to Jamaica's thriving art scene, it's her business endeavors that bring her into this very elite club.

Not only is she estimated to be a multi-millionaire, but she sits on the boards of several Jamaican companies, the most significant being Restaurant Associates Ltd, the company that holds the franchise for Burger King and Popeye's restaurants in Jamaica. Burger King is currently the second largest fast-food franchise in Jamaica, with 19 outlets in Jamaica, and one, the Half-Way-Tree restaurant, a particular prize catch, having been named the top selling Burger King in the world for several years on end.

Lois Lake Sherwood brings a quiet elegance to anything she touches, and under her quiet leadership her family has amassed a tidy fortune. But while she prefers to allow her children to be the public face of the companies, the immense power she wields in this country is like her, understated (*Jamaica Observer*, 2005).

DISCUSSION

Sherwood's early ambition was to be an artist, not an entrepreneur. Fortunately, she was able to pursue this dream while also becoming an entrepreneur. She is the chairman of two companies she founded and serves on the boards of several other businesses. Restaurants Associates is the most well known of these companies. With some 28 franchise restaurants, she has provided thousands of jobs with benefits to Jamaicans over the 26 years she has been affiliated with Burger King. She has also endeavored to purchase local supplies and services thereby contributing to the local economy.

Many Jamaicans have benefited from training and contributions provided by her restaurants; and the Rodwell Lake scholarships in honour of her first husband help many young students meet expenses in high school and college.

From an early age, Sherwood was known for her determination and perseverance, traits she credits as being important to her entrepreneurial success. She believes in "never taking no for an answer." This was evidenced when she refused to accept the rejection of their application for a franchise by Burger King, but went on to persuade them that she and her husband were the people that could run the Jamaican Burger King operations.

As a child, Sherwood was able to observe her parents in productive actions—she watched her mother design dresses that she would then sell to her customers realizing a profit from her efforts. She recalls her mother was very creative in her designs. Her father made all the furniture for their home and Sherwood would later parlay this early exposure to furniture making into her first venture in which she had furniture made by local craftsmen for her store the Mahogany House.

Her savings initially allowed Sherwood to start her first venture. She recalls that she saved most of the money that had been allocated to groceries. Later, when larger sums of money were required she approached the banks which were reluctant to loan to a woman at first but she persisted and convinced them she was a good credit risk. Later when her track record was established credit became more readily available.

An important lesson from Sherwood's success is the importance of perseverance, pushing back when necessary and doing your homework. Whenever objections were raised, Sherwood was prepared with facts and figures to counter any argument to the contrary. These traits have served her well on her entrepreneurial journey from pin-up girl to business magnate.

CHAPTER 10

George Yap

George Yap founded LEASA Industries, one of the largest growers, manufacturers, processors and packers of healthy food products across the southeastern United States. Company products are distributed to various retail locations throughout Florida, Georgia, Alabama, South Carolina, Tennessee, Alaska and the Caribbean.

The company has won numerous awards including awards and admiration for its location in the depressed inner city neighborhood of Liberty City, Miami, Florida; for offering jobs to welfare mothers and a second chance to residents with police records and troubled backgrounds.

George Yap was born in Kingston, Jamaica, in 1941. His mother and father, Mable and Patrick Yap, were immigrants who had migrated to Jamaica in the 1920s from Guangzhou, China. The Yaps had eight children. George was the seventh.

NATURAL DISASTERS

The family operated a small bakery but a fire engulfed the business and destroyed everything. His father then started a factory that bottled carbonated soft drinks at the corner of Matthews Lane and Barry Street in downtown Kingston. In 1951, Hurricane Charlie, the deadliest tropical cyclone of the season, hit Jamaica with category 3 intensity and caused widespread damage. The Yap's family business was completely destroyed. His father never completely recovered from these two setbacks but according to Yap, he was a generous soul and died a happy man.

NO FUNDS FOR SCHOOL

As a young boy, Yap developed an illness that kept him in the hospital for six months causing him to miss school for an extended period. He ended up not completing high school as the financial toll from the loss of two businesses left the family with insufficient funds to pay for his education.

After dropping out of Gaynstead High school, Yap sold lunches cooked by his mother to Chinese shops and other businesses downtown. When this proved profitable, he expanded to include dinners. Realizing that he enjoyed being a salesman, Yap soon developed a thriving business selling other items such as hot dogs, hamburgers and Jamaican patties to various high school canteens in Kingston.

NOT EVERYONE IS GOOD AT BAKING

Encouraged by his success, he looked to what seemed like the next logical step. He started a bakery. He soon realized that he was good at selling, but not baking. Products that he sold were usually returned for refunds. At one point, his delivery van was seized by a bakery supplier for nonpayment. An equipment supplier repossessed his ovens used for warming patties.

TAKING A RISK

When one door closes, another usually opens. But sometimes you have to look to see it. Yap saw an opportunity in Jukeboxes and "one-armed bandit" slot machines. It was a risky but profitable venture. And Yap loved a good risk. He would eventually own over 100 machines and go on to own several bars. He had become a successful Jamaican businessman.

POLITICAL AND ECONOMIC UNCERTAINTY

In the year 1977, Yap and his wife Einez are living in Florida having abandoned everything they owned in Jamaica by fleeing the political and economic upheavals of the 1970s. It was a time of political violence, crime and uncertainty. His cousin, Ferdie Yap, who was campaigning as a candidate for the opposition JLP was arrested and detained under a state of emergency declared by Prime Minister Michael Manley. Fearing for his freedom should he encounter a similar fate since he was also aligned with the opposition party, Yap made his escape to Miami, Florida. Yap was now an immigrant like his parents before him who had earlier fled political unrest in China. It was rough going in Miami initially. He recalls how he bought a Dodge vehicle for $700.

It was drivable, but he had to use a wire clothes hanger to keep the front door closed.

A GOOD WIFE

Yap credits much of his success to the sacrifices of his late wife Einez who died in 2005. She was of Chinese and Malaysian ancestry. Her parents were the Lee-Chows and lived in the town of Bath in the parish of St Thomas in Jamaica. They were married in 1965 and had two boys and two girls. Einez worked two jobs to provide food and shelter for the family after they left Jamaica. With limited education and unable to find employment, Yap realized he would have to start his own business but he had no capital having left Jamaica with almost nothing.

HYDROPONIC FARMING

Yap heard about a hydroponic food farm that had filed for bankruptcy. The owners had given up in defeat but Yap saw opportunity—although he knew nothing about farming. Yap admits he had "absolutely no idea" what he was doing. He was a city man and had never grown even a weed before. But he was desperate for a chance to do something. Yap borrowed US$15,000 from family and friends to purchase the farm. He named the company LEASA using the first initial of each member of the family including their three children, Andrew, Sean and Allison.

There was a moment of joy when the deal was signed and Yap was given papers to the new company. He was back in business. Elation soon turned to panic when the promised support and training from the previous owners did not materialize. The initial results of the farm were disastrous. The business only managed sales of US$175 per week in the beginning. It had only US$5,000 in sales the first year but losses were US$30,000 after only a few months of operation.

THE POWER OF PERSEVERANCE

Buying a business you know nothing about is a very risky proposition but Yap says. "I am a gambler. I love to take risks and I get excited by taking risks. The bigger the risk, the bigger the reward but it's also the harder you fall." Yap believes in perseverance and advises aspiring entrepreneurs, "You have to believe in yourself. And don't be a quitter." He recalls trying to get a loan to keep the business going early on--seven banks rejected him. Despite this discouragement he did not give up. Finally he walked into an African-American bank and made an application. When they asked what collateral he had, he smiled and said, "Me." The bankers laughed but he was able to walk out with a US$10,000 loan.

ADMIT YOUR MISTAKES

Another principle Yap espouses is, "Don't be too proud. Pride won't take you to the supermarket. Admit when you fail or make a mistake and learn from it." He adds, "We should not fear criticism. We should see it as a good thing."

LEASA INDUSTRIES INC.

Today, LEASA Industries is profitable with sales approaching US$10 million. It grows and sells vegetables such as bean and alfalfa sprouts, specialty sprouts, value added fresh cut vegetables, bulk vegetables, Chinese food items, and its famous soy line which includes firm, veggie, cilantro and spicy tofu. Also available are stir fry vegetable mixes, vegetable soup mixes, fresh herbs, sugar snaps, snow peas, shallots, specialty onions, egg rolls and won ton wrappers.

EVERYONE DESERVES A SECOND CHANCE

LEASA Industries Inc. employs people from the inner city neighborhood of Liberty City. Yap explains that, "these are rehabilitating drug addicts, ex-convicts and welfare mothers, who nobody else wanted to employ. I say to them: 'I am giving you a second chance because everybody deserves one.'"

A MAN WITH A GOOD HEART

People have told him, "George, you have a heart, but no head." He has even taken people out of jail and trained them to work in his business. And once, he hired an ex-con as a security guard. Asked why he would do this, "I just enjoy helping people," Yap replied. "I believe in giving before people ask."

His son Andrew is now president of LEASA Industries. Two of his brothers, a nephew and a sister-in-law also work in the business.

Yap returns to Jamaica often and donates to charities there and is currently involved in a project to help build homes for the very poor who are squatters.

AWARDS

LEASA Industries has won numerous awards including the following.

- 1989 Small Business of the Year Award for community service

- 1997 National Minority Manufacturer of the Year Award by the U.S. Department of Commerce and Minority Business Development Agency.

- 1998, Welfare to Work—Small Business Owner of the Year, South Florida SBA.

- 1999 and 2000, 100 Fastest Growing Privately Held Companies in America's Inner Cities from Inc Magazine and Harvard Business School Initiative for a Competitive Inner City.

- 1999 Manufacturer of the Year Award by the Florida Manufacturing Technology Center and the Florida Business Journal.

- 2007 Supplier of the Year Award—Florida Regional Minority Business Council.

DISCUSSION

George Yap left everything behind and fled to Miami with his family fearing political reprisals. In Jamaica he had been a serial entrepreneur, starting various businesses.

His father had two businesses and although both suffered from disasters it was enough to provide Yap with an entrepreneurial identity as well as an introduction to the entrepreneurial culture. Unable to continue in high school due to lack of funds, Yap showed his innovative side when he started selling cooked lunches door-to-door in Kingston's business district as a teenager. Yap is probably the entrepreneur with the highest propensity to take risks of all those studied. He bought a hydroponic farm when he had never even "planted a weed" previously. He saw an opportunity in a bankrupt business when others would have run in the other direction.

Lack of education forced Yap to become a "necessity" entrepreneur but his propensity for taking risks, his entrepreneurial mindset, and his ability to innovate and to recognize opportunities enabled him to make the transition and he became an "opportunity" entrepreneur.

CHAPTER 11

Robert Levy, CD

Robert Levy is the chairman of Jamaica Broilers Group Ltd, one of the most advanced and diversified agricultural producers in the developing world and operating at the highest levels of efficiency and quality. Through his inspired leadership, this company has been transformed into a vertically integrated operation that caters to both local and international markets. Levy is one of the most highly respected businessmen in Jamaica today and he has a long record of distinguished service to the country.

Robert Levy describes his childhood as, "tremendous, we had everything we needed." He was born in Kingston on May 1, 1940 and grew up with his brother and sister. His father Sidney was originally from Montego Bay and his mother, Hazel, was from Highgate in St. Mary. Levy recalls that his father was "the best dressed man in town. He was not religious, but he never once embarrassed his children in any way." His father and his uncles had a business in Kingston representing manufacturers of various products such as pharmaceuticals, foodstuffs and appliances.

DYSLEXIA ISSUES

Levy attended de'Carteret College and Jamaica College for high school but admits he was not a good student and gave a lot of trouble. By the time he was 20 years of age, he had cut off two of his fingers. He dropped out of high school without sitting the requisite exams. He later learned that he had dyslexia, a reading disability that occurs when the brain does not properly recognize and process certain symbols. Dyslexic people tend to be highly creative, intuitive, and excel at three-dimensional problem solving and hands-on learning.

JAMAICA BROILERS LTD

After leaving school, Levy worked for an uncle, but in 1959, at the age of 19, he joined his father at the recently formed Jamaica Broilers. Initially, the company imported finished poultry for sale to the Jamaican market. Later it was decided to grow and process chickens in Jamaica instead. Levy recalls that it took some time for the public to adjust to the "white chicken" having been accustomed to the local backyard raised domestic chickens that were darker in color and sold in the local markets.

THE EMPTINESS WITHIN

According to Levy, by age 30 he was living what appeared to be a very good life, "I had every single thing a young person could want, a beautiful wife, new cars, new house, two children but I was the most arrogant, ugly, unhappy guy you could possibly meet." He wondered how such a thing could be possible. One day, he changed his life by having a conversation with God on his knees, in his office. He began to study the Bible fervently and claims to have read it through at least 15 times. His life has never been the same. He gives God credit for all the extraordinary success he has achieved.

Once he had alignment with the almighty, Levy set about transforming Jamaica Broilers. He spearheaded new development and the company's drive to gain control of all elements of the supply chain.

THE BEST DRESSED CHICKEN

The Jamaica Broilers' Best Dressed Chicken is one of the best known brands in Jamaica. The company controls some 40 percent of the Jamaican chicken market and is the largest and most sophisticated poultry operation in the Caribbean. Jamaica Broilers introduced a free range product in keeping with the trends. The company's free range farmers were the first poultry growers outside the USA to obtain a Step 3 rating certification from the Global Animal Partnership (GAP).

VERTICAL INTEGRATION

Jamaica Broilers is vertically integrated in regard to their main business of poultry—they own each member of the supply chain, starting with fertile hatching eggs locally at Jamaica Poultry Breeders Ltd in St. Ann. They provide

Hi-Pro feed produced at the Best Dressed Feed Mill in Old Harbour, Jamaica to contract farmers who raise the chickens until maturity when they enter the Best Dressed Chicken processing plant.

CONTENT AGRICULTURAL PRODUCTS

Content Agricultural Products is the cattle rearing and beef producing subsidiary of Jamaica Broilers. It accounts for approximately 15 percent of the island's beef market. This subsidiary also produces salted pig's tail and pickled mackerel.

THE BEST DRESSED FISH

The Best Dressed Fish is farm raised tilapia of world-class quality, raised in the state-of-the art fish ponds of Aquaculture Jamaica Limited located in the parish of St Elizabeth. .

HI-PRO ACE DIVISION

The Hi-Pro ACE Division operates the Farm and Garden Supercenter and sells Hi-Pro Feeds and Hi-Pro Chicks. The garden center carries over 20,000 items and represents many well known brands such as Ace Hardware, Kawasaki, FG Wilson, Poulan, Carolina Skiff, Toro and Vetoquinol. The feeds are manufactured with specific diets for broilers, layers, pigs, cattle, horses and fish. The chicks are day old baby chicks hatched from fertile eggs in the Group's state-of-the-art hatchery in White Marl, St Catherine.

JB ETHANOL LTD

In 2007, JB Ethanol Ltd., a fuel ethanol dehydration plant was opened at Port Esquivel in the parish of St Catherine, to take advantage of ready markets for ethanol which exist in North America, Canada, some parts of Central America and CARICOM. The finished product from the plant is anhydrous ethanol.

The plant is capable of processing locally-produced hydrous ethanol from Jamaican sugar cane—thereby providing an outlet for this product and directly supporting the privatization strategy of Jamaican Sugar assets. It also sources hydrous ethanol from Brazil. According to Levy, "green ethanol can be produced from sugar cane and low energy production ethanol gets tax incentives. Our product is 99 percent pure ethanol—no water--and Jamaica has an advantage in producing the anhydrous ethanol."

OVERSEAS OPERATIONS

The group's overseas operations include Wincorp International which is based in Miami, Florida and ships mainly poultry-related products to businesses in the Caribbean and Central America. International Poultry Breeders is based in the state of Georgia and produces hatching eggs.

In Haiti, the company has invested in local production facilities comprising a Feed Mill, Hatchery and Poultry farm which were recently completed. The company has been focused on building the Hi-Pro brand in the country and Hi-Pro animal feeds and baby chicks are now available via distributors.

The company invested in Atlantic United Insurance Company which is incorporated in St Lucia with business offices in The Cayman Islands.

HARVARD BUSINESS SCHOOL

Levy has more than made up for his earlier encounters with the educational system. In 1986, he successfully completed the Harvard Business School Owner/President Management Program (OPM), a three-year intensive program that focuses on analyzing business opportunities, leading growth and planning future transitions.

FOCUS ON QUALITY

According to Levy, one reason for the group's success is their focus on quality. "None of us in this business is super smart nor are we workaholics. But we want to do things right and to the best of our ability—quality is who we are." Another reason he cites is the relationship they strive to maintain with the staff. They also have an approach to selecting managers that has worked well for them. The executive team interviews everyone being considered for a management position—and each member of the team has veto power. This ensures that anyone hired has the confidence of the entire team.

THE POWER OF PRAYER

In 2000, the Jamaica Broilers was US$20 million in debt and started a prayer project at the company in which four executives and their spouses would pray every Thursday afternoon. By 2002, the company had US$20 million in cash in the bank. According to Levy, "God turned things around. We can't explain it. We never 'tief' it. Business picked up some but not that much."

2012 RESULTS

In 2012 Jamaica Broilers reported that revenue increased by 11 percent—moving up J$2.4 billion from the J$21.3 billion recorded in 2010/2011 to J$23.7 billion in 2011/2012. However, due to market constraints and direct cost increases gross profits only increased by four percent from $4.6 billion in the previous year to J$4.8 billion during 2011/2012. Net profits attributable to stockholders at J$936 million reflect a two percent decrease when compared to the J$956 million realized in 2010/2011.

ECONOMIC TRENDS

Levy enjoys being the most successful agro business in the Caribbean and is considered an "entrepreneur par excellence." Although he admits he is fortunate to be in the food business as it offers the least amount of variance based on what happens in the economy, that doesn't mean it's not subject to jolts in the economy. The cost of grain which has been $2-3 per bushel over the last 50 years is now $8-9 per bushel. This has motivated them to start planting some grain which will be good for Jamaica, he explained.

PASSING THE TORCH

Levy's two sons are both involved in the business. Christopher, a Harvard graduate, is president and CEO of the group while Steven who just finished his master's degree runs WinCorp International based in the USA.

AWARDS

In 2002, Levy received national honours as Order of Distinction in the rank of commander.

A long-standing member of the Jamaica Agricultural Society, he is also a past president of the American Chamber of Commerce, a past director of the Rotary Club, and a past director of the Caribbean Christian Centre for the Deaf.

In 2008, he was bestowed with the honourary degree of Master of Arts, Honoris Causa, by the Caribbean Graduate School of Theology, In recognition of his exemplary life at home, in business, in the church and other levels of society.

In 2009, Northern Caribbean University conferred on him the honourary degree of Doctor of Laws, *honoris causa*, for distinguishing himself as a nation builder.

In 2010, he was inducted into the Private Sector Organization of Jamaica's Hall of Fame.

In May 2011, the company was recognized with the *Jamaica Observer Food Awards 2011*—Lifetime Achievement Award—in acknowledgement of the group's significant contribution to the local food industry.

DISCUSSION

Robert Levy is one of the most respected business people in Jamaica today. Evidence of his entrepreneurial prowess and impact on Jamaican agriculture is abundant. He heads one of the most advanced and diversified agricultural enterprises in the developing world.

From their core chicken business, Jamaica Broilers has vertically integrated to control hatchers and feed plus other aspects of the supply chain. He started new businesses in the beef, fish and other industries. When he saw opportunities for Jamaica in ethanol processing which is a foreign exchange earner for the island, he built a plant.

As good corporate citizens, Jamaica Broilers supports many community projects through the Jamaica Broilers Foundation which focuses on children and youth, at risk and disadvantaged groups, and other programs. Through their Hi-Pro Ace Supercentre, they sponsor the annual Tennis Jamaica Open Championship, and the annual gospel festival, "Best Dressed Fun in the Son" for example.

CHAPTER 12

Vincent HoSang

Caribbean Food Delights is the largest Jamaican frozen food manufacturer in North America. It is a multi-million dollar corporation which produces beef, chicken, vegetable, shrimp and other varieties of spicy Jamaican patties which are also known as empanadas or turnovers in its state-of-the-art, mechanized Safe Quality Food (SQF) certified plant in Tappan, New York.

Royal Caribbean Bakery is a sister company which is operated as retail restaurants selling assorted Jamaican baked products such as fruit buns, hard dough bread and pastries in addition to patties.

The companies are well known for their contributions to Jamaica and the Diaspora. They have won numerous awards for philanthropy including the prestigious Commonwealth Award.

Vincent HoSang was born in 1941 and grew up in the small town of Springfield in the parish of St James in western Jamaica. His parents, Nukelyn and Henry HoSang operated a general store typically referred to as a "Chiney Shop." They also had a rum shop and a bakery in the town. There was no electricity or running water in the Springfield at that time. But HoSang says he enjoyed a comfortable early childhood with his siblings, making their own toys and playing dolly house with his sisters. He had 13 siblings, nine brothers and four sisters. They learnt at an early age how to be resourceful and how to make do with what they had.

DOWN AND OUT IN MONTEGO BAY

According to HoSang, his father couldn't say no whenever his poor neighbors in the village asked for favors. There was no employment and money was difficult to come by. He gave so much; he eventually gave away the store. The family was forced to split up and live with relatives. HoSang was sent to live with an uncle who had a grocery store in Montego Bay.

CAREER CHOICE

As a teenager, HoSang was forced to make a critical decision that would impact the direction in which his life would unfold. He had been attending high school at Cornwall College for three years when his uncle requested that he quit school and help him by working fulltime in his shop. In return his uncle promised to help him get his own shop.

His ambition was to become a doctor and in order to accomplish that he needed to stay in school. He sought advice from his older brother, King, who advised him to stay in school and offered financial assistance. But HoSang, moved by the help he had already received from his uncle when it was sorely needed, decided to drop out and work in the shop. He now thinks that God had bigger plans for his life and was directing him in making that fateful decision.

HELLO, NEW YORK WINTERS!

After helping his uncle for several years, Vincent was asked by his brother, King, to go and help his father who had opened a new shop in Kingston, Jamaica's capital. He worked for his father for a while but in 1968 he decided to seek a better opportunity by migrating to the USA.

Although his first job in New York only paid US$60 per week putting hinges on briefcases, HoSang did not complain but worked diligently and put in extra effort which did not go unnoticed as his boss soon gave him a raise. His second job was a big improvement at US$148 per week delivering milk at night. He recalls that the winters were cold and the snow depressing.

JAMAICAN PATTIES

In 1976, HoSang married Jeanette who hailed from Spanish Town in Jamaica and they soon had the first of four children. He always wanted to start his own business but after a decade of working in New York, his American dream seemed quite far away. Once again he called on his big brother, King, for advice and counsel. King suggested that he try making Jamaican patties and offered to help him get started in business.

HoSang located a fried chicken restaurant in a great location in the Knightsbridge section of the Bronx, NY. He bought the business using his savings and assistance from his brother. He immediately saw several improvements he could make to achieve profitability.

The previous owners showed him the ins-and-outs of the business and how to comply with various government regulations. His brother taught him how to make patties while Jeanette developed Jamaican dishes for the menu. By focusing on providing good customer service combined with support from the Jamaican community, the business was soon thriving.

Vincent's timing could not have been better. Political upheavals on the island of Jamaica had resulted in an exodus of Jamaicans to the USA, and many settled in New York during the 1970s and 1980s. Among Jamaicans, patties—spicy meat pies in a flaky crust—are primarily eaten as a lunch item or snack. It was an easy way to satisfy the nostalgia they had for their home far away. The market for Jamaican products grew rapidly as other nationalities became captivated by the spicy island treats.

THE ROYAL CARIBBEAN BAKERY

The next step up the ladder of success for HoSang came when he bought a small bakery which he named the Royal Caribbean Bakery. The business kept growing and growing and eventually he bought a 10 acre property in Rockland County, New York, and built a 75,000 square foot manufacturing facility.

CARIBBEAN FOOD DELIGHTS, INC.

The manufacturing arm of the business was now named Caribbean Food Delights. Company products were being distributed all over the country in major supermarkets, wholesale clubs, military bases and their own retail outlets. It has now expanded into exporting products overseas.

As the business grew, Caribbean Food Delights was able to obtain bank financing for expansion. The most recent expansion in 2007 cost an estimated US$17 million and provided over 100,000 square feet to accommodate freezers, mixers, sheeting and packaging equipment, ovens, an X-ray machine, wrapping equipment and a holding freezer that holds 30 trailers of products.

A FAMILY BUSINESS

Now in his 70s, HoSang is still active and serves as president and chief executive officer (CEO) of Caribbean Food Delights. His wife, Jeanette, is CEO of the Royal Caribbean Bakery which manufacturers Jamaican breads, bullas, buns and pastries. His children are also involved in the businesses with daughter Sabrina serving as chief operating officer, son Damian, a mechanical engineer by training, keeps the plant humming and daughter Simone works in the food science department.

Both businesses sold to over 7,000 retailers worldwide, including Costco, BJ's, Sam's Club, and Wal-Mart, as well as many other national chains. They also serve 160 military commissaries worldwide. Caribbean Food Delights manufactures 40,000 patties an hour or over 83 million annually. In 2007, Caribbean Food Delights received the Forbes Enterprise Award for its visionary practices.

COMMUNITY INVOLVEMENT

HoSang has never forgotten where he came from. Despite his success he is very much a part of the Jamaican community. And, he gives God a lot of credit for the amazing path his life has taken and for blessing him every step along the way. He also believes in giving back.

For over 20 years Caribbean Food Delights has been feeding Jamaican high school athletes who travel to Pennsylvania each spring for the annual Penn Relays athletic meet. The program was recently expanded to feed some 600 and included athletes from other nations such as Trinidad & Tobago, The Bahamas, Grenada and Guyana.

THE VINCENT HOSANG FAMILY FOUNDATION

In 2002, the Vincent HoSang Family Foundation was established. Education and health care are two key areas that benefit from the philanthropy of the HoSang family. It also funds several scholarships at the UWI in entrepreneurship and donates to numerous institutions in Jamaica as well as in the USA.

A mobile medical clinic replete with examination rooms and equipment for doctors and dentists was built for use in Jamaica by the foundation in 2005. Another sizeable donation was made to Father Ho Lung's Missionaries of the Poor charity in Jamaica to build a home for abandoned children, people living with AIDS and others less fortunate. The foundation also provides scholarships to college students in the USA.

At the time of this writing, HoSang is busy with a project to acquire two multi-million dollar Linear Accelerator X-ray machines for Jamaican hospitals to use in cancer treatment.

DISCUSSION

Vincent HoSang is another product of the Jamaican "Chiney Shop." His entrepreneurial identity factors included his father and his uncle's shops in which he worked as a boy.

His first venture was as a small businessman buying a losing fried chicken restaurant which he converted into a Jamaican restaurant. As business improved, he expanded by purchasing a small bakery to make Jamaican products. He was not content to just provide an income to support his growing family; he wanted to pursue the opportunity he saw in selling Jamaican foods to the immigrant community. He is an example of a "necessity" entrepreneur who successfully made the transformation into an "opportunity" entrepreneur.

An important ingredient in HoSang's success was the social capital provided mostly by his brother King HoSang. At every step of his journey, King provided advice, emotional support and when necessary, financial support.

His entrepreneurial mindset was evidenced by his ability to take risks and start new businesses when he saw opportunities. For example, when the restaurant was doing well, he ventured into manufacturing, added new products and pursued new markets for his products.

CHAPTER 13

Gordon "Butch" Stewart, OJ

 *Gordon "Butch" Stewart is considered the Steve Jobs of the hotel industry—creating a product you didn't know you wanted and convincing you that you need it. He heads some two dozen diverse companies that are collectively Jamaica's largest private sector group, the country's biggest foreign exchange earner, and its largest non-government employer. He is best known for his creation of a tourism empire that started with one broken down hotel in Montego Bay, Jamaica and today spans the Caribbean with 19 resorts. Sandals Resorts International has won just about every award for high standards of excellence and customer service in the tourism industry.*

Gordon "Butch" Stewart was born in Kingston, Jamaica in 1941 and grew up "by the sea" in the resort town of Ocho Rios when it was still a small fishing village. His early life has been described as a "carefree one of fishing, swimming and sailing."

DROPPING OUT

School work was not Stewart's forte and he dropped out of school at age 14 because "he did not like homework." He was deemed "least likely to succeed" by his teachers. But he was known for "working harder than anyone else" and his eye for opportunity was demonstrated when he was able to use a boat he and a friend had built to earn money by recruiting a villager to use the boat to offer rides to tourists. The venture was short-lived as the boat sank shortly after. They had used regular plywood in its construction instead of marine plywood.

A JOB IN SALES

As a young man, he worked for the Dutch-owned Curacao Trading Company as a salesman when he returned to Jamaica after taking some courses in England. He did well at his job and rose to the position of sales manager. After several years, he had saved £3,200 and was ready to venture out on his own.

APPLIANCE TRADERS LIMITED

Stewart saw an opportunity in room air conditioners. Jamaican houses did not have central air conditioning and any cooling was done by room air conditioners. He walked the streets of Kingston soliciting orders door to door for window units. Being a skilled salesman, he soon had over 30 orders—but he had no air conditioners to sell. He contacted the Fedders Corporation in New Jersey to see if they would give him a distributorship.

Because he had no funding and lacked the stability of a big company, no one in the company was taking him seriously. Stewart bought an airline ticket and went to New Jersey to Fedders' offices. He met several executives and was getting nowhere until he met the president's nephew who listened to his presentation and decided to give him a chance.

Appliance Traders Limited was started in 1968 in the Cross Roads section of Kingston with limited funds. Stewart recalls that his desk was a plywood door retrofitted with legs. Although they were clearly outclassed by global brands such as Carrier, York, GE and Westinghouse, Stewart had a vision of being number one in the room air conditioner market. He differentiated himself from the competition by offering installation within eight hours of receiving an order. Within one year Appliance Traders was number one in the marketplace. His dedication to providing exceptional customer service had paid off.

A MASTER OF MARKETING

Before long, Appliance Traders Limited had expanded into the commercial air conditioning market. Stewart demonstrated that he was a master at marketing and promoting his business. He introduced mobile advertising on the island when he put the Fedders logo on the doors of his Mercedes Benz and all over his service vehicles. He set impossibly high standards for his employees to meet. They "worked hard but also had a ball" recounts one early employee.

158

Spurred by government restrictions on imports, Appliance Traders began manufacturing air conditioners, household appliances, water pumps, and other products. In 1975, they acquired Caribbean Brake Products Limited, a company that manufactured brakes, clutches and filter products for various makes of automobiles. They also began representing top appliance brands such as Amana refrigerators, Kitchen Aid dishwashers, and Panasonic fans among others.

BAY ROC AND CARLYLE ON THE BAY HOTELS

Seeking a means of generating foreign exchange—the government had placed restrictions on use of foreign exchange for imports to only those who were earners of foreign exchange—Stewart took a look at the tourism industry. He knew nothing about tourism and in the 1970s Jamaica's tourism had suffered under the government policies at the time. Investors were pulling out, the number of tourists was declining and things looked terrible. Nevertheless, he bought the dilapidated Bay Roc and Carlyle on the Bay Hotels in 1981. Despite the election of a new government with a different agenda, everyone thought he was crazy. It was thought to be "bad timing, bad property, wrong experience, etc."

> According to Pamela Lerner Jaccarino, in the book, *All That's Good*:
> Stewart wanted to develop a striking new concept for the Carlyle property, which had been a traditional European Plan Hotel. He sensed it wasn't going to work the way it was and recognized that he had to be as innovative as he had been in the early days at Appliance Traders Limited. (Jaccarino, 2005, P. 58).

And while others saw a "run-to-ground hotel" situated next to the runway of Montego Bay's airport, Stewart saw, "a magnificent beach and spacious rooms." The air conditioning man knew nothing about hotels but he understood marketing. He set about refurbishing and staffing the properties. And he checked with hoteliers to see what the industry wanted and what the customers wanted—his plan was to exceed the customers' expectations (Jaccarino, 2005, 58).

EXCEEDING THE CUSTOMERS' EXPECTATIONS

Stewart introduced many innovations that are now commonplace: he was first to include hair dryers, king sized beds and clock radios in every room. He recognized that most guests were couples and set out to design the "finest, most romantic resort for two people in love."

SANDALS RESORTS BEACH HOTEL

The Bay Roc name was changed to Sandals Resorts Beach Hotel, a name which suggested relaxation and vacation. On November 27, 1981 the first guests were welcomed to the hotel. Stewart had taken the "old battered up place and turned it around." Whenever planes took off from the airport their flight path took them over the hotel and made an awful noise. This was irritating to the guests. He found a way to turn that negative into a positive by starting a tradition of having couples kiss and wave in the air whenever an aircraft roared overhead.

The transformation of the Bay Roc into Sandals made the news in the world tourism circles. Stewart established personal relationships with travel agents and tour operators. He invited them to tour the property and threw parties for them. He went on to unleash groundbreaking upgrades to the hotel such as beachfront rooms, Jacuzzis, tropical Japanese fishponds, fitness centers, scuba diving and more. And then there was the never before seen swim-up pool bar which was such a big hit it became a standard at all Sandals properties. In a few years, Sandals had established itself as the place to be in Jamaica, especially for honeymooners. Within three years Sandals was profitable.

A COMMITMENT TO EXCELLENCE

By1987, the Appliance Trader attitude, work ethic and philosophy had been thoroughly inculcated in all aspects of the hotel operations. Innovation and the drive for superior service and quality were routine aspects of Sandals. Although they were not the first to offer the all-inclusive idea, they certainly revolutionized the concept.

EXPANSION IN PROGRESS

In 1986, Sandals acquired the highly regarded Royal Caribbean Hotel which was a short distance away and renamed it Sandals Royal Caribbean Hotel. They also renamed the Sandals Resort Beach Club to Sandals Montego Bay to avoid any confusion. In the 1980s, Jamaica's economy was on an upswing and "the climate of growth and booming business" encouraged Stewart to expand. In 1987, he acquired two old neighboring properties—Coconut Cove Beach and the Sundowner—in the resort town of Negril known for its legendary "seven mile beach." These two properties were merged into one that became Sandals Negril (Jaccarino, 2005, 119).

HURRICANE GILBERT

"Hurricanes? Oh, that's just the island's way of pruning trees." This is how Stewart has reportedly referred to the threat of hurricanes on the island. In 1988, hurricane Gilbert gave a major pruning to Jamaica when the category 5 hurricane slammed into the island at 175 miles per hour. It was the most destructive storm in the history of Jamaica. Widespread damage and loss of life was reported. Entire industries were wiped out. Twenty foot storm surges forced hotels in resort areas to evacuate.

Hurricane Gilbert was a major test for the Stewart organization. Reports of "total devastation" poured in from Montego Bay. Incredibly, all of Sandals employees in Montego Bay reportedly showed up for work the day after the hurricane. A major reconstruction project was begun while Stewart assured his travel industry partners that Sandals would be back better than ever. They were.

OVERSEAS EXPANSION

In 1981, Stewart made his first foray overseas with the opening of the opening of Sandals Antigua. He added several other hotels to the chain; some through management contracts which included Sandals Ocho Rios in 1989, Sandals Inn in 1990 and Sandals Dunn's River in 1991. In 1993, he added two properties in St Lucia. He also added wedding packages to his offerings that year. Sandals Royal Bahamian & Spa was added in 1996. By this time the hotel chain had become the largest in Jamaica and the entire Caribbean.

THE JAMAICA OBSERVER

In1993, Stewart started the *Jamaica Observer* as a weekly newspaper printing 50,000 copies. In 1994 it began to print a daily edition. It continues today as one of the major daily papers on the island.

AIR JAMAICA

In 1994 Butch Stewart formed the Air Jamaica Acquisitions Group (AJAG). The government of Jamaica had announced its intention to privatize the national airline, Air Jamaica. The airline had been a perennial money loser and was a drain on the island's limited funds.

Hotelier John Issa and former Jamaican mining minister Hugh Hart were the original bidders for Air Jamaica, but they reportedly withdrew their offer saying the government was laying down too many preconditions. Stewart's bid was accepted and he became majority shareowner with the government retaining 25 percent and employees five percent stakes in the airline. Stewart brought his "commitment to excellence" to bear on the airline and refurbishment and expansion plans were drawn up. A new motto, "on time, no line" was adopted to highlight improvements in a previously poor record of customer service and on-time departures. He also created the Montego Bay hub to optimize aircraft utilization.

Stewart made a host of improvements including new and expanded routes, adding state of the art and fuel efficient planes, establishing international alliances with other airlines, introducing a "flying chef," and champagne flights. Under his watch, the airline won several major international awards, including 'Best Airline Servicing the Caribbean'.

The first problem Stewart encountered with the airline was the downgrading of the island's air safety to a category II by the FAA just after a year after operations were taken over by AJAG. This was the responsibility of the island's Civil Aviation Department but it increased costs to the airline and for three years affected the airline's ability to operate as its new aircraft were essentially sidelined.

The second problem was the September 11 terrorist attacks. There was a drop in air travel plus higher fuel prices and other problems as a result of the gulf war, which drove many carriers into bankruptcy. Air Jamaica's planes were stuck around the world for weeks after being forced to land due to the attacks.

Stewart turned the airline over to the government in 2004 when government support was not forthcoming—he reportedly admitted that partnering Air Jamaica with the government had been a nightmare as all the problems were inherited from the government (Townsend 2006). The airline had lost an average of approximately US$67 million dollars each year during the 10 years it was run by AJAG. However, it would lose more than three times as much per year once the government took control. It was eventually sold to Caribbean Airlines in 2011.

BEACHES RESORTS

In 1997, the first Beaches Resort was opened in Negril, Jamaica. It offered a concept that catered to families who would be offered the same amenities as couples—several dining establishments, large pools, beachfront activities, as well as babysitting services and family-oriented fun. Beaches, like sibling Sandals resorts, would also be all-inclusive for a no-worry vacation. Other resorts were later added in Ocho Rios and Providenciales, Turks and Caicos.

THE ALL-INCLUSIVE CONCEPT

Club Mediterranee SA (Club Med), a French Vacation resort company, pioneered the all-inclusive concept in the 1950s. Sandals improved on the concept. According to Sandals everything is included "including luxury."

Today the Sandals Empire has earned a worldwide reputation for providing some of the most spectacular vacation experiences in the Caribbean. There are 19 Sandals Resorts International properties located in Jamaica, Antigua, St. Lucia, Turks and Caicos, and The Bahamas.

FAMILY TIES

Stewart's son, Adam Stewart, took over as CEO of Sandals Resorts International in 2006. Adam oversees all areas of SRI operations—he is one of the world's youngest CEOs. He was born on January 27, 1981, the same year his father purchased his first hotel and launched Sandals Resorts International (SRI) which would one day become the Sandals Empire. Jaime Stewart-McConnell, Stewart's daughter, managed the Royal Plantation Collection of very exclusive properties and Stewart's son, Brian Jardim, also worked for the company before venturing off on his own with the Margaritaville chain.

Stewart suffered a great loss when his son Jonathan was killed in a car accident in 1990.

THE SANDALS FOUNDATION

Adam Stewart founded the Sandals Foundation to coordinate the company's many philanthropic projects. Previously, the group had some 300 projects which were never publicized. The foundation's focus is on community, environment and education. It allows guests and corporate sponsors to contribute to local communities.

AWARDS

Sandals have dominated the travel industry awards over the years and received numerous awards such as World's Best All-Inclusive, Top Caribbean

Hotel Group, and World's Leading Independent Resort. At the 2012 World Travel Awards (WTA), the industry's most prestigious travel honours, Sandals claimed 15 of the 50 trophies.

Stewart has received numerous personal awards including, Hotelier of the Year, American Airlines award for Development of Caribbean Tourism, Caribbean Hotel Industry's Golden Conch Award and Destination Marketer of the Year. He has been honoured by the Jamaican Government with the Order of Distinction (OD), Commander Class, and the Order of Jamaica (OJ) awards. In 1995, he was inducted into the Private Sector Organization of Jamaica Hall of Fame.

DISCUSSION

Stewart is reported to have said that had he known what he was doing, he'd never have started the Sandals Hotel chain. What is clear is that he brought his passion for innovation and customer service to the tourism industry and as they say, the rest is history. He focused on execution which is what entrepreneurs tend to do instead of analyzing new ideas to death.

Stewart exemplifies many of the classic traits of the successful entrepreneur: he didn't like school, he took calculated risks, and he could see opportunity where others only saw problems. It's also interesting to note that his first business sold appliances and when he was growing up his mother owned a small appliance business.

Boldness is one adjective that describes Stewart. He is not afraid of bold decisive moves. He is also a non-conformist. He thinks "outside-the-box" and this has fueled many of the innovations he has implemented in his businesses.

CHAPTER 14

Norman Wright

Norman Wright is the Founder of Perishables Jamaica Limited, a manufacturer of Jamaican herbal teas under the TOPS brand. It is an example of a successful Jamaican small and medium- size enterprise (SME). The company packages teas under contract to other companies for the export as well as local markets. At a time when many Jamaicans eschew farming, Norman is encouraging the expansion of farming activities and making a positive contribution to the island's economy while earning valuable foreign exchange.

Norman Wight was born in Kingston, Jamaica on July 4, 1955 but grew up mostly in the garden parish of St Ann located on the north side of the island. He lived in the rural, hilly village of Coultart Grove, some 11 miles from the sea.

AN EARLY LOVE OF FARMING

Wright describes his childhood as, "lots of fun." He developed an early love of farming and learnt how to live off the land by planting crops and watching them grow to maturity. He recalls hunting birds with a sling shot, roaming the land in search of ripe fruits such as mangoes, naseberries, star apples, guavas, oranges and apples. There was no TV and radio was a luxury. Lighting was by lamp light and the refrigerator was powered by kerosene. He recalls that his responsibilities included milking cows, tending the goats and rabbits, and pumping water into the family tank. Many of these tasks were completed before heading off to school in the mornings.

An early introduction to business came when he spent time with his uncle who lived in Brown's Town and operated a haberdashery store. He worked in the store on holidays and vacations as a greeter directing customers to the appropriate areas or salespeople. He did some sales for his uncle also.

EDUCATION

Wright's education started at the age of seven at the Claremont Primary School and for high school he attended York Castle High School in Brown's Town, also in St Ann.   He then attended the College of Arts Science and Technology (CAST)—which later became the University of Technology—and completed a laboratory technician technology course.   Later on he would supplement his education with courses in accounting and industrial management.

WORK EXPERIENCE

His first job was at the Esso Refinery in Kingston in the Research and Development Department. In 1975, he started to work for sister companies Orion Sales and Tetley Tea Company (Ja) Ltd in the Quality Control Department.   He rose up the ranks holding such jobs as chief chemist, production manager, plant manager, general manager and finally managing director. According to Wright, it was at Tetley that he gained his basic experience in the tea business.

JAMAICAN AGRICULTURE

Wright recalls that he always had a desire to do something in farming as he had an interest in indigenous products. He grew up on farms, plus his father worked for the Ministry of Agriculture.

Jamaica is blessed with a wide variety of soil types and climatic conditions, allowing nearly every tropical product to grow there. The chief economic crops are sugar, bananas, citrus, cocoa and coconuts. According to *Geography and History of Jamaica*, published by the Gleaner Company, many of the major crops were introduced from other countries. Sugar cane, coconut, rice and ginger were introduced into the island from Far Eastern countries, bananas from the Canary Islands, cocoa from South America, limes and mangoes from India, the breadfruit from Tahiti and ackee from Africa.

PERISHABLES JAMAICA LTD

In 1980, Wright started Perishables Jamaica Limited with only US$300. It was impossible to get funding without a track record so he did consulting work and used the proceeds to help fund the new venture. His first product was a Jamaican peppermint tea and back then he contracted out the packaging and other processes that he has since brought in-house. Tops Pep'O'Mint (a blend of Jamaican peppermint and black tea), was first produced in 1985 and 'is the first Herbal Tea to be consistently made and marketed in Jamaica."

Today, the company produces 20 flavors of tea including, cerasee, ginger, bissy, turmeric, lemon grass, cola nut, cinnamon, sarsaparilla, cullenmint, sorrel and pimento. There are also bended teas such as cinnamint, a blend of cinnamon and mint, and gincin, a blend of ginger and cinnamon.

PEPPERMINT

According to Sylvia Lee, writing in the *Gleaner*, a new farming industry had developed when Perishables Jamaica Ltd created a demand for peppermint. She also explained some interesting characteristics of the peppermint plant:

> Peppermint in south Manchester is both unusual, in one sense, but attractive to those who grow the plant. It thrives on the marginal land in that area, which in some places has more limestone and honeycomb rock than soil. And the lateral roots of the plants weave themselves in between and at the base of the rocks, extracting the smallest amounts of moisture to feed the plant

> Those who cultivate the crop report that the leaves are always green, and the more the plant is cut (about six inches from ground level), the faster the young shoots grow. A major advantage is that the plant shows immunity to most viruses and is insect-resistant, thus rendering it unnecessary to use chemical control methods. It also is not eaten by goats, so it is possible to rear goats inside or alongside peppermint cultivation (Lee, September 9, 1989).

PRIVATE SECTOR DEVELOPMENT PROGRAMME

Perishables Jamaica Ltd, as an SME business enterprise, was able to access services through the Private Sector Development Programme (PSDP), a joint initiative of the Government of Jamaica and the European Union that included grant funding used to acquire a printer for packaging and to develop a website. The PSDP was a €26.17 million, five-year joint initiative established in 2004 between the Government of Jamaica and the EU, which operated out of the offices of the government's investment promotion arm, Jamaica Promotions Limited (JAMPRO), formerly Jamaica Trade and Invest (JTI).

The initiative was created to address specific challenges facing micro, small and medium-size enterprises (MSMEs) and their support organizations. JAMPRO/JTI, an agency of the Ministry of Industry, Investment, and Commerce, was the PSDP's lead implementer (JIS, 2011).

CONTRACT FARMING

Perishables Jamaica owns the farm on which they grow some of the plants used to make teas but most of the raw material used by the company is sourced from approximately 300 small contract farmers. To address issues in the consistency and quality of the products from so many different farms, Wright was instrumental in the establishment of the South Manchester Herbs and Spices Cooperative which works to develop pathogen free plants. Working with the Jamaica Social Investment Fund and the cooperative society, they built a centralized drying facility which ensures that all the plants are dried at the correct temperature and humidity for the proper length of time.

Contract farming is a system that has benefits for farmers and businesses alike. According to David Glover:

> ...a key feature of contract farming, which bears on production response, is risk sharing and risk reduction. In fact, contracting is fundamentally a way of allocating risk between the company and its growers. The latter assume most of the risks associated with production, while the former assumes the risks of marketing the final product. Total risk is reduced relative to a non-contract situation of that crop (Glover 1994).

Another benefit of contract farming is that it provides farmers with access to markets that would not otherwise have been available to them. Without the quality control and tight coordination offered by contract farming, it is frequently unlikely that smallholders would be able to sell perishable goods overseas through open market sales. The most significant income increases have been generated for those schemes in which smallholders gain access to lucrative export markets for labor-intensive luxury crops (Glover 1986). Important income increases have resulted from traditional crops as well, however, particularly tea. The Kenya Tea Development Authority's success in this field is often cited.

EXPORT FOCUS

From its inception, Perishables Jamaica Limited looked for "exports of indigenous Jamaican agricultural products and byproducts with the primary objective of being a net earner of foreign exchange."

Perishables Jamaica Ltd has about 15 customers, many of whom are distributors that work to get the products into supermarkets and stores. The list includes distributors in Canada, The Cayman Islands, CARICOM, the UK and USA. Very little inventory of finished product is maintained and they often struggle to produce enough product to meet the orders.

The company also does contract work such as the packaging of teas and grinding raw tea materials for other companies and individuals that produce teas but lack the necessary manufacturing facilities. Some of their contract customers include Jamaican Country Style, Caribbean Dreams, Facey Products and Tropical Blends.

THE CONCH CHOWDER DEBACLE

Early in the business, when he had only one product—peppermint tea—Wright decided to produce conch chowder in cans. He had traveled to The Bahamas where he saw tins of conch chowder and thought it would be a good idea to do something similar in Jamaica as a way to earn foreign exchange. No one in Jamaica was doing this. He developed a prototype and sent samples all over the USA and Canada where the product was wildly received. Enthused by the response, he decided to move quickly into production and bought up as much conch and other supplies that could be found.

On the verge of shipping trailers of the new product to the UK and the USA, he was informed by the Bureau of Standards that the product had a contamination problem and could not leave the island. The entire production run and shipment had to be dumped. Wright had invested all the money the business had accumulated up that that juncture—some US$150,000—in the conch chowder product. This concluded the foray into canning. Wright returned to what he knew best, teas, where there was minimal opportunity for spoilage.

The lesson says Wright is, "think outside the box but approach things in a less cavalier manner when you go to market." There have been other obstacles on the road to success but Wright says he has learnt to see them as "stepping stones and not obstacles."

ECONOMIC IMPACT

At the time of this writing, Jamaica is in negotiations with the IMF on a debt restructuring deal. Wright says, however, he is not too concerned because Perishables Jamaica is a net earner of foreign exchange because of its exports to the USA, Canada, The Cayman Islands, CARICOM and the UK. Although his company only employs about 12 people in the manufacturing plant, through his company hundreds of farmers have a market for their products. He feels most gratified by the number of lives that have been improved by his business and the feeling that he is making a contribution to the social fabric of the country.

Wright continues to expand the company's product line and has plans to add turmeric, guinea hen weed and Moringa leaf. He predicts increased revenue from these products to augment the existing earnings from Perishables' existing products. The company believes in sustainability and is making plans to go completely off the electric grid within a year. At present, rainwater is harvested on the farm and methane from a biodigester is used to warm the herbs.

DISCUSSION

Perishables Jamaica Limited is classified as an SME. Despite the size of his business, Wright's contribution to the Jamaican economy has been highlighted as an example of what can be done to help stimulate the local economy. In 2005, on the 25th anniversary of the company, the President of the Jamaica Methodist District Conference had this to say about Perishables Jamaica Ltd and Norman Wright:

> You have shown many fellow Jamaicans what hard work, sustained high standards and trust in God can achieve. By your efforts you have helped many of our nationals appreciate and use local raw materials for economic benefit and the opening of employment opportunities.

Wright was exposed to business at an early age. He worked in his uncle's store as a boy. His love of farming combined with education and work experience led him to conceive the company he eventually started on a shoe string budget. Perishables Jamaica is a success story that can inspire Jamaicans to make better use of the island's existing resources instead of always looking overseas.

Wright explains his desire to become an entrepreneur, "I always wanted to be in farming. I love it. My father and grandfather were involved in farming and I was always interested in indigenous Jamaican products."

Wright started his business, with a very small amount of cash since loans were not possible. He had to keep working as a consultant in order to provide more cash for the business. He cites his personal trait of "keeping focused on the goal" as being most important to his success.

How has Jamaica benefited from his success? Wright cites his use of Jamaican products and helping people in agriculture improve their lives. He also is a net producer of foreign exchange for the island. The company has given scholarships to students over the years and he feels Perishables Jamaica is helping to improving the social fabric of the Jamaican society. The Jamaican flag is proudly displayed on all the products and he feels goodwill is being accumulated for Jamaica.

CHAPTER 15

Abraham Elias Issa, OJ, CBE, JP

The late Abraham "Abe" Elias Issa was chairman and Director of E.A. Issa & Bros Limited, House of Issa Limited and a host of other Issa businesses that comprised the Issa conglomerate. Issa joined his father's dry goods business after completing college and soon emerged as a dynamic innovator and visionary. He expanded the family's business into a powerful conglomerate that included hotels, retail stores, manufacturing, distribution and imports. At one time, he was the chairman or director of 36 companies, a man with a "wealth of imagination and unquenchable drive." He is considered by many to have been the single most important contributor to the development of tourism in Jamaica. He saw the potential of the industry at a time when successive governments did not.

Abraham "Abe" Issa was born in Kingston, Jamaica on October 10, 1905. His father, Elias Abraham Issa, was born in Bethlehem, Palestine in 1876. His father and grandfather came to Jamaica after attending the World's Fair in Chicago in 1893 as merchants. It is reported they had a booth at the fair, but made no money there and were looking for another opportunity when someone who had been to Jamaica's Great Exhibition of 1891, which attracted some 300,000 visitors from around the world, suggested they try it (Issa, 1994).

Upon arrival in Jamaica, his father and grandfather opened a store at 11 Princess Street in downtown Kingston. They also sold goods door to door. His mother and other family arrived once things appeared settled. The business became known as E.A. Issa & Brothers and specialized in wholesale dry goods.

All did not go well with the business at the start. Within six years of its establishment, Jamaica was hit by the great earthquake of 1907 which destroyed a great deal of Kingston. The Issa business lost all its stock, and one of the brothers, Joseph, was killed. Undaunted, the bothers restarted the business that same year. It then began to improve. By dint of hard work and keen business sense a thriving business was built.

EDUCATION

Abe Issa attended St Aloysius Primary School in Kingston then went to high school at St. George's College (1916 -1922), at the time an all male Roman Catholic High School established in 1850 by Spanish Jesuits. Abe excelled and was a brilliant student and athlete. He was captain of the Manning Cup Football and Sunlight Cup Cricket teams and also ran track and played tennis.

He and his brother Joe went on to college at Holy Cross College in Massachusetts where he graduated summa cum laude in Spanish in 1926. After college, Issa joined the family business at his father's request. At the time, his father was sole owner having bought out his uncles when they left the business.

In 1931, Abe met the girl of his dreams, a beautiful Lebanese named Lorraine Shaouy in New York. When they met again years later, he proposed and they were married in Bethlehem, Palestine at his uncle's house.

A PROMOTIONAL GENIUS

One of Issa's first business strategies was to add a retail component to the business. He opened Issa's of King Street on December 20, 1930 at the corner of Barry and King Streets. It was Jamaica's first modern department store and it became the "Mecca for shopping in Jamaica" featuring Issa's exceptional customer service. He became famous for standing at the front of the store and greeting customers by name. He was also a "genius at promotions, displays and merchandising." He expanded from two to four floors and added escalators and cash registers. A marriage ceremony was even performed live in the store.

Issa added more stores on same block of King Street: Milady's, The Enterprise and The Budget. In 1958, he purchased the famous and most prestigious Nathan's Department store on King Street.

A STRING OF FIRSTS

Issa went on to achieve a number of firsts in Jamaica as he built the House of Issa into a leader in Jamaican commerce. He developed the first shopping center in Half-Way-Tree—Tropical Plaza. He also developed Liguanea Plaza. He opened the first supermarket, Hi-Lo, at Cross Roads in Kingston. In 1959, anticipating the shift in commerce from downtown to uptown, he bought out an entire race track, Knutsford Park, and developed New Kingston, which is now a modern banking and commercial center.

THE GREAT EXHIBITION OF 1891

The Great Exhibition of 1891 is considered to be the first effort to promote tourism on the island. The government raised funds and constructed an entire exhibition ground at the Kingston Race Course (now the site of National Heroes Park). The wooden exhibition building itself was built on lands now occupied by Wolmer's Schools by local architect, George Messiter. It covered 40,000 sq. ft., was of Moorish architectural style and cost close to £15,000 ("The Great Exhibition of 1891," *Gleaner*, January 14, 2002).

The Exhibition billed as "the most extraordinary commercial event in the history of the Gulf of Mexico and the West Indies," opened on time on January 27, 1891. It ran for four months and after receiving 302,831 visitors the Great Exhibition closed on May 2, 1891.

The government encouraged the building of accommodations for the Great Exhibition. So, hotels and resorts were set up in Kingston, Spanish Town, Moneague, Mandeville and Port Antonio, of which the most famous were the Titchfield, in Port Antonio and Myrtle Bank, in Kingston. Others included the Constant Spring, Queens, Rio Cobre, Moneague and Mandeville hotels. The Constant Spring Hotel is credited with being the first building to have electricity and indoor plumbing in Jamaica.

TOURISM

Issa wanted to buy the Constant Spring Hotel which was owned by the colonial government but was not profitable. His father advised against it since they had no expertise in operating hotels. The government sold the hotel to the Franciscan Sisters who were looking for a new home for their convent and school. The Immaculate Conception High School is still in operation at the same location.

In 1904, the feeling of the Jamaican 'working class' towards tourism was summed up in the following excerpt:

> Tourist! Cou yah sah! Dem is a confusion set of people. What we want dem for?— An what good dem going to do? All them idle buckra drive and ride over de mountains in dem buggy and harse wit all dem 'surance, and look down upon we poor naygurs. True dem say dey brings we money, but when time we eber see it? All de storekeepers dem in Kingston and the big tabern-keeper, dem is the one dat get the money out of dem.... An when de tourists come up to de country and see we working in de ground, dem is not goin' to do anything fa we, but take pitcha and laugh at we. Chu! Me bredder, only de buckra dem will profit. (*The Leader*, February 5, 1904 cited in Taylor, 1987-88, p.44).

Issa, however, saw the potential that tourism held for Jamaica but it is doubtful the average Jamaican at the time saw this. Certainly there were government leaders that needed to be persuaded of the benefits.

THE MYRTLE BANK HOTEL

The Myrtle Bank Hotel was originally a boarding house converted from a shipyard. By 1875 when downtown Christmas Bazaars became popular and drew large crowds, the Myrtle Bank became a recreational and social centre. A music stand was erected in the centre of its tropical garden and The West India Regiment Band entertained large crowds twice a week.

When the owner, a Scotsman named James Gall died, the property was acquired by the government and a modern hotel with long French windows that opened on all sides into verandahs, was built on the site in preparation for the Great Exhibition of 1891. The hotel was destroyed in the 1907 earthquake, reconstructed in 1918, and sold to the United Fruit Company. At that time, it was the largest hotel in Jamaica with 205 rooms and a filtered salt water pool.

In 1945, the Myrtle Bank hotel, which was still owned by the United Fruit Company (UFC), came up for sale. This time, Issa convinced his father to buy it and they negotiated to buy it for £35, 000. Issa opened up the hotel to all Jamaicans, regardless of color. Previously, non-whites had not been allowed under UFC policy.

The hotel had a free port and was the place to see and be seen. Marketed as a health resort because of several natural springs that flowed through the property, the Myrtle Bank attracted famous Americans, Britons and other celebrities such as Errol Flynn, Noel Coward, Joan Crawford, Peter Ustinov, Louis Armstrong, Winston Churchill, Walt Disney and Adlai Stevenson.

THE TOWER ISLE HOTEL

Issa's next tourism venture was the construction of the Tower Isle Hotel in Ocho Rios. In 1948 he was *Spotlight Magazine's* Man of the Year for undertaking and financing without foreign or government help the construction of the hotel. According to the Private Sector Organization of Jamaica, it was his vision to build a hotel in what was considered a mosquito infected swamp that was to lay the foundation for the transformation of Ocho Rios from a sleepy fishing village into a tourist haven. It sparked a wave of hotel building in Jamaica.

At that time, there were only a very few resort hotels and so when he decided to build his own it was a big risk as most people had never heard of Ocho Rios. There was no airport in Montego Bay and guests had to travel from the airport in Kingston to the hotel.

Tower Isle was the first resort hotel to operate all year round and include summer vacations. It was first to include an art gallery. Issa maintained a file on each guest and on their return visits they were welcomed with telegrams, flowers and champagne. He introduced the idea of taking photos of small town visitors and sending to their hometown papers. The hotel's famous clientele included the likes of Vincent Price, Eva Gabor and Debbie Reynolds (Issa, 1994).

Tower Isle later became the first Couples Resort when Issa created an all-inclusive concept in 1978 to cater to the vacationing couple. Today, there are several boutique hotels under the Couples Resorts umbrella "blending luxury, romance and value under one roof." They include Couples Tower Isle, Couples San Souci, Couples Negril and Couples Swept Away which are run by the Issa family including Abe Issa's son Lee and nephew John.

Successive governments had failed to see the value of tourism to Jamaica. Issa is quoted in the book, *Mr. Jamaica—Abe Issa*, as saying:

> I spoke to Busta, I talked to Sangster, I discussed it with Manley, I pleaded with Nethersole; they all said the same thing, tourism could only be small fry. I kept telling them they were wrong, tourism could be our biggest industry. And when they asked me why, I told them—the world is our market.

He spoke of Jamaica's "invisible export of sun, sea, beaches and scenery" and how "when it comes to beaches we could lend" other countries some (Issa, 1994).

JAMAICA TOURIST BOARD

Finally, the day came when Jamaica created the Jamaica Tourist Board. Issa was made chairman and served from 1955–1963 which became known as the "Golden Age of Tourism." His greatest achievement was building up tourism on the island. He became known as "Mr. Jamaica" throughout the travel circuit, operating on a very small budget and with no pay from the government, he worked to create happy visitors, traveling at his own expense to promote Jamaica.

He was responsible for introducing water skiing to Jamaica. From 1958 until 1959, he was president of the Caribbean Tourist Association which represented 29 countries. He is credited with developing the concept of "island hopping."

SERVICE TO COUNTRY

Issa had a long record of dedicated public service to his country. He headed the Development Finance Corporation and later the Development Bank of Jamaica. He served as a member of the former Legislative Council of Jamaica from 1958 to 1981 and was a director of Air Jamaica from 1964 to 1972. He loved Jamaica and called it "the greatest little country on earth."

According to his daughter, Suzanne Issa:

> He was a man of great character, his unshakable convictions and clarity of purpose showed in everything he did. He believed that anything was attainable with hard work and perseverance; and he never became discouraged because he also believed that behind every dark cloud was a silver lining. He was a man full of warmth, courage, intelligence and fun (Issa, 1994).

Others have referred to Issa as a "human dynamo" and a very demanding boss who pays "attention to detail and orderly thinking." He also educated Jamaicans about the value of the tourism to the island with campaigns such as "Tourism Matters to you."

He had two sons and two daughters.

AWARDS

In 1984, Issa received the Norman Manley award for Tourism.

In 1960, he was made a Commander of the most Excellent order of the British Empire (CBE) for his leadership role in tourism.

In 1980, the Jamaican Government awarded him the Order of Jamaica (OJ) for his pioneering role in Jamaica's tourism development.

TOURISM TODAY

The factors that contributed to the growth and development of Jamaica's tourism industry in the 1960s were:

- the introduction of air travel to the island resulting in improved transportation;

- close proximity of Jamaica to the large North American tourist market;

- rapid growth in disposable income in North America;

- the Cuban revolution of 1959 and the subsequent US embargo and travel restriction;

- development in 1969 of a national airline, Air Jamaica; and

- tax incentives and duty-free imports of building materials and equipment for hotels.

The image of Jamaica as a sun, sea and sand tourism destination continued and is evident in its spatial development. The main tourist centers or resort areas (Negril, Montego Bay, Ocho Rios and Port Antonio) were developed along the north coast because of the white sand beaches and pleasant weather. Apart from the north coast centers, Kingston, the capital of Jamaica and a major commercial and cultural centre, also attracts a substantial number of tourists. However, the ability for Kingston to attract international tourists has decreased over the years due to social problems in the city.

DISCUSSION

This profile of Abe Issa was compiled from published accounts of his life. He died in November, 1984. Issa led a remarkable life and his contributions to

Jamaica's economic development are legendary. His belief in tourism has paid off for Jamaica as it now accounts for some 10 percent of Jamaica's GDP. In terms of foreign exchange, tourism has routinely contributed upwards of 50 percent of the exchange earned by the island. In 2010, tourism contributed approximately US$2 billion to the Jamaican economy with over three million visitors to the island. Since 1980, tourism has shown tremendous growth in comparison to Jamaica's other major foreign currency earners (Stupart, 2012).

Issa saw opportunities where others could not and his determination kept him focused on developing the tourism product in Jamaica. As an innovator, he scored numerous firsts in Jamaican business and built a successful hotel in what was then a mosquito infected part of the island paving the way for others to follow.

CHAPTER 16

Cherry Miller

Cherry Miller is an example of a necessity entrepreneur or sole trader, small business owner or micro enterprise owner. She has operated a very small shop in the village of Port Sea, St Elizabeth, Jamaica for over 50 years. Her profile is included to provide a contrast to the other entrepreneurs who are opportunity entrepreneurs.

Cherry Miller was born in October 1937 in the rural district of Brown's Hill in the parish of St Elizabeth on Jamaica's south coast. This is the same area of Jamaica where General Colin Powell's family lived before migrating to the USA.

Miller's parents were Beatrice (nee Gordon) and Roland Myers. They had seven girls and four boys. Her father, who was of mixed White and Black descent, was a small tobacco farmer who also grew yams, cocoa, banana, corn and vegetables for the family's table. He also raised goats, chickens, sheep and the occasional cow.

According to the family's oral history, her paternal grandfather was Jewish and came to Jamaica on a ship arriving from Scotland. However, most of the people with the Myers surname claim descent from Germany. There is even a nearby town named Myersville in the parish. The first group of Germans to arrive in Jamaica were recruited by the brother of Mr. Solomon Myers—a Jewish German who owned a coffee estate on the island—from a town in Germany called Bremen in 1834 (Tortello, 2004).

Miller attended the Redbank primary school but explains that she was unable to continue her education beyond the primary level as her parents were poor and had to provide for 11 children. She learnt dressmaking from a neighbor and did some sewing to earn money. She dated Leonard Miller, a young man who had attended the same school but was a few years ahead of her. Leonard also dropped out of school when his father died unexpectedly. Miller became pregnant about the time when Leonard was selected as a temporary farm worker to the United States of America. He was away for two and a half years.

Upon Leonard's return from the USA the couple got married and rented a place to live. Using funds saved while Leonard was working in America, they bought a piece of land in a district known as Port Sea and there built a two room-house and also constructed a very small grocery store or shop near the street. Miller says it was a very hard life in the early days as they went on to have a total of seven children—four girls and three boys. But the little shop provided a small but steady income over the years.

While she focused on running the shop, her husband grew yams, beans, vegetables and other crops to supplement their income and supply food to their kitchen. Eventually, things settled down and life became a bit easier. They were able to buy a minivan which Leonard used to operate an airport service for residents of the village. The house and shop are in the same place as when first built except the house now has several more rooms.

The little shop sold basic food items like sugar, flour, oil, salted codfish, soft drinks and bread. Nowadays, they also sell prepaid cards for cell phones. One side of the shop served as a bar selling Jamaican white rum and beer. The shop benefitted when a small health clinic was built across the street by the local bauxite company.

The biggest problem they ever had with the business was once when there was a burglary. A burglar entered through the roof and stole several bottles of rum and several packs of cigarettes.

DISCUSSION

Cherry Miller fits the category of a small business owner, sole trader or micro enterprise owner. She is not an entrepreneur in the same sense as most of the others in this study. She is what the Global Entrepreneurship Monitor classifies as a "necessity entrepreneur," a person who typically starts a business out of necessity to provide an income with no interest in growing the business or developing an enterprise. This distinguishes her from an opportunity entrepreneur who starts a business by choice to pursue an opportunity.

She has maintained her grocery store in essentially the same state as when she started it and has never sought to expand it in over 50 years of operation.

In Jamaica, the micro enterprise owner comprises the majority of the micro and small sector players with approximately 37.6 percent of the employed labor force, averaging approximately 411,600 persons in the year 2010. Like the typical micro enterprise owner, Miller had no employees and did not create any additional jobs. She went into business because job opportunities were virtually non-existent in that area of Jamaica in the 1950s.

Miller's situation in regard to access to a high school education was the norm in Jamaica at that time. There were only a few high schools, spaces were extremely limited and the cost was prohibitive to most Jamaican families. This no doubt had some impact on her ability to move out of the "necessity" into the "opportunity" entrepreneur classification.

CHAPTER 17

Hazel Robinson

Hazel Robinson, as a single mother of two, quit her job to start a small manufacturing business that made clothing which she sold to tourist shops and cruise ships. Her business fell in the category of a small or medium enterprise (SME).

Hazel Robinson was born in November, 1940 in the village of Bethany, in the parish of St Ann. She is the last of the 12 children born to Vincent and Annie Chang. Her father was a Chinese immigrant and her mother a Jamaican.

MARBLES AND THE BEACH

Hazel grew up in the seaside town of Oracabessa, in the parish of St Mary on Jamaica's north coast where her parents owned a grocery store. She recalls playing marbles, cricket and jumping rope as a child. She and her siblings went to the beach every day as they were very close to the sea. But they had to walk five miles each way to school and once home they usually picked fruits, such as oranges and limes off trees on the family property to sell. Her mother sewed a lot and taught her to sew. She liked sewing and designed clothes for her dolls.

A FREE PLACE TO ARDENNE HIGH

At age 11, Hazel was sent to Kingston, the island's capital, when she won a tuition scholarship known as a "free place" to Ardenne High School. Her parents arranged for her to live in a boarding house with a lady in order to attend the new school. However, Hazel felt it was too restrictive compared to life in the countryside. Also she discovered that she did not like school. One day while visiting home on a holiday, her father announced he could no longer afford the cost of boarding and she had to come home and work in the grocery store.

ESCAPING THE SHOP COUNTER

Unhappy with working in the shop, Hazel accepted a job in Kingston to escape. She was 15 years old but claimed to be 19. The job required shorthand, typing and some bookkeeping which she did not know so she went to Durham College, a secretarial school, and took shorthand and bookkeeping courses at night.

In 1959, she married a Chinese man who was a friend of her brother, Donald. Immediately after being married, her husband stopped working, citing various reasons. They had two children and Hazel found herself working three jobs to maintain the family which at this point included her mother.

THE CURACAO TRADING COMPANY

By now she was working for Curacao Trading Company as a salesperson selling textiles, yarn and dyes. Robinson recalls that she was good at sales and often won trips to other islands as prizes.

To supplement her income, she designed some baby shirts and sold them to Woolworth's. They initially bought two dozen shirts. She was encouraged when they followed up with an order for six dozen shirts followed by one for 12 dozen. From this she realized there was an opportunity in manufacturing.

At work, she was assigned to sell a material that was made in Holland, a Java or African Print that would not sell–only one customer bought it. The customers did not know how to use the print and therefore did not buy it. She came up with the idea of using this fabric to manufacture garments such as dashikis that had become very popular at the time with the growing Black consciousness.

BOU BOUDIMA LIMITED

In 1969, she had been divorced for several years and was a single mother of two. She decided to quit her job and start her own manufacturing business. It was called Bou Boudima Limited. She approached suppliers she knew through her job and asked if they would give her sewing machines on credit and they agreed. She then rented a house on Balmoral Avenue in Kingston, hired a pattern designer and four workers. Funds were tight so she had to secretly borrow a cutter from another business to do her cutting at night, returning the cutter in the mornings. Her designs were an instant hit and sales were strong. One of the biggest problems she faced in the early years was obtaining a trade license to import the fabrics.

In 1970, with sales taking off, she moved to a house at 63 Westminster Road where she installed 50 machines and hired 70 workers. Business was so good she was able to pay off the mortgage on the building in full. Her designs were sold to cruise ships and stores in the tourist industry. They were also used on Air Jamaica for their in-flight fashion shows. Stores like the Morin Shop on King Street regularly advertised her designs in the newspaper.

She started another company, European Fashions Limited, which focused on sales and marketing. The main products were dashiki tunics.

A DAY IN COURT
One day, having had just returned from a trip to Canada, she came to work to find a summons in the mailbox. Her offense: operating a business in a residential area. She went to court with her attorney. She pleaded guilty with an explanation. Her explanation: there were six other businesses operating on the same street. The judge smiled and fined her £15. When she was escorted to the cashier to pay the fine, she realized she did not have any Jamaican money in her purse, only Canadian. By this time her attorney had already left, so she was placed in a holding cell until her sister arrived with cash.

MARRIAGE AGAIN
After 12 years, she remarried her first husband who joined the business as a partner and eventually took over operations. One day he told her that they had lost the garment business as the government had taken it over. And just like that she was out of business. Years later, she would discover information that led her to believe the company had been sold without her knowledge.

Robinson migrated to the USA and once more became a "necessity" entrepreneur. Having little education, she bought a beachwear store in Sarasota, Florida. She had no credit in the USA but the owner was gracious enough to do owner financing. She made many changes to the business including adding products for the winter months, more surfing lines, skateboards, other products for kids and expanding the shopping floor. Business grew and she was able to open a second store. She subsequently divorced her husband when he left for another country.

After several years, she sold the stores and entered retirement. With a new husband, and her children now fully grown, she moved back to Jamaica and started a new life.

DISCUSSION

In the 1980s the Jamaican apparel industry had more than 50 companies and business flourished under the quota-based Multi-Fibre Agreement (MFA) that governed the world trade in textiles and garments from 1974 through 2004. Jamaica and other Caribbean Basin countries took advantage of the generous quotas allowed by the USA to export clothing.

Robinson was a small business owner with some entrepreneurial streaks. She started a manufacturing company to make clothing and improve her income. And she made a good living doing this while the business lasted. What she did is something that was done by many other small apparel manufacturers at that time. However, her ability to see the opportunity in a fabric that no one else was using is entrepreneurial. Her ability to use social capital to get supplies and equipment on credit as well as taking the calculated risk of leaving her job to start the factory also demonstrated her entrepreneurial spark.

Many Jamaicans are forced to start businesses because of a lack of education, skills or the availability of jobs. They start businesses out of necessity. Most are "sole traders" who work alone and never go on to expand the original business or create jobs. Robinson was making the transition to "opportunity" entrepreneurship by starting a new business to market and sell her clothing designs. But this was derailed by the loss of the garment factory.

Today, Jamaica's apparel industry has been decimated by globalization. Cheaper imports flood the market and multinationals have left for cheaper production and labor costs in other countries such as Mexico. Efforts are being made however, to shore up the local fashion industry and help it compete on a global stage.

CHAPTER 18

Audrey Marks

Audrey Patrice Marks is the founder and CEO of Paymaster Jamaica Limited, Jamaica's first "one stop shop" multi-payment agency which serves customers in Jamaica, the United Kingdom and the United States of America. Bill payment collections are received on behalf of over 55 Jamaican client companies.

Audrey Marks was born in the parish of St Mary which is in Jamaica's northeast quadrant. Her parents were Claude and Olive Marks. Her mother owned and operated a grocery store while her father was a farmer.

EDUCATION

Marks attended Marymount High School in Highgate, St Mary. While working at Air Jamaica, she studied Management at UWI. She went on to obtain her Master's degree in Business Administration from Nova Southeastern University's H. Wayne Huizenga School of Business and Entrepreneurship in Florida.

In the early '90s, she decided it was time to move on from Air Jamaica. However, she felt the terms of separation were stacked against her. This was when Marks proved that she was no "shrinking violet." In her 20s, she hired her first attorney and negotiated a separation package (Lowrie-Chin, 2009).

While employed to Telecommunications of Jamaica she saw that the company anticipated an increase in the number of customers and that no allowance was being made for accepting those projected new payments. She realized there was an opportunity in providing access to bill payment facilities and the idea for Paymaster Jamaica was born.

PAYMASTER JAMAICA LIMITED

In 1997, Paymaster Jamaica Limited opened its doors to customers with one client company and two service locations, providing next day account updating. After several years of effort, Marks had inked an agreement with the Jamaica Public Service Company (JPS) to collect payment for electric bills. Marks had no background in technology but she was able to have a system designed, developed and implemented with all necessary hardware, software and network support in place within a three year timeframe.

There was turmoil in Jamaica's financial sector in the 1990s caused by a huge banking meltdown so it was difficult to find investors for Paymaster. Marks sold some real estate and a vehicle she owned to obtain capital.

The company has created some 150 agencies in Jamaica, providing services to over 1.4 million customers and employment for over 400 persons with annual transactions of over J$40 billion Dollars. It is the first multi-transaction agency in the Caribbean.

Today the company's client portfolio includes the major utility companies in Jamaica plus cable service providers, internet service providers, tertiary institutions and financial service companies. They also handle various other transactions such as check cashing, insurance, remittances, ticket sales, membership clubs, traffic tickets, property tax as well as US Embassy online applications and appointments.

OTHER BUSINESSES

Marks started and operated six businesses before embarking on Paymaster. These businesses, ranged from a 100-acre banana exporting farm, a transportation company, to a real estate sales and development company. She has also operated a venture capital company with diverse investments, including manufacturing, travel and entertainment companies.

Marks served on several private and public sector boards, including being deputy chairman of the Urban Development Corporation (UDC), chairman of the Central Wastewater Treatment Company Limited (CWTC), chair of the Tourism Product Development Company (TPDCo), director on the boards of RBTT Securities Jamaica Limited, Jamaica Trade and Invest (JTI), National Health Fund (NHF), the University of the West Indies (Mona School of Business).

She was the first female president of the American Chamber of Commerce of Jamaica (AMCHAM), an organization which promotes investment and trade between the United States of America and Jamaica.

JAMAICA'S AMBASSADOR TO THE USA

Marks served as Jamaica's Ambassador to the USA from 2010 until 2012. She was also Jamaica's permanent representative to the Organization of American States over the same period.

AWARDS

Marks is the recipient of numerous citations from her peers and various organizations for her pioneering work, entrepreneurial endeavors and commitment to social causes. She was an Ernest & Young Nominee for the "Caribbean Entrepreneur of the Year 2000"; Business Leader of the Year Award nominee for 2000; and recipient of the Florida International University Business Leader of the Year Award for 2003 and 2010.

She enjoys playing golf, mentoring young adults and spending time with her family. Marks and her husband, electrical engineering consultant Jassel Dunstan, have two daughters, Morgan and Madison.

DISCUSSION

There are places in the world where women do not have access to an education. Jamaica is not one of them. In 2007, 82 percent of the students who matriculated to the University of the West Indies were women. Although men continue to dominate at senior levels of governance and leadership in Jamaica, women have made great strides in the workplace.

Audrey Marks grew up in an independent Jamaica. By the time she attended high school, secondary education had become more accessible to the average Jamaican. She is one of the few entrepreneurs in the study with an advanced degree, having obtained a master's degree from the H. Wayne Huizenga School of Business and Entrepreneurship in Florida.

Her ability to recognize a business opportunity and to take the necessary actions to capitalize on the opportunity is a key aspect of her entrepreneurial success. Because of her entrepreneurial mindset, she was not distracted by the Jamaican financial sector collapse in the 1990s but remained focused on her goal. And her ability to innovate—by providing a one-stop bill payment system—is another highlight of that mindset.

Marks represents the new breed of Jamaican entrepreneur who is well educated and comfortable with digital media and technology. In fact, her business is based on the use of information and communication technology.

PART III

Review and Analysis

CHAPTER 19

The Entrepreneurs and their Industries

The entrepreneurs profiled in this book were selected from different industries, educational backgrounds and upbringings. One "necessity" entrepreneur was included to provide a contrast to the "opportunity" entrepreneurs.

The cornerstone of each profile was an interview with the entrepreneur, where this was possible. One entrepreneur is deceased and two were unavailable; their profiles developed from published information. The data obtained from interviews was supplemented by data from documents, publications, conversations with family and associates as well as media reports.

Many of the entrepreneurs have achieved success that has been recognized by the Jamaican community and government. Many of them have been bestowed with national honours by the Jamaican Government. Several different industries are represented and include: agriculture, insurance, investment banking, quick service restaurant, real estate, health care, tourism, manufacturing, hydroponic farming and banking.

Four of the entrepreneurs live outside of Jamaica and had achieved success in a foreign land. All four have been recognized in Jamaica for their successes and their contributions to the island. Some imported Jamaican products for use in their business and thereby contributed directly to the island's economy. Six of the entrepreneurs were women.

The good news is that Jamaican entrepreneurs are succeeding in Jamaica and on the world stage. They come from all walks of life, from the country and the city, with varied educational backgrounds and personality traits. But Jamaica needs to do more to foster an environment that encourages entrepreneurship. Children must be encouraged to think outside the box like entrepreneurs and to develop an entrepreneurial mindset. In the same way Jamaica has developed a sports culture, an entrepreneurial culture must be developed. One important step according to GEM is:

> A separation must be made between business failure and individual failure in the minds of Jamaicans. The stigma attached to business failure needs to be reduced and viewed instead as a stepping stone to ultimate success. Laws must be enacted to reduce the absolute risk to persons who engage in entrepreneurial activity by improving social safety nets and creating bankruptcy protection for firms (GEM Jamaica, 2011).

LIST OF ENTREPRENEURS, COMPANIES AND INDUSTRIES

The Table below provides a summary of the entrepreneurs profiled in this book, their companies and their industries:

TABLE 10	LIST OF ENTREPRENEURS, COMPANY AND INDUSTRY		
CASE#	NAME	COMPANY	INDUSTRY
1	Michael Lee-Chin	Portland Holdings Inc.	Diversified Investments
2	Vincent Chang	Tastee Patties	Restaurant
3	Rita Humphries-Lewin	Barita Investments	Securities
4	Lowell Hawthorne	Golden Krust	Restaurant
5	Dr. Paul Chen-Young	Eagle Financial Group	Banking and finance
6	Lois Sherwood	Restaurant Associates	QSR and real estate
7	George Yap	LEASA Industries	Hydroponic Farming
8	Robert Levy	Jamaica Broilers	Agriculture
9	Vincent HoSang	Caribbean Food Delights	Food manufacturing
10	Gordon "Butch" Stewart	Sandals Resorts, ATL Group	Hotels and Appliances
11	Norman Wright	Perishables Jamaica	Herbal tea
12	Abe Issa	House of Issa	Auto/Hotel conglomerate
13	Cherry Miller	Grocery store	Retail Grocery
14	Hazel Robinson	Bou Boujima	Apparel/Clothing
15	Audrey Marks	Paymaster	Bill payment services

CHAPTER 20

How Jamaica Benefits from Entrepreneurial Success

The entrepreneurs profiled have made significant contributions to Jamaica's economy and its social fabric. It was an entrepreneur who recognized the potential of tourism to the island's economy at a time when government leaders did not. The largest private employer is a company founded by one of these entrepreneurs, Butch Stewart. These entrepreneurs are committed to giving back and they provide support for worthy causes in Jamaica, so there is no doubt that entrepreneurship can have a transformative effect on Jamaica.

A COMPARISON OF BENEFITS TO JAMAICA

This section provides examples of the ways in which the entrepreneurs have contributed to the island.

TABLE 11	ENTREPRENEURS AND BENEFITS TO JAMAICA
NAME	**EXAMPLES OF BENEFITS TO JAMAICA**
Michael Lee-Chin	Rescued the failing National Commercial Bank and restored to profitabliity. His Foundadtion makes significant contributions to education including some 200 scholarships awarded in 2012. He also pays exam fees for all high school students taking business courses. In his home parish of Portland, he has built a new court house and civic center, bought hotels and other properties and plans to revive tourism in the parish. He also funded a nursing school at the Northern Caribbean University in Jamaica.
Vincent Chang	Is best known for sponsorship of the Jamaica Talent Trail, an annual talent search that identifies talented Jamaicans, Tastee is also a foreign exchange earner by means of exports to other countries. Thousands of jobs have been created and many businesses facilitated via the franchise and distributor operations. *(continued)*

TABLE 11	ENTREPRENEURS AND BENEFITS TO JAMAICA	(continued)

NAME	EXAMPLES OF BENEFITS TO JAMAICA
Rita Humphries-Lewin	Focuses on early childhood literacy and numeracy by hiring a staff of fulltime teachers who train the teachers for work in inner city communities. Donations to various worthy causes via the Barita Education Foundation.
Lowell Hawthorne	Contributes to the island's foreign exchange by purchasing Jamaican products for use in US-based restaurants and makes donations to education through the Mavis & Ephraim Hawthorne Foundation.
Dr. Paul Chen-Young	Provided jobs for hundreds in the over 12 businesses he established. Provided scholarships and bursaries for students at high schools, technical colleges, universities and the School for the Visual Arts. His group was one of the pioneers in the "homework hotline" call-in program. Commissioned an original work by the National Dance Theatre Company among other cultural contributions.
Lois Sherwood	Provides thousands of jobs to Jamaicans in her 28 restaurants and other businesses. Gives scholarships to high school and university students via the Rodwell Lake Memorial Fund.
George Yap	Makes donations to various charities in Jamaica. He is currently working with the government on a low-cost housing solution.
Robert Levy	Is recognized for a key role in contributing to the growth of the Jamaican agricultural industry. Earns foreign exchange via exports such as anhydrous ethanol sold to the USA. Hundreds of farmers do business with his various businesses. He is a sponsor of numerous programs such as the Jamaica Open Tennis Championship and the annual gospel festival, "Best Dressed Fun in the Son." Provides support for community projects through the Jamaica Broilers Foundation which focuses on children and youth.
Vincent HoSang	Focuses on contributions to health care—donated a mobile clinic and is currently raising funds for two multi-million dollar cancer X-ray machines for hospitals. He established the entrepreneurship challenge at UWI and gives numerous scholarships via the Vincent HoSang Family Foundation.
Gordon "Butch" Stewart	His group of companies is the country's biggest foreign exchange earner, and its largest non-government employer. He has created thousands of jobs and careers in Jamaica. The Sandals Foundation funds some 300 community projects especially in the area of education.
Norman Wright	Perishables Jamaica Ltd is a net earner of foreign exchange for the island. He has also provided opportunities for hundreds of small farmers who grow plants on contract to his company.
Abe Issa	He was a pioneer in many industries but he is especially noted for recognizing the potential of tourism as an industry—which is, today, one of the largest sources of foreign exchange for the island—and his tireless efforts in marketing Jamaica to the world.
Cherry Miller	Created jobs for herself and her husband at a time when none existed in that part of the island.
Hazel Robinson	Provided jobs for dozens of people and earned foreign exchange by selling her apparel to cruise ships and tourist shops.
Audrey Marks	Her innovation in creating a new way for Jamaicans to pay bills has provided hundreds of job opportunities.

DR. GLEN LAMAN

CHAPTER 21

Responses from Entrepreneurs to Selected Interview Questions

This chapter presents a selection of questions from the interviews with responses. The author's comments are provided where no response was available.

TABLE 12: SAMPLE QUESTIONS AND RESPONSES – QUESTION 1

Entrepreneurs take risks and sacrifice time, money and effort to go into business. But they do so for many different reasons. According to GEM, many Jamaicans start businesses out of necessity. This question sheds light on the antecedents and motivations that led to the entrepreneurs starting their own businesses.

TABLE 12	TO WHAT WOULD YOU ATTRIBUTE YOUR DESIRE TO BE AN ENTREPRENEUR?
NAME	**RESPONSE**
Michael Lee-Chin	His parents owned a small store in which he worked as a boy, sometimes alone, and had responsibility for running and closing it.
Vincent Chang	Growing up, he worked in several different stores. As a young man he had to work nights at the bakery where he was employed. When his wife complained about this, he looked for an opportunity to be his own boss.
Rita Humphries-Lewin	"Ironically, it was encouragement from male colleagues that led me to go into business. They had family and other responsibilities that made it too risky for them so they encouraged me to do it."
Lowell Hawthorne	"My mind kept going back to Border and the family bakery in Jamaica…the urge to engage in full time entrepreneurship became increasingly intense."
Dr. Paul Chen-Young	"My experience at the Workers' Bank where I was replaced by one of the directors I had selected convinced me to never again work as an employee for anyone or any entity." *(continued)*

TABLE 12	TO WHAT WOULD YOU ATTRIBUTE YOUR DESIRE TO BE AN ENTREPRENEUR? _(continued)_
NAME	**RESPONSE**
Lois Sherwood	"My husband was unhappy in his job and I just thought we could do better on our own."
George Yap	"My Father. He had a lot of losses but died a happy man helping people. He loved to work and showed me I can learn to do stuff."
Robert Levy	He joined his father's business at age 19 and learnt every aspect of the business working from the bottom up until he would eventually shape the business by directing its development into the conglomerate it is today.
Vincent HoSang	"My parents, my uncle and like many Chinese who like to be their own boss."
Gordon "Butch" Stewart	His mother owned a small appliance business in which he worked as a young boy. He was not a good student but demonstrated early streaks of entrepreneurism.
Norman Wright	"I always wanted to be in farming. Love it. My father was involved in farming and I was interested in indigenous products."
Abe Issa	His father asked him to join him in business after he graduated from college.
Cherry Miller	"There were no jobs at that time so I thought we had to do something for our selves."
Hazel Robinson	"I had a family to feed and was always looking for an opportunity to make more money. I loved to sew and had sold a few children's dresses to Woolworth's which showed me that there was an opportunity in clothing."
Audrey Marks	Her mother owned a grocery store and this no doubt influenced her to become the master of her fate.

TABLE 13: SAMPLE QUESTIONS AND RESPONSES – QUESTION 2

As discussed previously, many entrepreneurs have certain personal traits in common. Researchers list traits such as need for achievement, locus of control and propensity to take risks. This question provides insight into what the entrepreneur thinks are the important traits for their success.

TABLE 13	WHAT ARE THE PERSONAL TRAITS MOST IMPORTANT TO YOUR SUCCESS?
NAME	**RESPONSE**
Michael Lee-Chin	Took bold steps to get funding for his first venture and demonstrated that he is not afraid to go against the herd when necessary.
Vincent Chang	Loved baking and was especially fond of pastry and this was important in his transformation of the Jamaican patty.
Rita Humphries-Lewin	"Having respect for the client's wishes and money." She has been described as 'smart', 'brash and bold' and 'someone whose word is her bond'.
	(continued)

DR. GLEN LAMAN

TABLE 13	**WHAT ARE THE PERSONAL TRAITS MOST IMPORTANT TO YOUR SUCCESS?** (continued)
NAME	**RESPONSE**
Lowell Hawthorne	He had a strong work ethic and as an employee he was "reliable, punctual, disciplined and respectful." In five years working in the equipment section of the NYPD, he never once called in sick.
Dr. Paul Chen-Young	"The ability to pull together talented teams to organize new businesses was a key element of Chen-Young's success."
Lois Sherwood	"Never taking no for an answer and believing anything is possible."
George Yap	"I am not afraid to ask for help and work hard. I read about success stories of others and improve on it."
Robert Levy	He attributes all of the successes achieved to the fact that the group puts God first in everything, trusting the Lord to direct the right people with the right ideas and the right attitudes to the organization.
Vincent HoSang	"My personality: being courteous, helpful and honest to my customers as well as to others."
Gordon "Butch" Stewart	From an early age, Butch was known for working harder than anyone else. He also excelled at exceeding his customers' expectations and providing numerous innovations.
Norman Wright	"The ability to focus on the goal. I have done some of everything in the business, payroll, personnel, marketing etc. Also being a people person."
Abe Issa	He had "unshakable convictions and clarity of purpose" that showed in everything he did. "He believed that anything was attainable with hard work and perseverance; and he never became discouraged because he also believed that behind every dark cloud was a silver lining."
Cherry Miller	"You have to be a hard worker and able to deal with the public."
Hazel Robinson	She possesses boundless energy and has an incredible ability to connect with people from all walks of life.
Audrey Marks	"Persistence, resilience and looking beyond the immediate circumstances."

TABLE 14: SAMPLE QUESTIONS AND RESPONSES – QUESTION 3

Interest in entrepreneurship can be shaped by early life experiences. In this study, most of the entrepreneurs had a parent or relative who owned a business in which they were allowed to work as a child. In a British study, it was shown that for men, becoming an entrepreneur was predicted by having a self-employed father; for women, it was predicted by their parents' socioeconomic resources which points to conjoint influences of both social structure and individual agency in shaping occupational choice (Schoon & Duckworth, 2012).

| TABLE 14 | WERE THERE ANY EARLY LIFE EXPERIENCES THAT SHAPED YOUR ENTREPRENEURIAL JOUNEY? |

NAME	RESPONSE
Michael Lee-Chin	At an early age he was given responsibility for running his parents small dry goods store alone for several hours each day and closing it in the evening. This allowed him to assume responsibility for something important very early in life.
Vincent Chang	After the untimely death of his father, when he was 13, he and his three brothers were separated and sent to live with various relatives. He worked in several small shops while he was growing up.
Rita Humphries-Lewin	Humphries-Lewin's mother insisted that for the first six months after starting her first job she could shop as she pleased with her paycheck but thereafter she was required to pay for room and board. That taught her responsibility and the value of money.
Lowell Hawthorne	His whole family would wake each day at 4:00 am to get the bakery up and running. All the children had chores to complete before heading off to school. At the age of 10, he was raising rabbits and guinea pigs for profit. Soon this expanded to chickens, goats and pigs that his mother helped him sell.
Dr. Paul Chen-Young	"I worked in my parents shop where there was always work, whether it was sweeping the floor, cutting paper for wrapping codfish, flour, rice, cornmeal, sugar and bread, or dealing with customers."
Lois Sherwood	"My parents were both creative people. My father made all the furniture in our home and my mother designed dresses and sold them to earn money."
Robert Levy	His father and uncles had a business representing manufacturers on the island. Later his father started Jamaica Broilers importing chickens. He joined the business at age 19 and learnt all aspects of it from the bottom up.
Vincent HoSang	"The example of my parents who had their own business as well as my uncle who also had his own business."
Gordon "Butch" Stewart	As a teenager, he and a friend built a boat and recruited a villager to provide rides to tourists for a fee. The venture was short-lived as they had used the wrong type of wood in constructing it.
Norman Wright	"I worked in my uncle's shop in Brown's Town during school vacations as a greeter."
Abe Issa	His father and uncles had a business in downtown Kingston known as E.A. Issa & Brothers which specialized in wholesale dry goods.
Cherry Miller	"It was a very hard life in those days and my parents had to provide for 11 children. They rose early every morning to do as much work as possible before the sun got too hot. Every child had chores. Some tended the animals, some gathered wood for cooking, and some washed clothes. We got used to hard work from an early age."
Hazel Robinson	Her father had a small shop and as children they picked lime, oranges and other fruit that they would sell in the shop.
Audrey Marks	"My parents' resilience during a farming crisis."

TABLE 15: SAMPLE QUESTIONS AND RESPONSES - QUESTION 4

Prior work experience can provide entrepreneurs with knowledge and skills that are necessary in starting and running their venture. It can also provide valuable contacts in the industry. It is thought that individuals develop different stocks of knowledge throughout their careers, and that the knowledge gained from information about customers and markets influence their ability to recognize and exploit particular entrepreneurial opportunities (Shane, 2000).

TABLE 15	WERE THERE ANY WORK EXPERIENCES THAT HAD AN IMPACT ON YOUR ENTREPRENEURIAL LIFE?
NAME	**RESPONSE**
Michael Lee-Chin	He worked as a bellman on a cruise ship and as a lab technician at a bauxite company. After college, he returned to Jamaica and worked for the government on the Mandela Highway project as a civil engineer. In 1976, he returned to Canada and became a financial adviser.
Vincent Chang	One of his first jobs was at the Hannah Town Bakery where he did a bit of everything including sweeping the floors. The bakery made a good spiced bun and it was here he developed a love of baking which prompted him to take courses in baking.
Rita Humphries-Lewin	"My job with Annett & Company, a Canadian Stock Brokerage subsidiary is where I first became fascinated with the brokerage business. It was where I began to feel I had found my niche."
Lowell Hawthorne	After high school, he operated a minibus service from Border to Half-Way Tree via Lawrence Tavern and the Constant Spring market. He had sold some of his pigs, goats and chickens to purchase the used bus.
Dr. Paul Chen-Young	"My first job was in bookkeeping. It paid very little but I learned from each work experience. At the World Bank what I learnt was discipline and there I was exposed to the world of finance and the highest levels of professionalism. On trips to Malawi and east Pakistan I got to see how governments operated."
Lois Sherwood	"In my first job as a telephone operator, everyone loved me. Whenever, anyone called for someone who was not available, I offered to call them back when he became available. No one had done that before."
George Yap	"After I dropped out of school I started to go from business to business downtown selling lunches my mother cooked. I realized I was good at selling."
Robert Levy	When he joined his father at Jamaica Broiler's he learned all aspects of the business from the ground up.
Vincent HoSang	"I had worked for an ice cream and milk company where I saw some automation equipment in operation. It was impressive and that stuck with me."
Gordon "Butch" Stewart	He worked for Curacao Trading company, which sold a variety of products including appliances, in the sales department. In a few years he had saved £3,200 to start his venture.
	(continued)

TABLE 15	WERE THERE ANY WORK EXPERIENCES THAT HAD AN IMPACT ON YOUR ENTREPRENEURIAL LIFE? *(continued)*
NAME	**RESPONSE**
Norman Wright	"My job at Tetley Tea Company was where I received my basic training in all aspects of business."
Abe Issa	He joined his father's business after graduating from college and began to transform it.
Cherry Miller	After leaving school she started sewing to make some money.
Hazel Robinson	Working for the Curacao Trading Company as a salesperson allowed her to meet many people who had their own businesses and were important contacts when she ventured out on her own.
Audrey Marks	"Redundancies of coworkers"

TABLE 16: SAMPLE QUESTIONS AND RESPONSES – QUESTION 5

Entrepreneurs take risks. According to Tom Ashbrook writing on Entrepreneurship.org, "Entrepreneurship means risk... to seriously consider taking the entrepreneurial leap already sets a person apart from the vast majority of men and women, who will never come close to actually leaving the world of wages. But even for the brave-of-heart, the reality of risk that comes with that leap—when the last paycheck is left behind and life is reduced to a single do-or-die mission—hits like ice water. It is the most naked moment in a working life. It can be a powerful energizer. It can also be overwhelming if you are not, at some level, prepared" (Ashbrook).

TABLE 16	WHAT ARE YOUR THOUGHTS ON RISK-TAKING?
NAME	**RESPONSE**
Michael Lee-Chin	Took several key risks in his career. Borrowed money to buy $500,000 worth of stock in McKenzie Financial. The stock appreciated seven-fold in four years and he used the profits to make his first acquisition.
Vincent Chang	Does not like to take risks and never felt that any of the initiatives he took to enter and expand his business were particularly risky.
Rita Humphries-Lewin	"I have done some risky things. I once bought Argentinean notes when everyone else was running in the other direction. I have never lost money. When you are responsible for other people's money, it's not yours to play with—don't go there."
Lowell Hawthorne	"Calculated risk not taken is opportunity lost. Risks must be properly assessed, analyzed and evaluated. You must weigh the gains against the losses."
Lois Sherwood	"Risk is a function of how one relates to it—risk must be given proper attention and once you do that risk is manageable."
	(continued)

TABLE 16	WHAT ARE YOUR THOUGHTS ON RISK-TAKING?	*(continued)*
NAME	**RESPONSE**	
Dr. Paul Chen-Young	"My experience at Lai Corporation was quite valuable. The company was broke when I arrived—I could hardly make payroll. This forced me to be creative in using assets in generating cash flow. My appetite for risk was developed here."	
George Yap	"I am a gambler and love to take risk because I get excited by taking risks. The bigger risk, the bigger the reward but the harder you drop."	
Robert Levy	"You have to take risks but I wouldn't bet the store."	
Vincent HoSang	"I have taken a lot of risks and it helped me to get where I am today. Risk is good but be conservative."	
Gordon "Butch" Stewart	Not afraid to make bold moves that clearly involved risks. In starting Appliance Traders, he presold 30 air conditioners when he had no supplier and no units to sell. Later, he bought the Bay Roc hotel, a rundown property at the end of an airport runaway at a time when tourism was in decline in Jamaica and he knew nothing about the hotel business.	
Norman Wright	"Think outside the box but be careful."	
Abe Issa	He was not afraid of being a pioneer and achieved many firsts in Jamaica: the first shopping plaza, first supermarket, etc. He had a bold vision for tourism and built a hotel in a mosquito infested area confounding the conventional wisdom at the time.	
Cherry Miller	Took a risk in building a small shop in a tiny village but was generally very conservative and took very few risks.	
Hazel Robinson	"I believe you have to take risks but not gamble with everything you have."	
Audrey Marks	"A necessary part of living a life to fullest potential."	

TABLE 17: SAMPLE QUESTIONS AND RESPONSES - QUESTION 6

There are many obstacles that an entrepreneur must overcome along the path to success. Funding to start a business is a common obstacle and in a small country like Jamaica, obtaining startup funding can be a daunting process. Then there are numerous internal and external obstacles that must be addressed. And there is always an element of uncertainty, competition, government regulations and lack of knowledge to be overcome. Successful entrepreneurs know how to over obstacles.

TABLE 17	WHAT OBSTACLES DID YOU FACE IN YOUR VENTURE?
NAME	**RESPONSE**
Michael Lee-Chin	In 1999 when the internet boom was in full throttle the speculation from the press and others was that he would soon be selling to raise cash to pay shareholders cashing out of his fund. They were advising his clients to sell before he did. In a bold and contrarian move, instead of selling, he bought. He borrowed $50 million to buy McKenzie shares at discounted prices and quickly made millions when the price appreciated (Kostigen, 2012). *(continued)*

TABLE 17   WHAT OBSTACLES DID YOU FACE IN YOUR VENTURE?   *(continued)*

NAME	RESPONSE
Vincent Chang	After two years in business, illness sidelined him for several months. The business was in jeopardy, but his wife sprang into action. She took command of operations and rallied family members and staff to keep the business going until he recovered.
Rita Humphries-Lewin	"It was very difficult in those early days as a female stockbroker. Men did not respect your knowledge or expertise. I had the experience many times where men would come in and when I asked them if I could help, they would point to my male junior for assistance" (Boyne, 1993).
Lowell Hawthorne	In the early days, a shakedown by Mafia garbage contractors had them fearing for their lives if they did not pay exorbitant fees. Then there was panic when the supplier of patties decided to terminate their supply. He had to figure out how to make patties.
Dr. Paul Chen-Young	The 1990s financial sector meltdown caused many businesses to shutdown. His network was bought by the government for $1.
Lois Sherwood	"There were obstacles in getting loans from banks that had never lent money to a woman before. I had to do my homework to persuade them."
Robert Levy	"One year we found that we were $20 million in debt. We started a prayer group with several directors and their wives who would meet once per week to pray. Miraculously, two years later we were in the black with cash on hand."
George Yap	"I approached seven banks in Miami trying to borrow money. I had no collateral. They all said no. When I went to an African-American bank I walked out with $10,000."
Vincent HoSang	"Lack of capital to set up a plant in compliance with federal regulation in wholesaling a meat or poultry product. Eventually, I received financing from the bank and seller of the building I bought."
Gordon "Butch" Stewart	In 1988, hurricane Gilbert, a category 5 hurricane, slammed into the island at 175 miles per hour. It was the most destructive storm in the history of Jamaica. Widespread damage and loss of life was reported. Entire industries were wiped out. It was a major test for the Stewart organization. Reports of "total devastation" poured in from Montego Bay.
Norman Wright	"An early venture into canning conch chowder ended in disaster as we used up all our cash on it. Since then I have had tunnel vision for the tea business."
Abe Issa	Successive governments had failed to see the value of tourism to Jamaica. He spoke to Bustamante, Sangster, Manley and Nethersole; "they all said the same thing, tourism could only be small fry. "I kept telling them they were wrong, tourism could be our biggest industry. And when they asked me why, I told them—the world is our market." He spoke of Jamaica's "invisible export of sun, sea, beaches and scenery" and how "when it comes to beaches we could lend "other countries some (Issa, 1994).
Cherry Miller	"We were burglarized when a thief came into the shop through the roof and stole several bottles of rum and some cigarettes. But I didn't let it stop me. I just kept going."

(continued)

TABLE 17	WHAT OBSTACLES DID YOU FACE IN YOUR VENTURE?	(continued)
NAME	**RESPONSE**	
Hazel Robinson	"In the very beginning I was operating a factory in a residential neighborhood as I was short of capital and had to pay fines. I could not afford to buy a cutter and had to borrow one, use it at night and return it each morning."	
Audrey Marks	Lack of capital forced her to start out with a smaller operation. She also faced gender, class and urban bias--she was a female from a rural area of the island.	

TABLE 18: SAMPLE QUESTIONS AND RESPONSES - QUESTION 7

Raising startup capital can be one of the most daunting tasks in entrepreneurship. Insufficient capital is a barrier to growth and success. Many startup entrepreneurs tap personal savings and seek loans from family and friends; a few are able to get loans. But this is not easy to do. Most new businesses fail and entrepreneurs are risky bets for lenders because they usually lack business experience and collateral to secure the loan. Successful entrepreneurs find a way to get funding and oftentimes they have to "make a way where there is no way."

TABLE 18	HOW WERE YOU ABLE TO SECURE CAPITAL FOR YOUR VENTURE?
NAME	**RESPONSE**
Michael Lee-Chin	Borrowed money to buy $500,000 worth of stock in McKenzie Financial. The stock appreciated seven-fold in four years and he used the profits to make his first acquisition.
Vincent Chang	Used savings and was able to borrow $3,000 from family and friends to buy a snack shop.
Rita Humphries-Lewin	She started Barita Investments with $10,000 of her own savings.
Lowell Hawthorne	The family raised $107,000 by putting up homes as collateral, emptying savings accounts and getting loans.
Dr. Paul Chen-Young	"Commercial real estate was the nexus for creating wealth to establish the capital base for my businesses."
Lois Sherwood	"In the beginning, I used money I had saved from our grocery budget to get started but later I had to get bank loans which they were reluctant to make at first since I was a woman."
George Yap	"We borrowed from family and friends to buy the hydroponic farm. Later I was able to get loans from the banks."
Robert Levy	His father started Jamaica Broilers and he joined a couple years later at age 19.
Vincent HoSang	"Financial help from an older brother and savings from my wife and myself."
Norman Wright	"It was hard to get a loan with no track record so in the beginning I used my own money I had saved and kept working as a contractor."
	(continued)

TABLE 18	HOW WERE YOU ABLE TO SECURE CAPITAL FOR YOUR VENTURE? *(continued)*
NAME	**RESPONSE**
Gordon "Butch" Stewart	After several years of working at Curacao Trading Company, he had saved $3,200 to start his venture.
Norman Wright	"I had to use money I had saved. It was impossible to get a loan without a track record."
Abe Issa	He joined the business started by his father and uncles.
Cherry Miller	She used money her husband had saved while a farm worker in the USA.
Hazel Robinson	Through her contacts as a sales person at Curacao Trading, she was able to obtain lines of credit from various suppliers.
Audrey Marks	There was turmoil in Jamaica's financial sector in the 1990s caused by a huge banking meltdown so it was difficult to find investors for Paymaster. Marks sold some real estate and a vehicle she owned to obtain startup capital.

TABLE 19: SAMPLE QUESTIONS AND RESPONSES - QUESTION 8

Entrepreneurs are more likely to give back according to a study by Ernst & Young entitled *Entrepreneurs & Philanthropy: Investing in the Future*, a comprehensive study which examines how entrepreneurs apply their personal passion for giving to their corporate philanthropy. The study found that companies led by entrepreneurs allocate more than twice the percentage of their profits to charity than many of America's largest companies (Hall, 2010).

The Jamaican entrepreneurs are no different; they are very involved in giving back and this is what they find most gratifying.

TABLE 19	WHAT ASPECT OF YOUR SUCCESS HAS BEEN MOST GRATIFYING?
NAME	**RESPONSE**
Michael Lee-Chin	He enjoys giving back and his philosophy is captured in his motto "doing well and doing good." He has won awards for philanthropy and he likes to mentor young people and is willing to tell his story so others might be inspired by it.
Vincent Chang	He is known for being a kind and generous soul. He has been able to give back by donating to various charities but is best known for the popular Tastee Talent Search competition which has been around for several decades.
Rita Humphries-Lewin	"First, I think I have satisfied my passion by working in this business and also I have been able to help a lot of people improve their lives."
Lowell Hawthorne	Seeing the vision being realized to make Jamaican patties mainstream by 2020. Also being able to give back, to mentor others, and help kids go to college. It's very gratifying when I see someone graduating from college and I know I had a part in making it a reality. *(continued)*

TABLE 19	**WHAT ASPECT OF YOUR SUCCESS HAS BEEN MOST GRATIFYING?**	*(continued)*

NAME	RESPONSE
Dr. Paul Chen-Young	"It has been most satisfying pulling together talented Jamaicans in a way that helped Jamaica move forward. For example, we were the first to invest in the tourist industry. We did financing for Sandals Ocho Rios and helped the government to divest the hotels and we created numerous jobs."
Lois Sherwood	Being able to help people. I am most touched by how appreciative people are when they are able to purchase a home.
George Yap	When I can give back to society especially the children when they smile. I have been able to get people out of jail and train them. God is not blind. The one who you least expect can help you.
Robert Levy	One thing that has been a pleasure was coming to work knowing that there is no politics. Here we have teamwork and we enjoy working with each other.
Vincent HoSang	Giving back to the less fortunate and giving advice to others to start their own business. Also, receiving numerous recognitions from both government and private organizations.
Gordon "Butch" Stewart	It must be extremely gratifying to be the largest private sector employer in Jamaica and several other islands, the largest single earner of foreign exchange and funding over 300 community projects.
Norman Wright	The fact that he is helping to improve the social fabric of Jamaica through his ventures.
Abe Issa	He was known as a philanthropist and Jamaican extraordinaire but also received various awards for his work in tourism; in 1960 Queen Elizabeth II conferred on him the Commander of the Most Excellent Order of the British Empire (CBE). In 1980, he received the Order of Jamaica for his work in tourism. This was followed by another major Jamaican award, the Norman Manley Award for Excellence in 1984.
Cherry Miller	"Being able to provide for the family and make a good life."
Hazel Robinson	"Making a contribution, providing jobs and helping others has been satisfying."
Audrey Marks	"Impacting millions of lives in Jamaica via increased productivity, savings and employment."

CHAPTER 22

Comparison of Characteristics, Traits and Ideas

Entrepreneurship can only exist when the entrepreneur exploits opportunities that allow new goods, services, raw materials, and organizing methods to be introduced and sold at a higher cost than their costs of production (Casson, 1982) or when a person can create or discover "new means-ends relationships" (S. Shane & Venkataraman, 2000).

TABLE 20: ENTREPRENEURS AND OPPORTUNITY RECOGNITION

The following Table provides examples of opportunities that were recognized by the Jamaican entrepreneurs.

TABLE 20	ENTREPRENEURS AND OPPORTUNITY RECOGNITION
NAME	**OPPORTUNITY RECOGNITION**
Michael Lee-Chin	Saw growth opportunity in buying stock of McKenzie, a company whose products he was selling to his clients. He bought the troubled National Commercial Bank in Jamaica when no one else would touch it.
Vincent Chang	Saw the opportunity to improve the taste and texture of the Jamaican patty.
Rita Humphries-Lewin	There were opportunities to create a Jamaican securities firm when foreign firms were leaving the country after independence. While others were hesitant, she stepped forward and did it.
Lowell Hawthorne	Realized there was a demand for Jamaican food products among the Jamaican immigrant community in New York and acted on it.
Dr. Paul Chen-Young	Realized it was easier to start a merchant bank than a commercial bank. He went on to create a dozen related companies when he saw complementarities.
Lois Sherwood	She bought antique furniture and real estate when British expatriates began leaving Jamaica after independence in 1962.
George Yap	Bought a bankrupt hydroponic farm although he knew nothing about farming.
	(continued)

TABLE 20	ENTREPRENEURS AND OPPORTUNITY RECOGNITION	*(continued)*

NAME	OPPORTUNITY RECOGNITION	
Robert Levy	Recognized that he could improve his poultry products business by vertically integrating into the feed and hatching businesses. Later he expanded into beef and fish. Ethanol production is another opportunity he exploited.	
Vincent HoSang	After working in the USA for several years he asked his brother, King for suggestions on how to move to the next level. He suggested, "Why don't you try doing something with Jamaican patties?"	
Gordon "Butch" Stewart	He recognized the opportunity in selling room air conditioners in Jamaica and established his first venture Appliance Traders Limited. Later he ventured into tourism at a time when others only saw problems.	
Norman Wright	While working for a tea company he realized the opportunity in using Jamaican indigenous plants and herbs in teas.	
Abe Issa	Was one of the first to recognize the potential of tourism as an industry that could be a major contributor to the economy in Jamaica.	
Cherry Miller	Saw an opportunity to buy land and build a small shop at the junction of two roads in her village.	
Hazel Robinson	Saw an opportunity to manufacture clothing using a material no one else saw was exploiting.	
Audrey Marks	Saw opportunity for bill payment facilities when she reviewed plans for customer growth at the utility where she worked.	

TABLE 21: EXAMPLES OF INNOVATION

According to Drucker, "innovation is the specific tool of the entrepreneur, the means by which they exploit change for a different business or service." The following Table lists some of the innovations by the Jamaican entrepreneurs.

TABLE 21	EXAMPLES OF INNOVATION	

NAME	EXAMPLES OF INNOVATION	
Michael Lee-Chin	After acquiring the NCB, developed his own credit card and so eliminated paying bank fees to a card company. His mutual fund company introduced many new products and services for clients. In Jamaica, he has diversified into media and healthcare by buying TV stations, a cable company and a hospital which he plans to develop into a "health care tourism" center.	
Vincent Chang	Redesigned the Jamaican patty and created the first restaurants that focused only on patties.	
Rita Humphries-Lewin	New financial instruments and accounts like "Tuition Builder" and "Barita Bridal Registry."New services such as FX trading.	
Lowell Hawthorne	New products, new recipes, new menus, combo meals	
Dr. Paul Chen-Young	New products: first to pay interest on current accounts with low balances; Eagle workers mortgage plan; created a one-stop financial services center. Established new Companies where he saw complementarities. Pioneered consortiums to finance Jamaica's hotel development during the 1980s. *(continued)*	

TABLE 21	EXAMPLES OF INNOVATION	*(continued)*
NAME	**EXAMPLES OF INNOVATION**	
Lois Sherwood	She started selling her subdivision lots on a hire-purchase basis, something she had done in her furniture business to make it easier for customers to buy.	
George Yap	Specialized in health focused vegetables. Offered customized ethnic products.	
Robert Levy	New products: added beef and fish to the brand. New Processes: contract with farmers to raise chickens and took control of the supply chain. New Business: added new businesses such as ethanol production as opportunities were identified.	
Vincent HoSang	New products: additional varieties of patties; Sabrina's puff pastry, added frozen and microwaveable products.	
Gordon "Butch" Stewart	Introduced many firsts in hotel industry: hair dryers in bathrooms, radios, swim-up bars, specialty restaurants, free weddings, "everything included," "Luxury included." He is considered the Steve Jobs of the hotel industry—creating a product you didn't know you wanted and convincing you that you need it.	
Norman Wright	Developed new products from indigenous herbs such as guinea hen, cerasse, and combining ginger and mint as "gingermint' teas.	
Abe Issa	He bought out an entire race track, Knutsford Park, and developed New Kingston, which is now a modern banking and commercial center. He developed the first shopping center in Half-Way-Tree—Tropical Plaza. He also developed Liguanea Plaza. He opened the first supermarket, Hi-Lo, at Cross Roads in Kingston.	
Cherry Miller	As a small business owner or sole trader did not focus on innovation as her primary motivation was to make a living by earning a regular income.	
Hazel Robinson	Created apparel designs for a material no one else saw a way to use.	
Audrey Marks	Introduced a one stop bill payment center which was a new service to Jamaica	

TABLE 22: ENTREPRENEURIAL IDENTITY FACTORS

Most of the entrepreneurs studied grew up in families where their parents either had a small business or were involved in some entrepreneurial activity that may have been the nexus of their later pursuits. And it is widely believed that children take on many of the same attitudes toward work as their parents.

The following Table shows possible identity factors for each entrepreneur.

TABLE 22	ENTREPRENEURIAL IDENTITY FACTORS
NAME	**IDENTITY FACTORS**
Michael Lee-Chin	His parents had a small shop in which he often worked alone after school and had responsibility for closing at end of each day.
Vincent Chang	As a child he lived with various relatives who all had grocery stores in which he worked.
Rita Humphries-Lewin	She grew up on a farm her parents owned in St Andrew.
Lowell Hawthorne	His father owned a bakery in the village of Border, St Andrew, and the whole family was involved in the operation of the business. *(continued)*

TABLE 22 ENTREPRENEURIAL IDENTITY FACTORS	*(continued)*

NAME	IDENTITY FACTORS
Dr. Paul Chen-Young	His father owned a grocery store in the village of Smithville, Clarendon and the children all worked in the store. He worked for the World Bank and other financial institutions before starting his own financial companies.
Lois Sherwood	Her mother designed and sewed dresses; Her father made all the furniture for their home.
George Yap	His father owned a soft drink business and later a bakery.
Robert Levy	His father had his own business as a manufacturer's agent and started Jamaica Broilers.
Vincent HoSang	His father had a grocery store. He also worked in his uncle's store.
Gordon "Butch"Stewart	His mother had a small business as an appliance dealer. His first business was in appliances.
Norman Wright	His father worked in agriculture. His uncle had a haberdashery store in which he worked on holidays. He was able to combine his love of agriculture with business at Perishables Jamaica.
Abe Issa	His father and his uncles operated a wholesale dry goods store in downtown Kingston.
Cherry Miller	Her father grew and sold tobacco and other crops for a living.
Hazel Robinson	She worked in her father's grocery store.
Audrey Marks	Her mother had a grocery store while her father was a farmer. She also completed graduate school at a school of entrepreneurship

TABLE 23: ENTREPRENEURIAL MINDSET EXAMPLES

According to McGrath & MacMillan (2000), people with an entrepreneurial mindset execute—that is they get on with it instead of analyzing new ideas to death…. They also engage the energies of everyone in their domain—both inside and outside the organization—in pursuit of an opportunity. They create and sustain networks of relationships…making the most of intellectual and other resources people have to offer. Entrepreneurs have the drive to start new businesses, to take risks, to innovate, and create value by producing new products, new processes or improvements.

TABLE 23 ENTREPRENEURIAL MINDSET EXAMPLES	

NAME	ENTREPRENEURIAL MINDSET EXAMPLES
Michael Lee-Chin	When his $500,000 investment in McKenzie Financial stock quadrupled, he didn't just sit on the cash but embarked on his first acquisition, AIC Limited. He has since made numerous other acquisitions including Jamaica's National Commercial Bank, Advantage General Insurance Company; CVM Communications Group; Reggae Beach and Blue Lagoon; and Medical Associates Limited (Hospital). *(continued)*

TABLE 23 ENTREPRENEURIAL MINDSET EXAMPLES	*(continued)*
NAME	**ENTREPRENEURIAL MINDSET EXAMPLES**
Vincent Chang	He was persistent in experimenting and creating a new crust and filling for his product and when he saw improvement in sales he dropped all other products and focused entirely on selling patties in his store.
Lowell Hawthorne	Tapped the home equity in his house, borrowed from a friend, quit his job to help start Golden Krust. Later he realized he could grow faster using other people's money via franchising.
Dr. Paul Chen-Young	He saw linkages between his original merchant bank and other businesses into which he expanded. His was the first Jamaican and Caribbean owned bank to set up operations in the United States and the first Caribbean Financial Institution to own a US-based brokerage or investment bank.
Lois Sherwood	She had local furniture makers copy antique designs which she then sold as "period reproductions." She was first to sell land on a hire-purchase basis in Jamaica.
George Yap	He endured rejection by many banks when he applied for a loan. He was willing to take risk with a business he knew nothing about.
Robert Levy	He set up a plant to process locally-produced ethanol from Jamaican sugar cane—thereby providing an outlet for this product—and selling to the USA. He spearheaded initiatives that expanded Jamaica Broilers product line into beef and fish.
Vincent HoSang	He started out with a small restaurant but soon entered into manufacturing as Caribbean Food Delights which supplies restaurants, supermarkets and wholesale clubs with products.
Gordon "Butch" Stewart	He bought a run-down hotel near an airport runway and turned it into an exciting concept that revolutionized the industry. Introduced many innovations to the hotel industry and now operates some 24 resorts plus other businesses.
Norman Wright	He leveraged the efforts of 300 farmers to grow herbs and plants instead of trying to grow all the raw materials himself. Saw the opportunity in using Jamaican indigenous products to earn valuable foreign exchange.
Abe Issa	He had a strategic vision for Jamaica in the tourist industry and pursued it at a time when few others saw the potential. In his other businesses, he was the first to do many things in Jamaica.
Cherry Miller	Realizing that jobs were virtually non-existent in her section of rural Jamaica, she and her husband built a small shop that is still operational 50 years later.
Hazel Robinson	She loved to sew and by selling some children's dresses to Woolworth's she realized money could be made in apparel. She seized the opportunity to venture on her own when no one else saw the potential in a new fabric her employer was unsuccessful in selling.
Audrey Marks	Although she had no background in technology, she was able to have a system designed, developed and implemented with all necessary hardware, software and network support in place within a three-year timeframe. And she soon inked a deal with a major utility to collect their bills via her Paymaster system.

TABLE 24: ENTREPRENEURS AND EDUCATION LEVELS ACHIEVED

Several studies indicate a correlation between education and entrepreneurship. But many of the entrepreneurs interviewed recalled having problems in a formal school setting. Several of them dropped out of high school. Some of the world's richest entrepreneurs were dropouts—Apple Computer's Steve Jobs, Microsoft's Bill Gates, Dell Computer's Michael Dell and Virgin Group's Richard Branson among others.

Amancio Ortega shuns publicity and never gives interviews but he is the third richest man in the world according to Forbes. Born into a very poor family, he dropped out of school at age 13 but went on to build a fashion empire and a net worth of some US$56 billion.

Li Ka-shing, the richest man in Asia, was born in Chaozhou in Guangdong province, China, in 1928. He was forced to drop out of school before the age of 15 due to the death of his father. He went on to build an empire comprising plastics, telecommunications, real estate, banking, airports, shipping and a myriad of other businesses. Forbes lists his wealth at $31 billion making him the eighth richest person in the world (*Forbes Billionaires*, 2013).

Education is an equalizing force, allowing people from the humblest backgrounds to move up the economic ladder. Nowhere has this been more true than China where the influence of Confucian teachings stresses the primacy of education. And yet, as the story of Li Ka-shing illustrates, it is possible to become quite rich without a formal education. This is also borne out by some of the Jamaican entrepreneurs who despite dropping out of high school went on to enjoy extraordinary success.

TABLE 24 ENTREPRENEURS AND EDUCATION LEVELS ACHIEVED	
NAME	EDUCATION LEVELS ACHIEVED
Michael Lee-Chin	He completed college with an engineering degree.
Vincent Chang	He had some high school education and took courses in baking and pastry making.
Rita Humphries-Lewin	She completed high school and certifications in the securities industry.
Lowell Hawthorne	He completed high school and college.
Dr. Paul Chen-Young	He gained a PhD in economics, worked at the World Bank in the prestigious Young Professional Program (YPP) and at the Jamaica Development Finance Corporation.
Lois Sherwood	She completed high school and art school.
George Yap	He dropped out of high school but felt he could learn how to do stuff. *(continued)*

TABLE 24 ENTREPRENEURS AND EDUCATION LEVELS ACHIEVED	*(continued)*
NAME	EDUCATION LEVELS ACHIEVED
Robert Levy	He dropped out of high school due to dyslexia issues but years later completed a Harvard Business School course for owner/managers.
Vincent HoSang	He dropped out of high school and later learned how to make patties from his brother.
Gordon "Butch" Stewart	He dropped out of high school at age 14 but took additional courses later.
Norman Wright	He had some college education. He later learned much about tea production while working at Tetley Teas.
Abe Issa	He completed high school and college.
Cherry Miller	She had primary school education but could not afford high school which was beyond the reach of the average Jamaican at that time.
Hazel Robinson	She dropped out of high school and started working at age 15.
Audrey Marks	She completed an MBA degree.

TABLE 25: ENTREPRENEURS AND EXAMPLES OF SOCIAL CAPITAL

Social capital, as discussed earlier, includes the many resources available to us through our personal and business networks. These resources include information, ideas, leads, business opportunities, financial capital, power, emotional support, goodwill, trust and cooperation. Adler and Kwon (2002) define social capital as:

> …the goodwill available to individuals or groups. Its source lies in the structure and content of the actor's social relations. Its effects flow from the information, influence, and solidarity it makes available to the actor" (Adler and Kwon, 2002).

TABLE 25 ENTREPRENEURS AND EXAMPLES OF SOCIAL CAPITAL	
NAME	EXAMPLES OF SOCIAL CAPITAL
Michael Lee-Chin	*When asked what success provided that he wouldn't have had otherwise he replied:* Access. That's a function of having built a good reputation, of differentiating myself and serving customers well. For example, when we visit Mexico City, I am able to get us an audience with the most prominent businesspeople in Mexico, the most relevant policy-makers, even the president. No one would have met with us if I had a bad reputation (Portsmouth, 2011).
Vincent Chang	He was able to get information on possible businesses for sale and access to financial capital via his network of family and friends. When he was ill for an extended period, family and friends pitched in and kept the business operating until he recovered.
Rita Humphries-Lewin	Her former associates encouraged her to start her own brokerage house and supported her so she was able to hit the ground running with 10 clients.
Lowell Hawthorne	His large close knit-family was a source of encouragement and support. They also raised over $107,000 in startup capital by using their homes as collateral, emptying savings accounts, etc.. *(continued)*

TABLE 25 ENTREPRENEURS AND EXAMPLES OF SOCIAL CAPITAL *(continued)*

NAME	EXAMPLES OF SOCIAL CAPITAL
Dr. Paul Chen-Young	He was well connected and knew many talented Jamaicans whom he could recruit in starting new businesses.
Lois Sherwood	She learned of the Burger King plan to offer a franchise in Jamaica at a party Americans attended in Jamaica. She had built up a reputation for success in her other businesses prior to working with Burger King.
George Yap	He borrowed from friends and family to purchase a hydroponic farm.
Robert Levy	He had a powerful board of directors and was well respected and highly regarded in Jamaican business community for high values and integrity.
Vincent HoSang	He had an older brother who was always ready to provide guidance and it was he who suggested starting a business as well as helped him with startup capital.
Gordon "Butch" Stewart	When a massive hurricane left his hotel in shambles and the whole island in devastation, all of Sandal's employees showed up for work the day after the hurricane in a display of unprecedented goodwill and social capital.
Norman Wright	"The management of Tetley Tea Company Jamaica Limited (now Jamaican Teas Limited) were helpful in the development of our first product TOPS Pep O Mint tea bags and they contract packaged our products until we established our own facility...Mr. Peter Cleare, Managing Director, Orion Sales Limited, Dr. Alfred Sangster, past principal of CAST/ Utech, and Mr. John Mahfood, managing director of Jamaican Teas Limited served as my mentors."
Abe Issa	He served as a member of Parliament, chairman of the Jamaica Tourist Board, and was an undisputed giant of Jamaican commerce.
Cherry Miller	She came from a large family of seven brothers and four sisters who provided support, encouragement and helped in whatever way they could.
Hazel Robinson	She was able to start her business with several lines of credit from suppliers with whom she had done business previously. When she couldn't afford a cutter, she was able to borrow one, use it at nights and return it to its owner each morning.
Audrey Marks	As an MBA graduate from a school of entrepreneurship she knew the importance of social capital and how to acquire it. Social capital can be acquired through investing in relationships developed in your networks and by adding value to the networks. Marks serves on many public and private sector boards which are important reservoirs of social capital.

CHAPTER 23

Recommendations

This book provides a baseline for continued research on the characteristics and traits relevant to entrepreneurship in Jamaica. It corroborates much of the existing understanding of the role of entrepreneurial traits or characteristics in entrepreneurship. And, it strengthens the belief that Jamaicans possess the same entrepreneurial qualities found elsewhere in the world.

Although several studies show a "direct, positive relationship between level of education and entrepreneurial performance" (Brush & Hisrich, 1991), this study of Jamaican entrepreneurs shows that lack of education does not have to be a barrier to entrepreneurial success. Some of the entrepreneurs profiled experienced difficulties in the traditional school setting, yet went on to demonstrate the innovation, creativity and other characteristics that defined their success.

RECOMMENDATIONS

According to the Global Entrepreneurship Monitor (GEM), Jamaica is one of the most entrepreneurial countries in the world. However, most of its entrepreneurs are of the necessity type. Jamaica needs to develop more opportunity entrepreneurs for these are the entrepreneurs who can innovate, create wealth, jobs and enterprises that drive economic growth.

One way to stimulate the opportunistic entrepreneurial mindset is to implement programs that expose children at an early age to the idea of business or to people who have businesses. The vast majority of the Jamaican entrepreneurs in the study had either a parent or a relative who owned a business in which they were allowed to work. At the age of 12, billionaire Michael Lee-Chin was allowed to operate his parents shop and close up in the evenings by himself. Most Jamaican children do not have parents who own a business but they could still benefit by participating in programs that expose them to the inner workings of a business and early responsibility.

On a recent visit to the Research Triangle area of North Carolina—an area known for its universities, high tech companies and enterprises—I heard of a school—Cedar Fork Elementary in Morrisville—where students in the second grade are asked to develop a business plan and create a product or provide a service that they can market to other students and the public. This early introduction to starting a business will no doubt pay dividends later in life for these second graders.

Existing programs that expose young people to entrepreneurism should be expanded. One such program is Junior Achievement Jamaica which was registered in 2009. It is part of the worldwide Junior Achievement (JA) organization which was started in the USA nearly 100 years ago. It includes programs that:

> ...allow young people to experience the entire company life cycle: conducting market research, creating viable product, marketing and selling the product ...and in many cases continuing as viable businesses.

Parents can help their children by being entrepreneurial themselves, even if only in small ways. They can make business games available; encourage initiative; help their children see opportunities instead of problems and encourage them to follow through on their ideas. Give them responsibilities at an early age.

Teachers and schools should start encouraging the entrepreneurial mindset from an early age. Schools can add entrepreneurship courses to the curriculum. They should realize that many successful entrepreneurs did not do well in the traditional school setting and respect the students that "think different."

According to Dr. John Kelly, one of the researchers who conducted the Entrebraineur study that was discussed earlier, teachers need to recognize the existence of right brain and left brain learners in class. The current educational system in Jamaica does not do this. Students like Butch Stewart, who left school at age 14 but went on to found Sandals Resorts International, did not fit into that system which does not value out-of-the-box thinking and non-conformity—important characteristics of entrepreneurs.

Entrepreneur and lecturer, Marguerite Orane, who taught entrepreneurship at the University of the West Indies, wrote that:

> ...entrepreneurship is essentially a creative act. Therefore, education that is exclusively or heavily science-driven gives short shrift to the development of right-brained thinking that is essential to identify new ideas and convert them to opportunities and then new and growing ventures. In our British-based system the underpinning of which was the development of cogs in the industrial wheel, the curriculum still focuses on rote learning, multiple-choice exam formats, and regurgitation of the "right" answer. In entrepreneurship, there is no 'right' answer (Orane, 2009).

We also need to help our children develop an internal locus of control early in life. Entrepreneurs have an internal locus of control. They believe they are responsible for their success and take actions to achieve that success. People with an external locus of control blame others for what happens to them and often are not motivated to achieve as they feel that the outcomes in their lives are controlled by chance or others and not by their own efforts.

Jamaica has developed a great system for producing world champions in track and field and is often referred to as a "sprint factory." Track and field training is part of the national culture and begins at an early age in primary school. High schools vie for athletic supremacy at the annual ISSA/GraceKennedy Boys and Girls Championships which attracts media from around the world. There is even a college dedicated to training coaches and trainers—the G.C. Foster College of Physical Education & Sports.

Jamaica should now develop the culture and systems to produce entrepreneurs in the same way it now produces sprinters.

LIMITATIONS

This book focused on a selected subset of Jamaican entrepreneurs, for the most part an older and more successful group. Most of them grew up in colonial Jamaica and therefore their life experiences are in many ways different from those born after independence. There are other groups of Jamaican entrepreneurs that could further illuminate our understanding of Jamaican entrepreneurs.

SUMMARY

The Jamaican entrepreneurs have demonstrated that success is possible in many different fields and by many different routes. A few were highly educated, but many did not go to college and some dropped out of high school. Some grew up in a rural Third World like environment while some had a relatively comfortable childhood lacking nothing. As the world's fastest man, Jamaican Usain Bolt would put it, "It's not how you start but how you finish."

According to Casson (1982) most studies of entrepreneurs relies on stereotypes. It is hoped that the profiles developed in this study will expand our thinking about Jamaican entrepreneurs beyond the stereotypes as we understand what they have accomplished and how they did it.

The book highlights some of the many benefits that the success of the profiled entrepreneurs have brought to Jamaica. These include foreign exchange earnings, development of personnel, creation of jobs, productivity improvements, donations to worthy causes, and contributions that improve the overall social fabric of the island.

It would be simplistic to conclude that all Jamaica needs is people with certain traits and behaviors and all its economic problems would be solved. There are external factors that also play a key role in spurring the nation's economy. However, there is no doubt entrepreneurship can play an important role in jumpstarting the economy. But, they also need the proper environment in which to thrive. Recommendations for promoting entrepreneurship on the island abound and it would be beneficial for policymakers to take heed.

Resources

List of Jamaican Honours

TABLE 26: JAMAICAN HONOURS

Several entrepreneurs in this book have been recognized by the Jamaican government for their contributions to the country. The complete list of Jamaican honours is shown in the Table below:

TABLE 26 JAMAICAN HONOURS	
ABBREVIATION	DESCRIPTION
N/A	Order of National Hero. Conferred on any Jamaican or naturalized citizen who has rendered the most distinguished service to Jamaica.
ON	Order of the Nation. Conferred on the governor-general and prime ministers, upon whom the Order of National Hero was not previously conferred.
OM	Order of Merit. Conferred upon any citizen of Jamaica who has achieved eminent international distinction in his or her field of endeavor.
OE	Order of Excellence. Reserved for foreign heads of state or heads of government.
OJ	Order of Jamaica. Bestowed on any Jamaican national or any distinguished citizen of a foreign country other than Jamaica, who has demonstrated outstanding distinction in service to Jamaica.
CD and OD	Order of Distinction. Has two ranks: higher class—Commander; and, lower class—Officer.

Source: Jamaica Information Service (JIS)

Maps of Jamaica and the Caribbean

Figure 1: Map of Jamaica

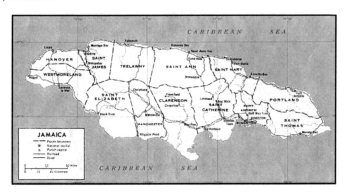

Figure 2: Map of the Caribbean

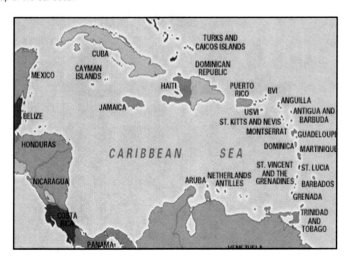

The Jamaican Flag and Coat of Arms

Figure 3: Flag of Jamaica

Figure 4: Jamaican Coat of Arms

DR. GLEN LAMAN

References

Acs, Zoltan J, and David B. Audretsch. 2003. *Introduction to the Handbook of Entrepreneurship Research*. Norwell, MA: Kluwer Academic Press.

Acs, Zoltan J. 2006. "How Is Entrepreneurship Good for Economic Growth?" *Innovations,* Winter.

Acs, Zoltan J, Arenius, Pia, Hay, Michael, and Maria Minniti. 2005. *Global Entrepreneurship Monitor - 2004* executive report. Babson Park, MA: Babson College.

Acs, Zoltan J, and David B. Audretsch. eds. 2003. *Handbook of Entrepreneurship Research.* New York, NY: *Springer Science.*

Adler, Paul S, and Kwon Seok-Woo. 2002. "Social Capital: Prospects for a New Concept." *The Academy of Management Review* 27: 17-40.

Ashbrook, Tom. *Risk in Entrepreneurship*. Entrepreneurship.org.

Associated Press. 1999. "Developing countries seek economic checks globalization needs rules, leaders insist." *Chicago Tribune*, February 13, 1999.

Baker, Wayne. 2000. *Achieving Success through Social Capital*. Jossey-Baaas Inc.

Bandura, Albert. 1977. "Self-efficacy: Toward a unifying theory of behavioral change." *Psychological Review*, 84: 191-215.

Bandura, Albert. 1992. "Exercise of personal agency through the self-efficacy mechanisms." In *Self-efficacy: Thought control of action.* ed., R. Schwarzer Washington, DC: Hemisphere.

Bandura, Albert. 1994. "Self-efficacy." In *Encyclopedia of human behavior*, 4. ed.V. S. Ramachaudran, 71-81. New York: Academic Press.

Bank of Jamaica. 2012. *Balance of Payments—Remittance Report.* External Sector Statistics Unit, Economic Information & Publications Department, Research and Economic Programming Division, Bank of Jamaica.

Baron, Robert and Thomas Ward. 2004. "Expanding Entrepreneurial Cognition's Toolbox: Potential Contributions from the Field of Cognitive Science." Entrepreneurship Theory and Practice, 28(6).

Baxter, Pamela and Susan Jack. 2008. "Qualitative case study methodology: Study Design and Implementation for Novice Researchers." *The Qualitative Report*, 13(4), 544-559. Retrieved from http://www.nova.edu/ssss/QR/QR13-4/baxter.pdf.

Bennett, Kimala. 2009. *Starting a Business in Jamaica*. Kingston: The Business Lab.

Bernstein, Andrew. 2011. "Nature Vs. Nurture: Who is Interested in Entrepreneurship Education? A Study of Business and Technology Undergraduates Based on Social Cognitive Career Theory." Thesis.

Bertram, Arnold. 2006. "Revisiting Michael Manley's social revolution." *Jamaica Gleaner*, April 9, 2006. Retrieved January 31, 2013, http://jamaica-gleaner.com/gleaner/20060409/lead/lead8.html.

Black, Clinton V. 1958. *History of Jamaica*. London: Collins Educational.

Black, Clinton. 1960. *Spanish Town - The Old Capital*. Spanish Town, Jamaica: The Parish Council of St Catherine.

Boyne, Ian. 1993. "From Secretary to Stockbroker: Rita Humphries-Lewin Story." *The Financial Gleaner*, January 11, 1993.

Branson, Richard. 2010. "Is Education the Key to Success?" *Livemint.com*. retrieved March 30, 2013. http://www.livemint.com/Opinion/jgm5G041LTKc885TrJJQdO/Is-education-the-key-to-success.html.

Briguglio, Lino. 1995. "Small Island Developing States and Their Economic Vulnerabilities." *World Development*, 23(9); 1615-1632.

Brockhaus, Robert. 1980. "Risk Taking Propensity of Entrepreneurs." *Academy of Management Journal*. 23(3); 509-520.

Brockhaus, Robert and Pamela Horwitz. 1986. "The Psychology of the Entrepreneur," in D.L. Sexton, R.W. Smilor (eds.) *The Art and Science of Entrepreneurship*, pp. 25-48. Cambridge, MA: Ballinger.

Brouwer, Maria. 1991. *Organizations, Individualism and Economic Theory*. New York. Routledge.

Buddan, Robert. 2004. "Universal Adult Suffrage in Jamaica and the Caribbean since 1944." *Social and Economic Studies*, 53(4), Special Issue on Government and Politics, 135-162.

Byrne, John A. 2011. *World Changers: 25 Entrepreneurs Who Changed Business as We Knew It.* USA: Penguin Group.

Casnocha, Ben. 2008. "Definition of Entrepreneurial Judgement." Casnocha.com. Retrieved March 28, 2013. http://casnocha.com/2008/07/definition-of-e.html.

Cassel, Andrew. 2001. "Free trade - the movie version - is pure fiction. A television documentary's look at Jamaica's plight fails to ask key questions, and demonizes globalization." *Philadelphia Enquirer.* Retrieved December 02, 2012, from ProQuest database.

Casson, Marc. 2003. *The Entrepreneur: an Economic Theory* (2nd ed.). Cheltenham: Edward Elgar Publishing.

Chan, K. K. 2010. "The Ancient Art of Chinese Business Savvy." *Timaru Herald,* August 10, 2010.

Chell, Elizabeth, Jean M. Haworth and Sally Brearley. 1991. *The entrepreneurial personality: concepts, cases, and categories.* London, New York: Routledge.

Chell, Elizabeth. 2008. *The Entrepreneurial Personality: A Social Construction.* New York: Routeledge/The Psychology Press.

Collins, Orvis F. and David G. Moore. 1970. *The organization makers; a behavioral study of independent entrepreneurs.* New York: Appleton-Century-Crofts.

Collister, Keith. 2012. "Debt to GDP won't exceed 150% in 2012—IMF. *Jamaica Observer.* June 10, 2012.

Coven, J. G. and M. P. Miles. 1999 "Corporate entrepreneurship and the pursuit of competitive advantage.." *Entrepreneurship: theory and practice,* 23(3), 47-57.

CIA. 2011. *The World Fact Book.*

Chung, Dennis. 2009. *Charting Jamaica's Economic and Social Development: A Much Needed Paradigm Shift.* Printed in USA by Dennis Chung.

Cross, John M. 2002. "Mahogany in Jamaica was like Gold in the Reign of Solomon." *The Meeting of East and West in the Furniture Trade. Sixth International Symposium on Wood and Furniture Consevation.* Amsterdam, Netherlands.

Cummins, Brian and John Kelly. 2010.Entrebraineur: Investigating Entrepreneurial Learning Preferences. June, 2010.Retrieved on January 15, 2013 from: http://www.stran.ac.uk/informationabout/research/entrebraineurproject/filetoupload,214627,en.pdf.

Dellape, John. 2012. "What is entrepreneurship?" *Mises Daily*, September 28, 2012.

Dinger, E. 2005. "Golden Krust Caribbean Bakery, Inc." International Directory of Company Histories, Encylopedia.com.

Drennan, J., J. Kennedy and P. Renfrow. 2005. "Impact of childhood experiences on the development of entrepreneurial intentions." *Entrepreneurship and Innovation*, (November). Drucker, Peter. 1985 and 2006. *Innovative and Entrepreneurship Practice and Principles*. New York: Harper & Row, Publishers, Inc.

Drucker, Peter. 1993. *Innovation and Entrepreneurship*. New York, Harper.

Eisner, Gisela. 1961. *Jamaica 1830-1930: A study in Economic Growth*. Manchester: University Press.

Flyvberg, Bent. 2006. "Five misunderstandings about case-study research." *Qualitative Inquiry*, 12(2); 219-245.

Forbes, Steve. 2005. "A Tribute to Peter Drucker." *Wall Street Journal*. Asia.

Forbes. 2013. *Forbes Billionaires*. Retrieved April 2013; http://www.forbes.com/ profile/li-ka-shing/.

Gardner, William James. 1873. *A History of Jamaica: from its discovery by Christopher Columbus to the year 1872*. Frank Cass & Co. 2005.

Girvan, Norman. 1999. "Jamaica's Internal Debt Trap: An Interpretation." Presentation to the Financial Sector Symposium.

Girvan, Norman. 2012. Pan-Caribbean Perspective: Colonialism, Resistance and Reconfiguration. Retrieved October 11, 2012 from: http://www.normangirvan.info/ wp-content/uploads/2012/06/girvan-paper-for-jornadas-bolivarianas11.pdf.

Gladwell, Malcolm. 2008. *Outliers: The story of success*. New York, NY: Little, Brown and Company.

Gleaner. 2005. "When Manley embraced democratic socialism." *Jamaica Gleaner*, June 20, 2005. Retrieved January 31, 2013 from: http://jamaica-gleaner.com/ gleaner/20050620/lead/lead6.html.

Glennie, Alex and Laura Chappell. 2010. "Jamaica: From Diverse Beginning to Diaspora in the Developed World." Institute for Policy Research. Retrieved January 31, 2013. http://www.migrationinformation.org/feature/print.cfm?ID=787.

Global Entrepreneurship Monitor. 2011. *Jamaica Report 2011. Retrieved on January 20, 2013 from* http://www.gemconsortium.org/docs/2596/gem-jamaica-2011-report.

Glover, David. 1994. "Contract farming and commercialization of agriculture in developing countries." In *Agricultural commercialization, economic development and nutrition.* ed.Von Braun, J and E. Kennedy. Baltimore, MD: Johns Hopkins University Press.

Goltz, Jay. 2012. "Six Attributes of Successful Entrepreneurs." *The New York Times,* February 23, 2012. Retrieved from: http://boss.blogs.nytimes.com/2012/02/23/six-attributes-of-successful-entrepreneurs/.

Golafshani, Nahid. 2003. "Understanding reliability and validity in qualitative research." *The Qualitative Report,* 8(4), 597-606. Retrieved July 13, 2012 from: http://www.nova.edu/ssss/QR/QR8-4/golafshani.pdf.

Gray, Obika. 2009. "Jamaica, 1938 Labor Riots." *International Encyclopedia of Revolution and Protest,* ed Immanuel Ness.

Habiby, Anne S. and Diedre Coyle Jr. 2010. "The High Intensity Entrepreneur." *HBR* (Sept.).

Hall, Holly. 2010. "Study Explores Charitable Habits of Entrepreneurs." *The Chronicle of Philanthropy,* (November).

Hart, Richard. 2002. "Labour Rebellions of the 1930s in the British Caribbean Region Colonies." London: Caribbean Labour Solidarity and the Socialist History Society.

Hawthorne, Lowell. 2012. *The Baker's Son.* NY: Akashic Books.

Herbert, Robert and Albert Link. 2009. *A History of Entrepreneurship.* London: Routledge.

Henderson, R. and M. Robertson. 1999. "Who wants to be an entrepreneur? Young adult attitudes to entrepreneurship as a career." *Education & Training,* 41(4/5); 236.

Hill, Brian. nd. Difference between Entrepreneurship & Small Business Management. Smallbusiness.chron.com. Retrieved April 17, 2013 from: http://smallbusiness.chron.com/difference-between-entrepreneurship-small-business-management-53370.html.

Hisrich, R., M., Peters and D. Shepherd. 2010. *Entrepreneurship.* (8th ed.). New York, NY: McGraw Hill.

Hodkinson, H. and P. Hodkinson. 2001. "The Strengths and Limitations of Case Study Research." Making an impact on policy and practice, LSDA Annual Conference, Cambridge.

Hofstede, Geert. 1980. *Culture's Consequences.* London: Sage Publications.

Hofstede, Geert. 1991. *Cultures and Organizations.* London, UK: McGraw-Hill.

Holden, Stephen. 2001. "Film review: One love, One Heart or a Sweatshop Economy?" *The New York Times,* June 15, 2001.

Hyatt, John T. 1990. Historical Evolution of the International Banana Trade. Retrieved January 20, 2013 from: http://www.ibrown.com/Thoughts/Banana%20 Trade.pdf.

International Meeting to Review the Implementation of the Programme of Action for the Sustainable Development of Small Island Developing States. Port Louis, Mauritius. 10-14 January 2005.

Issa, Suzanne. 1994. *Mr. Jamaica: Abe Issa—A Pictorial Biography by Suzanne Issa.* Published by S. Issa, Kingston, Jamaica

Jaccarino, Pamela Lerner. 2005. *All That's Good: the Story of Butch Stewart the Man behind Sandals Resorts.* Sandow Media.

Jackson, S. 2012. "Tourism Hits New Record." *The Gleaner,* April 11, 2012.

Jamaica Observer. "Jamaica's Five Most Powerful Women." *Jamaica Observer,* August 15, 2005.

Jamaica Observer. "Air Jamaica: End of an Era. The Little Piece of Jamaica that Cries." *Jamaica Observer,* July 08, 2011.

Jamaica Observer. "High brain drain bolsters strong remittances to Jamaica." *Jamaica Observer,* November 10, 2010.

Jamaica Observer. 2011. "EU to appraise Private Sector Development Programme in Jamaica." *Jamaica Observer,* April 15, 2011.

Jamaica Observer. "Maybe Jamaica Should Leave CARICOM." *Jamaica Observer,* June 7, 2012. Retrieved from http://jamaica-gleaner.com/gleaner/20120607/ cleisure/cleisure1.html.

Jamaica Observer. "Burger King Awards over $1 million in scholarships." *Jamaica Observer*, October 18, 2012.

Johnson, Anthony. 2008. *The Brave May Fall but Never Yield: A History of Kingston College*. Kingston, Jamaica: ISKAMOL Ltd.

Johnston, Jake and Juan Montecino. 2012. *Update on the Jamaican Economy*. Center for Economic and Policy Research.

Katz, Jerome and Dean Shepherd. 2003. "Cognitive Approaches to Entrepreneurship Research." *Elsevier Science Ltd*.

Kirby, David. 2003. *Entrepreneurship*. UK: McGraw Hill Education.

Kirk, Jerome and Marc Miller. 1986. *Reliability and validity in qualitative research*.

Newbury Park, CA: Sage Publications.

Kirzner, Israel. 1973. *Competition and Entrepreneurship*. Chicago: University of Chicago Press.

Koeppel, Dan. (2008). *Banana: the fate of the fruit that changed the world*. Published by Penguin Books Ltd.

Kohn, Linda. 1997. "Methods in Case Study Analysis." *The Center for Studying Health System Change*.

Kong, Jeanette. 2012. *The Chiney Shop*. A documentary short film.

Kostigen, Thomas. 2012. "Beating the Odds." *Financial Adviser*, July 1, 2012.

Kuratko, Donald F. 2005. "The emergence of entrepreneurship education: Development, trends, and challenges." *Entrepreneurship Theory and Practice*, 29, 577-597.

Laaksonen, Kalle, Petri Maki-Franti and Meri Virolainen. 2007. "Mauritius and Jamaica as Case Studies of the Lomé Sugar Protocol." Pellervo Economic Research Institute Working Paper.

Laeven, Luc and Fabian Valencia. 2008. "Systemic Banking Crises: A New Database." IMF working Paper.

Learning and Skills Development Agency. 2001. "Making an Impact on Policy and Practice." Paper presented to the Learning and Skills Development Agency conference, Cambridge, December.

Lee, S. 1989. "Peppermint—a new farming industry." *The Gleaner*, September 9, 1989.

Lewis, W. Arthur. 1966. *Development Planning: The Essentials of Economic Policy.* Harper & Row.

Lewis, W. Arthur. 1973. "The Shortage of Entrepreneurship." Statement by Sir Arthur Lewis, President Caribbean Development Bank, to The Board of Governors at The Third Annual Meeting held In Jamaica, April 26, 1973.

Lowrie-Chin, Jean. 2009) "Audrey Marks' Amazing Story." *Jamaica Observer*, June15, 2009.

Luton, D. 2012. "Put T&T In Its Place - MP Says Jamaica Should Decide On Leaving CARICOM." *Jamaica Gleaner*, May 31, 2012.

Manley, Michael. 1987. *Up the Down Escalator: Development and the International Economy, A Jamaican Case Study.* Howard University Press.

McClelland, David. 1953. *The Achievement Motive.* Appleton.

McClelland, David. 1961. *The Achieving Society.* D. Van Nostrand.

McGrath, Rita and. Ian MacMillan. 2000. *The Entrepreneurial Mindset: Strategies for continuously Creating Opportunity in an Age of Uncertainty.* Harvard Business Press.

Meditz, Sandra and Dennis Hanratty. eds. 1987. "Caribbean Islands: A Country Study." Washington: GPO for the Library of Congress.

Miller, Errol. 1990. "Jamaican Society and High Schooling." *Institute of Social and Economic Research*, Kinston, Jamaica: UWI.

Misner, Ivan. 2004. "Investing in Your Social Capital." *Entrepreneur*, August 23, 2004.

Morrison, Dennis. 2009. "Bumpy ride after remittance bonanza." *Jamaica Observer*, August 2009.

Mueller, Stephen and Anisya Thomas. 2001. "Culture and entrepreneurial potential: A nine country study of locus of control and innovativeness." *Journal of Business Venturing*, (January).

Murnieks, Charles and Elaine Mosakowski. 2007. "Who Am I? Looking Inside the 'Entrepreneurial Identity." Babson College Entrepreneurship Research Conference (BCERC).

Nicolaou, N., S. Shane, L.Cherkas, J. Hunkin, and T. D. Spector. 2008. "Is the tendency to engage in entrepreneurship genetic?" *Management Science*. 54(1), 167-179. doi: 10.1287/mnsc. 1070.0761.

Okhomina, Donatus. 2010. "Entrepreneurial orientation and psychological traits: the moderating influence of supportive environment." *Journal of Behavioral Studies in Business*; June, (3).

Orane, Marguerite 2009. "Thoughts on Entrepreneurship in Jamaica." Retrieved on May 23, 2013 from http://growthfacilitators.blogspot.com/2009/02/thoughts-on-entrepreneurship-in-jamaica.html.

Patterson, Orlando. 2001. *The Roots of Conflict in Jamaica. New York Times* Op-Ed.

Patton, Michael. 2002. *Qualitative Evaluation and Research Methods*. Newbury Park, CA: Sage.

Peverelli, Peter and Jiwen Song. 2012. *Chinese Entrepreneurs*. Springer.

Portes Alejandro and Ruben Rumbaut. 2006. *Immigrant America*. University of California Press.

Portsmouth , Ian. 2011. "Michael Lee-Chin: Do well. Do Good. Be Happy." Retrieved on February 10, 2013. From ProfitGuide.com, October 11, 2011.

Reynolds, C. Roy. 2000. "The Lord Moyne Commission" *Jamaica Gleaner* Commentary.

Reynolds, Jerome. 2013. "Finsac'd Entrepreneurs Saddened by Mandeville Couple Suicide." *Jamaica Gleaner*, January 2, 2013, Retrieved January 20, 2013. http://jamaica-gleaner.com/latest/article.php?id=42048.

Rodney, Walter. 1972. *How Europe Underdeveloped Africa*. London: Bogle-Louverture Publications.

Rodrik, Dani. 2011. *The Globalization Paradox*. New York: W.W. Norton & Company.

Rohter, Larry. 1997. "Blows From Nafta Batter the Caribbean Economy." *The New York Times*, January 30, 1997.

Sandefur, Timothy. 2008. "Innovation." *The Concise Encyclopedia of Economics*.

Sangster, Alfred. 2007. "The social and political context." Book Review Pt I. *Jamaica Gleaner*, November 19, 2007.

Seaga, Edward. 2009. *My Life and Leadership Volume 1 Clash of Ideologies.* MacMillan Caribbean.

Seaga, Edward. 2012. "50 Years Backward and Forward." University of Technology Annual Lecture, March 12, 2012.

Santos, Jeremy. 2008. "The Musical and Social Impact of Reggae." Yahoo Voices.

Say, Jean-Baptiste. 1836. *A Treatise on Political Economy.* Cosimo Press.

Scott, M., P. Rosa and H. Klandt. 1998. *Educating Entrepreneurs for Wealth Creation.* Stirling School of Management.

Schmid, Allan and Lindon Robison. 1995. "Applications of Social Capital Theory." *J. Agr. and Applied Econ*, 27 (1):59-66.

Scheff, David. 1985. "Interview with Steve Jobs." *Playboy.* www.allaboutstevejobs.com

Schoon, I. and K.Duckworth. 2012. "Who becomes an entrepreneur? Early life experiences as predictors of entrepreneurship." *Dev Psychol.* 48(6):1719-26.

Schumpeter, Joseph. 1943. *Capitalism, Socialism and Democracy.* United Kingdom: George Allen & Unwin Ltd.

Shane, Scott and S.Venkataraman. 2000. "The promise of entrepreneurship as a field of research." *Academy of Management Review*, 25(1); 217-226.

Shane, Scott. 2008. "Born Entrepreneurs?" *Small Business Trends.* February 25.

Sherlock, Philip and Hazel Bennett. 1998. *The Story of the Jamaican People.* Kingston: Ian Randle Publications.

Solomon, George T, and Erik K. Winslow. 1988. "Toward a descriptive profile of the entrepreneur." *Journal of Creative Behavior*, 22:162-171.

Spaulding, Gary. 2012. "Burger King Serves up Scholarships for Students." *The Gleaner*, August 31, 2012.

Stephenson, Madeline. 2011. "Michael Lee-Chin: Renaissance Man." *Dolce Vita Magazine*, June 10 2011.

Stewart Jr, Wayne and Philip Roth. 2001. "Risk propensity differences between entrepreneurs and managers: A meta-analytic review." *Journal of Applied Psychology*, 86(1); 145-153.

Sun, Ted. 2007. *Survival Tactics: The Top 11 Behaviors of Successful Entrepreneurs*. Praeger Publishers.

Swaby, Neville. 2011. "Zooming In On The '90s Meltdown." *Jamaica Gleaner*, June 12, 2011.

Thomas, Martin. 2008. "The Political Economy of Colonial Violence in Interwar Jamaica." 'Terror and the Making of Modern Europe' conference, Stanford University.

Tignor, Robert. 2006. *W. Arthur Lewis and the Birth of Development Economics*. Princeton University Press.

Tortello, Rebecca. 2003. "The Arrival of the Indians." *Jamaica Gleaner, November 3, 2003.*

Tortello, Rebecca. 2004. "The Arrival of the Africans." *Jamaica Gleaner*, February 3, 2004.

Tortello, Rebecca. 2004. "The Arrival of the Germans." *Jamaica Gleaner*, March 2, 2004.

Townsend, Abigail. 2006. *Gordon* "Butch" Stewart: It's been a Great 25 years, man." *The Independent*, December 17, 2006.

Teoh, L. 2011. "Difference between an Entrepreneur and a Small Business Owner." BizTechDay.com.

The Abolition Project. "Why was Slavery Abolished in the British Empire?" Retrieved 1/20/2013 from http://abolition.e2bn.org/slavery_111.html.

Tracy, Brian. 2005. "The Role of the Entrepreneur." *Entrepreneur*. June 20.

UN Background Paper: "Special challenges facing SIDS in trade and economic development."

Warmington, Delroy. 2013. "What to expect from the IMF agreement." *Jamaica Observer*, Sunday, February 03, 2013.

Welsch, Harold. 2004. "Entrepreneurship: The Way Ahead." *Psychology Press*.

Williams, Eric. 1944. *Capitalism and Slavery*. University of North Carolina Press.

Williams, Eric. 1970. *From Columbus to Castro: The History of the Caribbean*. United Kingdom: Vintage Books.

Wint, Alvin G. 1997. *Managing Towards International Competitiveness. Cases and Lessons from the Caribbean.* Kingston: Ian Randle Publishers.

Witter, Michael. 2012. "Lessons from the IMF Experiences." *Jamaica Gleaner,* July 8, 2012.

Wong, Tony. 2012. "Jamaica 50: Chinese Jamaican Tony Wong remembers growing up in a Chiney shop in Montego Bay." *The Star,* June 8, 2012. Retrieved January 31, 2013.

Wood, L. 2006. "The Travel and Tourism Industry in Jamaica Contributes US$870 Million to the Economy." *Business Wire.*

World Bank. "Ease of Doing Business in Jamaica." *Doing Business 2013.*

World Bank. *Migration and Remittances Factbook 2011.*

WTO. "Lamy hails accord ending long running banana dispute." Press Release September 15, 2009.

Yin, Robert. 2008. *Case Study Research: Design and Methods.* Sage Publications.

Zachary, G. Pascal. 2007. "The Silver Lining to Impending Doom." *The New York Times,* May 26, 2007.

About the Author

Glen Laman is a graduate of the University of Management and Technology (UMT) in the USA with a doctorate in Business Administration (DBA). He is also a certified Project Manager (PMP) and has an extensive career in corporate America as an Information Technology and Business Project Manager. He has worked for major corporations such as the Coca-Cola Company, JC Penney and AT&T.

He first encountered the entrepreneurial world as a young boy when his father operated a grocery store and later "Claudette's Ice Cream Parlour and Restaurant" in Kingston, Jamaica's capital. As a teenager, he worked in his brothers' whole foods store, Fruit-O-Rama, on weekends and vacations.

Despite an exciting career in the corporate world, he responded to the call of entrepreneurship and opened a franchised restaurant in a shopping mall. He later started a business which imported frozen coconut water, juices and other products from Jamaica for distribution to businesses in the US.

Much of the research for *Jamaican Entrepreneurship* was completed as part of his doctoral work at UMT. He enjoyed meeting the Jamaican entrepreneurs who were happy to share their stories and participate in the study, the first of its kind on Jamaican entrepreneurs.

There are many lessons to be gleaned from his analysis of the characteristics and traits of successful Jamaican entrepreneurs and it is hoped that readers will apply and share them.

CPSIA information can be obtained at www.ICGtesting.com
Printed in the USA
LVOW12s0632270614

391994LV00004B/5/P